British Nannies and the Great War

British Nannies and the Great War

How Norland's Regiment of Nannies Coped with Conflict & Childcare in the Great War

Louise Heren

PEN & SWORD
HISTORY

First published in Great Britain in 2016 by
Pen & Sword History
an imprint of
Pen & Sword Books Ltd
47 Church Street
Barnsley
South Yorkshire
S70 2AS

ISBN 9781473827530

Typeset in 11.5 pt Ehrhardt MT by
Replika Press Pvt Ltd, India
Printed and bound in the UK by
CPI UK

Pen & Sword Books Ltd incorporates the imprints of Pen & Sword
Archaeology, Atlas, Aviation, Battleground, Discovery, Family History,
History, Maritime, Military, Naval, Politics, Railways, Select, Social History,
Transport, True Crime and Claymore Press, Frontline Books, Leo Cooper,
Praetorian Press, Remember When, Seaforth Publishing and Wharncliffe.

For a complete list of Pen & Sword titles please contact
PEN & SWORD BOOKS LIMITED
47 Church Street, Barnsley, South Yorkshire, S70 2AS, England
E-mail: enquiries@pen-and-sword.co.uk

For Louis, without whose arrival we would not have
needed so many nannies.

And in memory of my father, who led me to believe
I could write.

For the long nights you lay awake
And watched for my unworthy sake;
For your most comfortable hand
That led me through the uneven land;
For all the story-books you read;
For all the pains you comforted;
For all you pitied, all you bore,
In sad and happy days of yore—
My second Mother, my first Wife,
The Angel of my infant life—
From the sick child, now well and old,
Take, nurse, the little book you hold!

And grant it, Heaven, that all who read
May find as dear a Nurse at need,
And every child who lists my rhyme,
In the bright fireside, nursery clime,
May hear in it as kind a voice
As made my childish days rejoice!

Robert Louis Stevenson

Contents

Picture Credits

The author and publisher wish to express their thanks to the following archives and individuals who have granted permission to reproduce photographic material within this book. Every effort has been made to trace copyright holders, but if any omissions may have occurred, please contact the publishers.

The Royal Archives © Her Majesty Queen Elizabeth II:

- Front of postcard from Marion Burgess to Kate Fox, 3 January 1913, depicting Princess Marie Kirillovna and Princess Kira Kirillovna of Russia.
- Postcard from Nurse Marion Burgess ('Burgie') to Nurse Kate Fox, 3 January 1913, sending Christmas and New Year greetings.

Churchill Archive Centre:

- Identity papers of Nurse Kathleen Wanstall, 1916, (Miscellaneous Collections 98).

Courtesy of Andrew Jennings:

- Photograph of Nurse Mary Faulconer's charge, Miss Marion Jennings, 1913.

Courtesy of the Mackarness family:

- Photograph of Nurse Eileen Godfrey, prior to her marriage and departure for India, 17 November 1913.

All other materials are reproduced by kind permission of Mrs Liz Hunt, Principal, Norland College, Bath.

Foreword

Norland College was established in a very different world, and yet the role of the nanny in modern family life is perhaps more vital today than it was back then. It is now common for both parents to work in an interconnected world, which moves so quickly. In such times, the support offered by an excellent nanny is of considerable value.

A nanny is a friend and role model for children, able to foster an ethos of calm and politeness and have that quiet sense of organization, the extra gentle touch of comfort to both parent and child.

I believe parenting is one of the world's most important skills, and sometimes one of the most challenging. Childhood is the time to enrich our children and to teach them the values they will carry with them into the next stages of their lives. Anything that helps you as a parent at this important time is worth its weight in gold.

Being a mother to five children, a daughter and four boys and all at distinct stages of age and education, is and has been an incredible joy. My belief has always been that children learn through osmosis and that a calm home is a happy one. I must say that without the help of our wonderful nanny I wouldn't have been able to fulfil my role and life's demands with such a calm head.

In the late Victorian era, when Norland College was established, children were often left 'seen and not heard' in the sole care of nannies, while parents prioritised their decisions and lives. Norland College has been strikingly good at adapting its traditions for the modern age, where parents are now so involved with their children and where a nanny works much more closely with the parents. Through such a close and positive relationship, the parents can still go out and work, but they can also play their most essential role in parenting.

The world-famous expertise offered by Norland College in training such figures who will eventually be so important in the lives of so many children, is part of a wonderful and crucial tradition of excellence. I am delighted that this fascinating book has now come to completion and will act as a documentary not only of that tradition but of how Norland College will continue to offer so much to a new generation as they discover the joys of being a parent.

HRH Crown Princess Marie-Chantal of Greece, 2015

Foreword

The Norland Institute and Norland College, as we are now, has an enviable reputation for the quality, integrity and loyalty of the young women it has trained to become children's nurses and in recent times, early years practitioners. We were the first, and have remained the foremost establishment for the training of young women who have a passion for the care and development of our youngest citizens. For over a century, our reputation has been maintained by adherence to three mottos.

When our founder, Mrs Emily Ward, began her life's work in 1892, she instilled the words 'love never faileth' into each of her probationer nannies. She encouraged them to love one another, to support and nurture each other. They should have an unfailing love for their vocation, a passion for raising children using the latest educational thinking of the time. And of course, a deep love for small people whom they would guide through their younger years, steered by the values of their age. Mrs Ward's motto has never left us. It is as relevant for the young women, and occasional young man, training at Norland today.

However, Mrs Ward had another motto: *Fortis in Arduis* – strength in adversity. Working with small children can be a lonely profession. All day long a children's nurse is surrounded by budding intellects, enquiring minds, requests and questions. And when those leaders, inventors and teachers of the future are all tucked up in bed, a nanny's job is not done because planning and preparing for tomorrow has only just begun. It takes strength and stamina to care for infants and toddlers day after day.

Reading the accounts of our forebears in this book, it is apparent that Mrs Ward's motto held especial significance for the Norlanders caught in Europe in August 1914. It is difficult to comprehend today the strength of character required, their determination to return home or to find an accommodation with their altered circumstances as the war ground on. Kate Fox's hazardous adventure through Germany to a safe haven in Holland; Kathleen Wanstall's decision to remain in Austria under the protection of her German employers; and Muriel Bois' bravery in travelling the length of the Mediterranean at the height of the war; all are remarkable stories of a group of women that today's Norlanders can only revere and hope never to endure what they experienced.

The third motto, which has long fallen into disuse at Norland, belongs to our first principal, Miss Isabel Sharman: 'in quietness and confidence shall be your strength'. She taught her students as we do today, not to judge, to offer childcare advice not opinions, and to go about their work to the best of their ability. With such quietness, Norlanders acquired quickly the confidence to travel the world, often working in remote areas of the British Empire and at the frontiers of what was then termed 'civilised society'. From Nigeria to Afghanistan and the Far East, in the early twentieth century Norlanders had the confidence to work thousands of miles away from home and the quietness of spirit to fit into the cultures in which they found themselves. No telephone, no email, no social media – something that would give today's Norlanders pause for thought before accepting a remote position.

Sadly, the world is a changed place and I believe Mrs Ward would agree with me, that there are some countries to which I cannot send our young women today, although before the Great War they sound like they were terribly exciting places to work.

However, there are many things about Norland that Mrs Ward would recognise: our insistence on a distinctive uniform perfectly worn; our approval of only the highest standards in childcare; and our teaching of the most enquiring group of young women I have had the pleasure to work with. Unfortunately, I do not receive inked letters and postcards from far-flung lands as she did. Email and social media have replaced the personal note from our students and I wonder what researchers of the future will make of Norland's history copied to computer drives that may not be viable in 50 years let alone 100.

One thing at Norland that has been an innovation forced upon us by our increasingly glittering client list is the requirement for the College's, our students' and working practitioners' absolute discretion. I have read with envy through the annual lists of employers, which Mrs Ward published. Recorded there are some fabulous royals, titled families and eminent politicians who have become household names in British history. I am sure today's client list is equally as impressive. However, even as principal, I am not allowed to know who employs Norlanders and it is probably best that I do not know. Mrs Ward's contacts book and search for royal approval were effective tools to promote her work in 1900. They have set us on a path that I hope will continue long into the future, but they would never do for a modern Norland in this century.

Liz Hunt
Principal, Norland College, 2015

Introduction

I t is a well-known phrase that history is written by the victors. This
is a point-of-view that encompasses political, diplomatic and military
history, but in the past twenty years or so, there has been a trend
towards social history – the history of the people. Social history tells the
same story, but from the perspective of those who really experienced it:
the people at the front line. Social history brings to life the true voices of
those who were there, although their presence was not officially recognised.
This is where primary sources come into their own.

Having moved from London via the home-counties, the twenty-first
century home of the Norland Institute (now Norland College) is a Georgian
building neighbouring a supermarket in central Bath. This is the modern
face of the world's oldest and most famous training college for nannies.

I first encountered Norland College in 2005, when producing an
observational documentary series for television about the Norland students'
daily life and studies. In the course of a year of filming at Norland, not
only did I take a crash course in childcare – very useful because my
own child was then six months old and I needed all the advice I could
get – but I also discovered copies of the Norland *Quarterly* tucked away
in a huge ottoman chest. Published four times a year, each copy of the
Quarterly begins with a lengthy missive from Mrs Ward, a letter from the
principal and then letters from Norlanders from all over the world offering
news, advice and nursery anecdotes. At Christmas a comprehensive list
of Norlanders and their places of work was published. Leafing through
editions of the *Quarterly* and early twentieth century correspondence from
the Norlanders, I knew I had found a brand new voice and a fresh story
to add to our understanding of women's experiences in the Great War.

These young women were not munitions girls emancipated by the war
or society ladies working as nurses on the Continent; my Norlanders were

educated, working- and middle-class young women with strongly-held opinions, who had experienced world events since 1892 from a privileged grandstand. They were describing a unique set of experiences because of who they were and for whom they worked. How they documented what they witnessed – the phrases they used and the comments they made – is social history in itself, but their letters described a version of the Great War that I had never encountered elsewhere.

Today, the students who enter the College come to Bath in order to take an honours degree in early years childcare and education, a qualification that establishes these young people as childcare practitioners, who may go on to become teachers, policy-makers and leaders in child welfare.

In 1892, when the Norland Institute first opened its doors, the course was equally as innovative. Never before had anyone offered or received training to become a children's nurse. It was a new career for young women, earning them a diploma, which would become a professionally recognised qualification. Previously, uneducated girls had entered domestic service, working their way through the household ranks of maids to eventually become a nanny in a private nursery, having learned from older women who had trodden the same path. The pay was poor, working hours were long and the daily routine highly disciplined. Naturally, the job did not attract educated young women from the middle-classes.

A 'training school for ladies as children's nurses' was the brainchild of Mrs Emily Ward, a devotee of Froebel's educational methods and an experienced school-mistress. She had already established the Norland Place School in 1876, where young women could train to become school teachers. Born in 1850, Mrs Ward grew up in a society growing increasingly aware that in order to combat urban poverty, education of the masses was the solution. A life-long interest in philanthropy and education set her on the path that would lead to the formation of the Norland Institute, shortly after her forty-second birthday.

As headmistress of Norland Place School, she had noticed that not all young women were intellectually suited to become teachers, but felt that children deserved better than girls of the 'domestic class' to raise them. Training young ladies to be children's nurses not only provided a new career for otherwise under-occupied young women, but also raised the standard of childcare in private homes. The young ladies she sought to recruit were not suitable for 'the school desk, the hospital ward or emigration', and were disinclined to marry. In order to qualify for entry to her new venture, Mrs Ward required candidates to have an all-round education; to be skilled in music and art; ideally to possess some previous experience with small children and a strong desire for independence, balanced by a temperament to serve others. Preferably they would already have suffered the gamut of childhood diseases and proved their resilience.

In the closing decades of the nineteenth century, Britain looked to the health of the nation to maintain its Empire. This was the beginning of the hugely popular Eugenics movement aimed at improving the genetic stock of the country through government policy, and among the movement's more fervent adherents, through selective breeding to eradicate the 'worst' traits of the so-called 'under-class'. Apart from improving the health of the lower orders, one of its aims was for well-educated and nicely raised children to become imperial officers overseas. Mrs Ward recognised the *zeitgeist* and decided to become part of it.

Recently married to a wealthy and philanthropically minded businessman, by 1892 Mrs Ward had the financial support behind her to establish the Norland Institute. Her first step was to ask Miss Isabel Sharman to assist her. Miss Sharman had been a pupil teacher at the Norland Place School under Mrs Ward and the two women deeply respected one another. Their teaching methods focussed on placing the child at the centre of its care – a pioneering concept which remains at the core of Norland's teaching and today is universally practised. Children's nurses were to be trained to care solely for the child and to educate it. Norland's young ladies would not be distracted by any additional domestic duties in an employer's home. In the class-ridden society of the late nineteenth century, recruiting genteel young ladies who would seamlessly fit into society families was Mrs Ward's and Miss Sharman's first task.

A round of drawing-room meetings in smart houses with a personally invited clientele established that properly trained children's nurses were very much desired in the best social circles. Mrs Ward received further interest in her project through articles placed in the daily papers and ladies' magazines – a precursor to today's advertorials; in the early days

Norland did not stoop to advertising. The first employers arrived by recommendation as word travelled around upper-class salons that having a 'Norlander' in the household was the latest thing.

The Institute opened in September 1892, under the same roof as the Norland Place School (separate premises at 29 Holland Park Avenue were found within a year) with just five probationers, each paying £36 for their six-month course. The fees were the equivalent of an unskilled working man's annual wage. To gain a place, candidates not only had to exhibit some interest in and previous experience with children, they also underwent a rigorous medical, which included a chest X-ray – an examination that was not without risk in the 1890s. At the turn of the twentieth century, tuberculosis was prevalent throughout society, spread by close contact with an infected person. Mrs Ward needed to be certain that she would not be responsible for introducing this killer disease into a smart family nursery.

The initial three months' domestic training included nursery cookery and children's laundry, as well as kindergarten games and educational lectures. For Norland probationers used to relying on servants in their parents' home, Miss Sharman demonstrated 'the washing of flannels and the care of hair brushes', the latter being silver so that a Norlander entering a new home could lay out her expensive toiletries and thus distinguish herself from the ordinary domestic staff.

A further three months were then spent in a children's ward at a hospital, where matron instilled self-discipline and routine. Girls were sent to matrons Miss Dunn, Miss Lobb and Miss Garrard at hospitals in the home counties where Mrs Ward had forged relationships. After a short holiday, the students were then placed for six months with a potential employer family to learn from the mother how to set-up their nursery; the family would pay reduced fees for the probationer's services in their home. At each stage of the course a student's marks were written up in their testimonial book, a leather-covered notebook that would follow a Norlander to every engagement for the rest of her career. They became a precious record of a nanny's service, treasured by Norlanders into old age and many have been returned to Norland on the nanny's death, along with their Norland Badge awarded after three years' 'loyal and dedicated service to Norland and the children in their charge'.

The service expected from a Norland Nurse is summed up in one family's testimonial written in 1919:

She came to me in September 1910; young, tall, quiet, capable. My eldest son was inclined to be delicate; my second son was three months old. I had been unwell since his birth, and [sic] we were settling into new quarters, so the Norland Nurse took charge, and from that day to this has fully deserved the early won title of 'Angel of the House'. In travelling invaluable, in sickness invaluable; always level-headed, always knowing where to find everything, ready, able and willing to knit a sweater, make a fancy dress, bind a cut, start a car, drive a pony, cook a meal, or lure sugar from a grocer, always merry.

Colonel and Mrs Burton had appreciated Nurse Margaret Gates' presence in their home for nearly a decade until their children had outgrown her services. There are numerous equally glowing tributes in the testimonial books now preserved in the Norland College Archive.

By 1893, Norland had recruited twenty-five students, after which numbers increased annually as did the fees, which had risen to £80 by 1904. At a time when household domestic servants' wages ranged between £12 to £28 per annum, Norland's fees were beyond the reach of most young women. Those who trained in the early years had private means, being the daughters of vicars, merchants, lawyers and doctors, but Mrs Ward also wished to extend her philanthropy to girls with the right credentials who lacked funds.

The 'maiden scheme' established in 1904 allowed a tiny group of girls to enter Norland on greatly reduced fees of only £12, in return for a year's service as a domestic servant at the Institute before starting their training. However, Mrs Ward was steeped in Victorian social etiquette and insisted that her 'maidens' joining the Institute every year were called by new names, 'Honour, Verity, Prudence and Mercy' and wore a special uniform to distinguish them from full fee-paying Norlanders.

Today, distinctions of class and money have receded into the past. Most Norlanders now have student loans, but two things have not changed in over a hundred years. From caring for toddlers on board a round-the-world yacht tour to keeping young children happy, occupied and insect bite-free while staying at a family estate in Africa, Norlanders can still be found in homes and schools all over the world. In 1921, Nurse Anna Miller and her sister worked their way around the world, picking up temporary engagements and replenishing their purses as they travelled from England to Canada and finally to New Zealand. Their coveted Norland Badges and testimonial books were sufficient to open doors in private homes, orphanages and schools across the Empire.

In the first two decades of the Institute's existence, Norlanders were undeterred by the prospect of travelling even to the remotest regions of the world. Operating a register of all trained Norlanders, the Institute posted its young ladies to Japan, China, Afghanistan, India, South Africa, Jamaica and even Uruguay. It is a tradition that has endured. Careful matching of the right nanny to a family continues into the twenty-first century.

As well as the myriad opportunities available to today's Norlanders, such as becoming primary school teachers or nursery managers, many continue to work as nannies. Often they are employed by the smartest and wealthiest families, among them royalty and celebrities; HRH The Duchess of Cambridge currently employs a Norlander to care for her children. Commanding high fees in recognition of their pedigree and training, a Norland nanny will cost a family upwards of £25,000 a year and the most experienced nannies can earn more than twice that figure. A hundred years ago, the expense of a children's nurse represented about the same proportion of a household's income. The early Norlanders earned £40 in their first year and those who acquired a royal position could attract more than £100.

A year after opening, Mrs Ward had enticed the Duchess of Bedford to employ one of her newly trained Norlanders. Rumour quickly spread of the quality of training provided by the Institute and the social standing of its nurses. Word travelled from one aristocratic nursery to another; royalty took up recommendations of this nurse or that, until Norland

Nurses were employed by Spanish, Greek, German and Russian royals, all requiring the polish that could only be achieved by hiring an English nanny from Queen Victoria, their grandmother's homeland. Across Europe, Norlanders in charge of royal nurseries frequently met one another as their employers' families travelled from palace to palace to visit relations.

Empress Frederick of Germany made one of the earliest royal appointments, when in 1893 she employed a Norland Nurse to care for her grandchild, recently born to her daughter the Crown Princess of Greece. It was the start of a relationship with the Greek royal family that would extend into the middle of the twentieth century and would consume the adult life of the most royal of royal nannies, Nurse Kate Fox.

Prologue
Nurse Kate Fox:
The Making of a Royal Children's Nurse

O f all the tales of the early Edwardian Norland nurses, the personal story of Nurse Kate Fox is not only the best preserved but probably the most compelling. Her letters to the Institute survive printed in the Norland *Quarterly*, although those to her employer have been lost. However, having spent the majority of her adult life among Europe's royals, Kate knew the correct etiquette and on her death her family deposited the letters, notes and cards received from royal personages in the Royal Archive at Windsor Castle. This detailed correspondence records a life-long relationship between a children's nurse and a royal lady that would withstand the tumult of both the First and Second World Wars. Their extraordinary correspondence would continue long after Kate's royal charges had become married ladies themselves.

Kate's career spans the decade before the war and completes Norland's Great War history in the years immediately after the conflict. The details of her rise to the position of 'royal nanny' and her return to England without her beloved royal charges neatly book-end the wider history of how the Norland Institute and its nurses coped with conflict and childcare during the Great War.

* * *

Born on 9 May 1870, Kate Fox was the elder of two sisters who entered the Norland Institute in London to train as children's nurses. They were the daughters of Charles Fox, noted in their Norland entrance records as a 'gentleman' from Middlesex. Jessie, the younger of the two women, completed her training the year before Kate, who finished the course in November 1895, aged twenty-five.

As nurse 113, Kate was among the earliest cohorts of Norland nurses to enter this new profession. The course had cost Kate's father £36 for her year's training, but her future was promising. Thanks to Norland's growing reputation, Kate could expect the very best employment opportunities with well-to-do families around the United Kingdom, who eagerly sought out this new kind of children's nurse.

The 1897 list of Norland nurses and their current appointments, published annually at Christmas in the *Quarterly*, mentions Kate working at Alderley Edge in Cheshire. She was still there the following year, but had moved to Mrs Reid Sharman's home in Wellingborough by Christmas 1899. This was the Norland Institute Principal Miss Isabel Sharman's family home and Kate had come to care for the latest addition to the family. Being asked by the Principal to become nanny to one of her relations was a privilege. Obviously, Miss Sharman had recognised something special in Kate and had duly rewarded this promising young children's nurse.

Kate remained with the Reid Sharman family until early 1900, when a new situation came up with the Ruspoli family. Having personally witnessed Kate's nursery practice and progress with her brother's child, it is likely that Miss Sharman had intentionally groomed Kate to take up aristocratic employment when a position became available. The Ruspolis were an ancient Italian noble family with three children aged between nine and five, and on 5 June 1900 another son, Emanuele Costantino was born. Kate had her hands full with four children to care for, but she was living with the prince and princess at their Monte Carlo home on the French Riviera. It was her first taste of what Norland's training had promised: travel, luxury and privilege.

Writing to Norland in November 1901, Kate described her first year of working with the Ruspolis:

We have no settled home, but are always travelling, which (in spite of the advantages and the greatest, I think, is the exquisite scenery one sees) is getting a little tiring, more especially on account of luggage,

*which, when one has no house in which to leave things, accumulates,
and is very costly.*

Kate did not have to worry about paying for the porterage of her luggage,
but the constant packing and unpacking of trunks for four children, with
all the paraphernalia required to set up a nursery in every house they
visited, was her responsibility and must have been an arduous task. She
never knew for how long they would stay and therefore, whether she
ought to unpack absolutely everything.

By late 1901, Kate and the family had settled at the family seat: Villa
Simeon, Oberhafen on Lake Thun, in Switzerland. The two elder boys
had an Italian tutor who taught them during the day, so that Kate only
had charge of them once lessons were finished. Six-year-old Edmondo,
whom Kate described as 'extremely delicate', and baby Emanuele were
in her constant care.

Emanuele had an Italian wet nurse to feed him and Kate had made
some effort to learn Italian, so that she and the wet nurse could chat while
they worked throughout the day. Kate acknowledged that 'she has been a
great comfort to me, as she is such a trustworthy and nice woman'. Kate
was amazed at the differences between British and Continental children,
noting that the latter were treated 'in a very grown up way':

[I] *was horrified when I arrived to find Edmondo, aged five, eating
a three or four course dinner immediately before going to bed; he was
never asleep till 10 or 11 o'clock, and the two elder ones dined at eight
with their parents, and went to bed at ten or half-past.*

None of this fitted into the regime Kate had learned at Norland,
and she was attempting to implement a timetable more in tune with
her training. With the wet nurse only speaking Italian and her nursery
maid only conversing in French, Kate was stretched to the limits of her
linguistic ability as well as her patience while organising her nursery.

Kate remained with the Ruspolis until September 1903, when a position
with the Greek royal family became available. Kate left for Greece,
intending only to stay for a year to nurse back to health the delicate baby

Princess Olga, then three months old. Compared to the luxury of the Ruspoli villas, Kate described the Greek royal palace as 'very primitive'. The family for whom she worked might have gone up in status, being royalty rather than nobility, but the surroundings were less salubrious. However, Princess Olga quickly 'bound herself' into Kate's heart, and with her parents, Prince and Princess Nicholas expecting another child, Kate was won over.

At the outset of their relationship, Princess Nicholas began her letters to her children's nurse 'My dear Miss Fox', but very quickly such formality diminished to 'My dear Foxie' and 'Foxie darling'. Their intimacy was almost immediate and despite the disparity in social rank, clearly the two women got along exceptionally well.

The first years of Kate's royal engagement were spent travelling between the family's palace in Athens, the Princess's own family home at Zarskoe Selo, St Petersburg and the Princess's mother's seat at Mecklenburg-Schwerin in Germany. The Norland Institute's Christmas list of nurses' whereabouts would always refer to Kate's employer with her full title: Her Royal and Imperial Highness, Princess Nicholas of Greece, in acknowledgement of her position as a Grand Duchess of Russia, sister to Grand Duke Kirill and grand-daughter of Tsar Alexander II.

In late October 1905, while travelling in England, staying at Windsor, Buckingham Palace and Sandringham, Princess Nicholas wrote to Kate at St Petersburg, seeking her advice on blankets and travelling bags for her two infant daughters.[1] Kate had quickly established herself as indispensable to the Princess and their correspondence was already so frequent that the Princess could write to Russia about tiny details and anticipate a response within days to help complete her shopping in London.

By mid-November, Kate and Princesses Olga and Elisabeth were staying at their grandmother's home, Schloss Schwerin, in Germany. Princess Nicholas thanked Kate for writing almost daily updates on the welfare of her 'darling angels'.[2] As Princess Nicholas travelled across Europe, she often caught up with other royal nurseries in the charge of Norlanders. Kate's colleague Nurse Marian Burgess was nanny to the Princess's nieces, the Kirill princesses. While in Paris, Princess Nicholas gladly passed on news of 'Burgie' and another royal nanny, Nurse Irene Collenette.[3]

Kate was certainly in the thick of European royalty and she shared her experiences readily with fellow Norlanders through the *Quarterly*, boasting: 'I have had the honour of having been addressed by members of almost all the Royal Families in Europe.' During 1905, she travelled by ship with her royal charges to the Yildiz Palace to visit the Sultan of Constantinople. Instructed to remain on board the royal boat, Kate waited to hear if she should prepare the baby princesses for bed when 'a private launch came up and I was told that the Sultan had sent for the little Princesses and all the suite to go to his Palace for the night'.

Kate described a magical drive through Constantinople at dusk, but complained that her dinner had not arrived in her room until 11.15pm and 'was very Oriental':

Two men brought a huge silver tray containing about twelve silver plates, each loaded with food of various kinds (there were only two rusty knives and forks to eat all with!) and though I tasted everything they were very worried because I did not eat it all!

Kate appreciated the luxurious bed linens 'too good to lie on', scent and Turkish cigarettes on her dressing-table, but resented the long walk to the bathroom in the morning.

The following day was spent in wandering the palace and sight-seeing around the city, but as evening fell the Sultan demanded the baby princesses' attendance at court, so Kate prepared swiftly for a personal interview with him, which was conducted in French through an interpreter. Later that night, she learned 'through the kindness of Princess Nicholas in coming herself to my cabin to tell me' that she had been presented with 'a beautiful order, called the Shepacat'.[4] Kate's employers were distinguished guests and conferring an order on Kate was an acknowledgement of their status, but Kate had evidently given a good account of herself too because the order was awarded also in recognition of the Sultan's regard for her.

Their journey continued through Russia to the imperial village at Zarskoe Selo, St Petersburg where one afternoon Kate's princesses were invited to tea with the Tsar's four daughters and his heir, the Tsarevitch.

Kate supervised the cousins' tea party and was thrilled when the Empress sent a lady-in-waiting to ask Kate personally for details about the Norland Institute. The Empress had started a similar venture, which was not doing well and she wanted to know more about Norland's special approach.

Kate revelled in her new post, offering details of royal parties and name-dropping at every opportunity in her letters to the Institute. The only discomfort Kate could muster was that the travelling was trying, although 'all trouble possible is taken off my hands, and I only have the actual looking after of my two little Princesses, who are perfect models during our journeys'. Kate recommended foreign life to her fellow nurses as 'such an education,' adding, 'I have found foreign employers exceedingly kind in every way'.

Throughout 1906, Kate remained in Greece with her charges because the Princess was pregnant again with her third child and was also required to attend the Greek Olympics in May. Kate went several times to the Games and enjoyed watching the final of the marathon, but all the excitement of life overseas could not stop her pining for English fare. Back in southern Europe where customs were very different, again she complained of late meal times and the impossibility 'even where there are many cooks to get just what one wants for the babies'.

In early autumn 1906, Kate managed to take two months' holiday in England, her first visit in three years. In Kate's absence, her sister Jessie took over her charges. Leaving her own well-ordered nursery in such safe hands gave Kate a deep sense of reassurance. With the arrival of Princess Marina in December 1906, Kate asked Jessie to stay on to help her through the first months with the new baby and the two older princesses. It was the first time since the sisters joined the Institute that they had been able to spend a significant amount of time together.

Less than a year later, the Greek royal family was travelling again and Kate was in Zarskoe Selo with her three babies while the Princess stayed in Paris where she met her brother, Grand Duke Kirill and his wife, Grand Duchess Kirill, a grand-daughter of Queen Victoria. The Grand Duchess had just given birth to a daughter, Maria, and the two royal women compared their babies like any new mothers. The Princess passed on a description of baby Maria to Kate:

She is a fine, big fat baby, bigger I should say than Marina, very good,
never cries & not a bit frightened of strangers, but ... As far as beauty
goes, she is not to be mentioned in the same breath as our babies![5]

If Kate had shared the contents of the Princess's letter, she could have
caused her employer great embarrassment, but the Princess trusted Kate
beyond the discretion required of their employment relationship – Kate
had become her confidante. Five years into their friendship, the Princess
was ending her letters to Kate with 'best love Foxie dear' and happily
gossiped about 'Miss M and Capt P' from Franzensbad.[6] It appeared
that committing her gossip to paper was deemed perfectly safe when the
letter was intended for Kate's eyes only. The young princesses also wrote
frequently when the household was separated, addressing their letters to
'my darling sweet nursie'. The oldest, Princess Olga wrote with news of
her dolly Daisy, having put her to bed 'just like a real nurse'.[7]

When Princess Nicholas's father died in 1909, Kate was presented with
a brooch made from 'one of papa's pins' as a remembrance.[8] Truly, Kate
was an adored member of the family's inner circle.

The Princess wrote to her freely, naming European royals as if they
were Kate's own close acquaintances and now closed her letters 'with
fondest love from Ellen'.[9] On one occasion when Kate was on holiday,
she missed the princesses sorely, eliciting a letter of sympathy from their
mother:

I can understand so well your feeling of loneliness & longing for the
children – you must feel like I do when I leave the Prince – it is a
horrible feeling which nothing can really remedy, one has just got to
keep up an outward appearance of cheerfulness not to make others sad.[10]

In the first six months of 1910, Kate travelled between Cannes, Frankfurt
and Bognor where she had taken the princesses for a holiday at Norland's
seaside house. Before starting their sixteen-week stay, Kate orchestrated
a visit by Princess Nicholas to Norland, much to Mrs Ward's delight.
This was exactly the kind of royal benefaction the Institute had long
desired.

Correspondence between Kate and the Princess over the summer of 1910 included details of Burgie's care of Princess Maria Kirill and discussion of a potential stay for Kate and the Greek princesses at Buckingham Palace. However, the invitation came with a hint of warning concerning royal etiquette:

> *It will be very nice if you can spend a night at Buckingham Palace and Princess Victoria is very kind to suggest it, only don't do it if you see there is the slightest reluctance; ask Prince Christopher to find out if you are* really *welcome.*[11]

A fortnight later, Kate had written with details of their visit, to which the Princess replied:

> *Thank you so much for yr Buckingham Palace letter, which was most interesting – I am very pleased you didn't ask to spend the night there – if Princess Victoria had* really *wanted it, she would have arranged it – like this they can't say that we are indiscrete* [sic] *or pushy.*[12]

It was Kate's first lesson in royal etiquette and she had behaved appropriately. The Princess's desire not to appear brash was also an indication of the status of the Greek royals in the European hierarchy. Princess Nicholas followed her advice on royal invitations with news of her sister-in-law's second daughter, Princess Kira Kirill. Suspected measles had turned out to be teething trouble and she commented on witnessing Princess Maria Kirill swimming in cold water and Burgie standing by, unable to advise against these inappropriate activities for such a young child.[13]

The Princess was openly competitive, often comparing her girls' behaviour with that of her brother's children. Titbits about nursery practice maintained a friendly rivalry between Kate and Burgie, and often the Princess solicited Kate's opinion on her sister-in-law's family. In October 1911, when Kate was holidaying again with the princesses, this time at Westgate-on-Sea, Princess Nicholas requested that she take the girls to London to be photographed so that she could share the pictures with her sister-in-law, Grand Duchess Kirill.[14] The competition even extended to comparing the girls' beauty as they grew up.

Since her birth in 1906, Princess Marina, known affectionately among the family as 'Baby', had suffered with a twisted foot, which by 1910 could no longer be kept secret. Kate administered daily massages to loosen the joint, but the child needed medical intervention and a supportive boot was designed to rectify the condition. Princess Nicholas was an attentive mother, sharing the medical care of the toddler with her nanny, but royal appointments required her to travel constantly from one palace to another and so the two women wrote frequently with updates on the child's foot.

Baby was under the care of a specialist at a clinic at Berck-Plage in France and Kate rushed there during a medical emergency in autumn 1912, to be met by Princess Nicholas. Princess Marina's foot was put in plaster and, after some toing and froing between Berck-Plage, Paris and London, finally the Princess's mother, Grand Duchess Marie Vladimirovna, demanded that the three girls along with their nurse journey with her to St Petersburg, where she would care for the youngest child. Princess Nicholas was powerless to refuse.

War had been declared between Greece and Turkey in October 1912, requiring Princess Nicholas to return to Athens to minister to wounded Greek soldiers along with the other royal ladies. Kate packed her belongings and headed to St Petersburg with the girls and their grandmother. She and the Grand Duchess were not on intimate terms, Kate having crossed the Grand Duchess a few years earlier concerning the care of the princesses, and now Kate wrote from Russia complaining that the Grand Duchess had accused her of always doing the opposite of the doctor's orders.

For Kate to write so begrudgingly of her employer's mother is testament to the strength of her relationship with the Princess, who replied quickly and sympathetically, acknowledging the overbearing behaviour of the 'naughty' Grand Duchess.[15] In Paris, Burgie had heard news of the rift between Kate and her employer's mother, and sent her a Christmas card expressing how sorry she was not to be with her in St Petersburg.[16]

The situation increasingly deteriorated until the Grand Duchess ordered Princess Marina to a family property in Crimea for her health. Kate accompanied the child, but not without complaining first to the Princess and bemoaning her separation from Princesses Olga and Elisabeth. Within days, Princess Nicholas was writing from Salonika to Kate consoling her: 'Of course you are right to tell me everything & I must know all that is going on, but I think that you take things too much to heart & get too easily upset, afterall most of what you hear is servants' gossip.'[17] Without the protection of her royal employer and intimate confidante, Kate had been relegated to the status of nursery servant while in Russia. She might be a Norlander, but that counted for little in the Grand Duchess's household.

In early January 1913, Princess Nicholas's attentions were still caught up in the Greco-Turkish war. She corresponded every few days with Kate but her letters, suggesting advice on how to handle her mother and asking for constant news of her daughters, were equally concerned with her desire for peace[18] and the terrible outbreak of typhoid fever among the troops she was nursing in Salonika.[19] Seven thousand refugees, who had fled the Bulgarians for fear of being massacred, were now in Greek camps. Yet, within a few sentences, Princess Nicholas changed the subject, describing how the 'King is quite enchanted with Olga's letter', and how much he liked his grand-daughters to be learning English from an English nanny.

The Princess also spilled her heart to Kate on hearing court gossip that: 'If Baby had been left to us, she would have become a cripple – all this I must hear & say nothing, & not only must I swallow it all but I must write amiable, charming letters.'

The Princess relied on Kate for news of her daughters, as well as using the nanny as her eyes and ears at the Russian court. However, she was very understanding of Kate's predicament, telling Kate that she was beside herself that the children had been separated from their loving nurse and encouraged Kate to 'cheer up, it's not for long now'.[20]

In Berck-Plage with the Kirill princesses, Kate's Norland colleague Burgie had heard of her stressful predicament and felt the situation sufficiently grave to send a telegram: 'think of you and feel for you'.[21] In a few words, the sympathy of one royal nanny to another conveyed all the anxieties Burgie too had experienced as a lone British nanny at the Russian court.

By mid-April 1913, Kate and Princess Marina were back at Berck-Plage, accompanied by Baron Offenburg, where Baby was having her boot changed daily by her doctor. Baron Offenburg was the official in charge of the royal children's administration, in lieu of their grandmother or mother.

In Greece for her father-in-law, the King's funeral, Princess Nicholas told Kate that she had received a letter from her mother demanding Kate's dismissal:

> *The Grand Duchess wants me* <u>*absolutely*</u> *to send you away, if not, it means that I love you more than her & that things will never be the same again between her & me; this means of course a serious quarrel with my mother. I* <u>*can not*</u> *for the children's sake & for their future specially let it come to this – fancy what consequences it might have! ... If you don't go she will have nothing more to do with me. I am bound to tell you all this, Foxie dear, for you to know how things are.*

The Princess had consulted her sister, who advised her that Kate should go; she wrote to her: 'Think it all over, put yourself in my position & try & help me through this hard moment as you have often done during the past nine & a half years that we have spent together.'[22] Kate did not take the hint. Although her departure could have resolved the bitter battle ensuing between mother and daughter, Kate either did not think to or could not bear to resign.

Finally, Baron Offenburg was requested to telegram Princess Nicholas, instructing her to give Kate her marching orders.[23] The Princess was forced to comply with her mother's demand. Not only was there the consideration of filial devotion and respect, but also of royal protocol. The Grand Duchess out-ranked the Princess, a situation exacerbated by Princess Nicholas's dependence on her mother's annual stipend to maintain the lifestyle she and her husband enjoyed.

At Christmas 1912, despite growing tension at the Russian court between Kate and her charges' grandmother, Kate had informed Norland that her postal address for the coming year was 'c/o H R and I H Princess Nicholas of Greece, Palais Vladimir, St Petersburg', the Grand Duchess's address. This implies that Kate did not understand the severity of the rift or the Princess's inability to intervene in her defence.

When the moment came, Kate's dismissal was peremptory in the extreme. Kate began to write a letter to the Princess while still at Berck-Plage with Princess Marina, but it was finished at home in Surrey. She described the bitter experience of handing over Baby to another Norlander, Nurse Margaret Alison, who had been engaged secretly by the Grand Duchess. Clearly, plans for Kate's dismissal had been in place for sufficient time to allow Norland to find a suitable replacement and for her to travel to Berck-Plage.

Kate was distraught after almost ten years' service, having raised all three princesses since birth. She had not even been allowed to say farewell to the older girls. The Princess remained powerless to reinstate Kate, but in a letter dated mid-May, she suggested that Kate would only be away for a 'rest' period, until the Grand Duchess saw sense.[24]

Nevertheless, a further letter received a week later explained the terms of Kate's dismissal and detailed her annual pension of £75 for the first year and £50 thereafter. The money would be paid by the Grand Duchess's estate at Schloss Schwerin, on the proviso that Kate ceased all communication with the princesses. It was a cruel detail to add to an already emotional and painful situation, but it was a measure of the Grand Duchess's dislike of Kate and her childcare methods.[25]

Princess Nicholas had lost a friend as well as a nanny, but she did not dare to see Kate again until the sour atmosphere had blown over, for fear of irritating the Grand Duchess any further.[26] A week later, news came, via the Princess, of Norland's agreement to award Kate her silver bar for ten years' continual service in one situation, although strictly Kate was a few months short of the required decade.[27]

By 1913, numerous Norlanders were sprinkled throughout Europe in royal households, but Kate's career so far had eclipsed all others for royal acquaintances, privileged access to palaces and royal gossip, and extensive travel criss-crossing Europe every few months with a train of servants behind her. News of Kate's demise spread around Norland's royal nannies overseas, but was never declared formally by the Norland Institute in

England. At Christmas 1913, Kate's entry in Norland's register gave no address at all, she was not even listed as 'at home'.

Kate did not learn the reasons for her dismissal until August 1913. She had spent the intervening months in turmoil, longing for the princesses whom she loved as her own. Having grown so close to the children and their mother, and believing herself beyond reproach, her instant dismissal had cut her to the quick. Too comfortable with her Greek royals, she had failed to understand how precarious a nanny's existence was, even one seemingly so essential to the fabric of her employer's family. She had been reminded that she was simply a hired servant whose employment carried the professional danger of having her heart broken when an engagement finished, or if she was sacked.

Finally, news filtered through royal channels and Princess Nicholas received a fourth-hand account of what had happened. For Kate, the explanation was most unsatisfactory and the hot topic of her dismissal would thread its way through her and the Princess's correspondence, a stream of letters that remained unbroken throughout the four years of the Great War.

Now back at home, it seemed doubtful that Kate could put the experience behind her. How would she ever find another family to replace them?

Chapter 1

A New Century

By 1900, the Norland Institute at Pembridge Square, London had been in existence for eight years under the administrative and financial guidance of founder Mrs Emily Ward and her hand-picked principal, Miss Isabel Sharman. It was the first training establishment of its kind, but Mrs Ward's idea had been such a success that rival organisations had already been set up in Manchester, Liverpool and at Sesame House, also in London.

The competing training centres had structured themselves along the same lines as Norland, copying the course syllabus, yet according to Mrs Ward there was one thing her competitors had failed to grasp: 'our least capable nurses can nearly always obtain situations, because the demand is far greater than the supply.' From the outset, Norland nurses were regarded as the *crème-de-la-crème*, becoming highly sought-after as word spread that having a Norlander to run one's nursery was the best care a mother could provide for her children.

Norland's reputation for quality of education and career prospects was also spreading through its graduates, whose sisters, cousins and friends were flocking to Mrs Ward's door. They applied to Pembridge Square, having heard the stories of Norland nannies living in comfortable nurseries and earning good salaries. The tales of foreign travel – something from which many single women in the opening decade of the century were barred – attracted high quality, ambitious candidates.

Probationers came from all over the country and generally from more well-off walks of life, although some prospective students seem to have felt the need to make their backgrounds sound grander in their entrance documents than they really were. Nurse Cicely Colls's father was a 'high-class tradesman'; he carried out skilled manual tasks, albeit at the top end of his craft. Cicely's upper working-class background as the daughter of a tradesman later influenced the political views she developed during the First World War. Nurse Marian Burgess's career would be one of the most glamorous among the early Norlanders, but she had relatively lowly beginnings, born in Newcastle to a 'whole-sale provision merchant'. And Nurse Ianthe Hodges, an ironmonger's daughter from Plaistow, East London became children's nurse to the Earl and Countess of Dudley. She spent many years travelling with her employer, as the Earl became successively Lord Lieutenant of Ireland and Governor-General of Australia.

Like Kate and Jessie Fox, several probationers were listed as daughters to 'gentlemen'; some had spent their early adulthood overseas attending music and art courses for their personal advancement, while others had already gained experience with children, travelling with family acquaintances as a mother's help. On the whole, the late nineteenth and early twentieth century Norlanders came from the upper working- and middle-classes. They were accomplished young ladies with aspirations beyond marriage and children of their own, who considered themselves a 'cut above' even before they had completed their training at Norland.

So far, Mrs Ward had not needed to advertise for probationers or employers, unlike her competitors. Reputation alone had built up an enviable client list, with a scattering of titled ladies mentioned among the well-to-do employers on the annual nurses' roll, but one ambition proved elusive until June 1902. In the summer *Quarterly*, finally Mrs Ward was able to report that the Institute had received royal recognition:

> *One little scrap of news will interest you. I had the honour of going to Buckingham Palace to see the Princess Henry of Prussia about a Norland nurse. She received me with the gracious courtesy which is always to be found amongst the truly noble – and subsequently Miss Sharman had the pleasure of taking two nurses for interview.*

This was the best form of advertisement; a simple statement of fact that Norlanders would pass on to other nannies. Nurse Beatrice Todd was the 'lucky girl' chosen by Princess Henry. Beatrice's previous engagement had been with a family in Lewes, on England's South Coast, but in one leap Mrs Ward had catapulted her into the Institute's highest profile position so far.

Princess Henry of Prussia, a grand-daughter of Queen Victoria, was married to Prince Heinrich of Prussia, the Kaiser's younger brother. Mrs Ward was quick to point out the pros and cons of royal employment: '"Lucky girl," I hear some of you saying, but you must not forget that a royal nursery is as much of a nursery as any other, only naturally there is more restriction and stricter discipline.'

The daughter of a clerk at the Ecclesiastical Commissions Office, Beatrice was thirty years old when Mrs Ward plucked her out to become nanny to royalty. Obviously, Mrs Ward thought she was mature enough, and sufficiently steady and discreet to be suitable for employment in an overseas royal household. Beatrice had qualified only six years earlier and now she was nanny to three Hesse princes aged thirteen, six and two. The family travelled frequently with an entourage fitting for a royal couple, which meant that for the next two years Beatrice would be constantly on the move.

Her job was particularly stressful because two of the princes were haemophiliacs and consequently required special medical care. Beatrice remained with the Hesse family for two years until the early death of the youngest boy, Prince Heinrich. The four-year-old fell whilst playing and hit his head, causing a brain haemorrhage. Because of his inherited disease, the flow of blood could not be staunched and the boy died the following day. For Beatrice, it was a terribly emotional end to her royal position. She had become particularly fond of the child, calling him 'my Baby', but with his death, a nurse was no longer required for the two older boys and her employment was terminated. She returned to England to care for her sister's family.

Mrs Ward was eager to publish royal and aristocratic news of every kind in the pages of the *Quarterly*. In 1902 Nurse Ianthe Hodges reported that she had another charge to care for. There had been a new addition to the Earl of Dudley's family, a boy named Roderick John, taking the number of children in Ianthe's nursery to four. In the same edition, Nurse Maud Seppings, who cared for a little girl in London, reported having witnessed the coronation that summer of King Edward VII and Queen Alexandra from a front-row seat on the House of Commons stand in Palace Yard. She described how pleased her charge was to have seen the King and Queen, and that the Lord Mayor's coach had reminded the child of the Cinderella fairy tale, leading her to ask, 'Where are the mice?'

Nurse Kate Fox wrote frequently and her letters were always afforded space in the *Quarterly*; they were superb publicity to the wider readership of Norland's increasingly high-profile credentials. Later, when Nurse Marian Burgess took up her position in the Russian Imperial household, her letters often took pride of place immediately after the principal's address.

At Christmas 1910, Mrs Ward boasted that 'in seventeen years of existence three Royal Employers have expressed a wish to visit the Institute'. Kate had already brought Princess Nicholas of Greece and her daughters to visit; they had been followed by Her Royal Highness The Grand Duchess of Hesse and her two sons. Due to a spring cleaning at the Institute, Mrs Ward had had to postpone a visit by Princess Alfonso of Orleans Bourbon, but a year later the Grand Duchess of Mecklenburg-Schwerin and Princess Maximilian of Baden, both of whom already employed Norlanders, visited the buildings in Pembridge Square.

Norland had achieved royal recognition for the quality of its children's nurses, but as the Institute's twenty-first anniversary approached, simultaneously Mrs Ward hoped to win official royal patronage. She anticipated that this mark of approval would set Norland above its competitors for good. However, although the list of royal employers continued to grow up until the declaration of war in 1914, official royal sponsorship never materialised.

As a woman of her time and class, Mrs Ward naturally looked to her superiors for elite approval of her Institute; everyone from charities to the capital's grocers sought royal patronage. Yet, Mrs Ward also encouraged philanthropy and a sense of social responsibility among her nurses. Whatever their background, they were entering a privileged lifestyle and she urged her nannies not to forget those less fortunate.

The daughter of a clerk in Holy Orders from Moseley, Nurse Maud Seppings completed her training in 1896. She so enjoyed her job as a children's nurse in London that she wanted to help other young women to experience the same joy too. In December 1897, Maud wrote to her sister nurses through the pages of the *Quarterly*, proposing a plan for a 'foundation fund'. She wished to allow a young girl who was less well-off than those who usually paid to train at Norland, to attend the year-long course free of charge. Maud hoped Norlanders would raise the money through subscription, donating a shilling every quarter. The first collection got off to a slow start with subscriptions raising only £5 7s 0d, but donations picked up and by December 1902 the fund had already financed one probationer's training, leaving a surplus of £12.

On leaving for a post in New York, Maud handed the reins to Nurse Jessie Fox, who became secretary and treasurer, and sent out another call for subscriptions so that they could support a candidate 'who will be a credit to the Institute, and who, though a lady, is unable to pay the fee'. Her sister Kate, then still working with the Ruspoli family, immediately donated £1. Kate had been one of the earliest proponents for the Foundation Fund, and even after her dismissal and return to temporary work in England, Kate remained one of the Fund's most generous contributors. She appreciated the privileged way of life to which her Norland training had opened doors and wished to support another young woman, 'who would perhaps otherwise not find a suitable occupation in life' to enjoy the same status.

However, the Foundation Fund had strict rules. After training at the Institute, a nurse had to remain on the Norland register in employment vetted by the Institute for at least three consecutive years. In summer 1904, Jessie reported that the most recent candidate for the bursary had failed to complete her three years and subsequently was repaying half of her fees by instalments. This boosted the Fund's coffers and Jessie advertised for another suitable young girl, aged over twenty-one, to be proposed as the next recipient. Even during her sojourn in Athens with her sister in early 1907, Jessie continued to remind subscribers to pay their dues and to cajole new Norlanders to sign up. The Fund was obviously a charitable venture close to the Fox sisters' hearts.

Dedication to charity also led the Principal, Miss Sharman, to set up an alternative to an assisted place at Norland. In 1904, Miss Sharman announced the 'Maiden Scheme' under which suitable young women, who could not afford the full course fees, which had now risen to £80, would work as domestic servants in the Institute buildings for a year in return for reduced fees of £12. Miss Sharman impressed upon her nurses that the success of the scheme would rely on their attitude towards the 'maidens':

> When you come to the Institute after Easter the door will be opened to you, and your meals served to you by a maiden in a special dress, who will tell you (if you ask her) that she is a Norland maiden, in the same social position as yourself, earning her training by undertaking for a year a portion of the domestic service of the house.

Four women were taken on in April 1904, distinguished by their different uniform, designed to be more suited to domestic work than the nursery. Miss Sharman had the best intentions in arranging to train this latest cohort of young women, but the casualties of her charitable actions were the existing domestic servants, who were given notice to leave, and Jessie Fox's Foundation Fund. By Christmas 1906, subscriptions to the Fund had fallen, and Jessie believed that nurses no longer saw the point in funding a probationer for free when the Maiden Scheme allowed reasonably affordable entry to Norland.

The scheme proved to be successful. After serving for a year as unpaid household servants, maidens were trained in the usual fashion and by 1913, Mrs Ward happily declared that 'some of the very best nurses' were former maidens. It was a title that never left them, a subtle social distinction with nurses writing to the *Quarterly* later in their careers still signing themselves 'maiden'.

The Foundation Fund did not suffer for long, however. As Jessie pointed out, 'in many cases a girl could enter as a probationer who could not do so as a "Maiden" for various good reasons'. Class distinctions were one reason. Some families would not allow their daughters to enter into domestic service under any circumstances, for whatever future rewards. However, for other girls even the reduced fees remained out of reach and the Foundation Fund continued to be their sole route to Norland training.

The role of nanny to the wealthy offered many perks, but it was not for shrinking violets. In the early 1900s, any Norlander would have fulfilled the definition of the 'Edwardian lady': caring and nurturing, yet robust, with stamina and an attitude that could command authority, whether confronted with recalcitrant children or non-English speaking natives. However, despite her background and training, a Norlander was compelled to remember her place as socially inferior to her employer. An early entry in Nurse Christine Tisdall's testimonial book described her as 'performing the duties of a servant in the spirit of a lady'. This was not an easy path to tread and sparked the first of many arguments to fill the pages of the *Quarterly*.

In March 1901, Nurse Maud Seppings started the trail of letters, entitled 'Difficulties'. Maud had been a Norlander for five years and she outlined 'three chief subjects of complaint'. Having spoken to fellow Norlanders, she felt nurses were 'overworked, despised and unappreciated'. She understood that her role did not usually require the long hours worked by household servants nor the same physical labour, but her daily tasks were still monotonous and without respite from them, she felt that a nurse could easily become 'strung up and worn out'. While other household staff might get Sundays off or a half-day during the week, Norlanders were expected to work for eleven consecutive months, generally with no designated day off, before earning a four-week holiday. Maud felt it was too much to ask and she longed for evenings out, a chance to 'get right away from... her usual surroundings'.

Being a middle-class lady in uniform was an anomaly until the First World War, when uniforms became all the rage, identifying the women who were 'doing their bit for king and country'. In 1900, although other nannies wore their own clothes, Norlanders were encouraged to wear their uniform. Some did wear 'private dress', but pride in their Institute led many to don a type of uniform attire that was 'neat and close fitting, with linen collar and cuffs, with a cape... hood lined with silk'. Yet, in her Norland uniform, Maud felt she was perceived as an equal by tradesmen, cabmen and railway officials; they despised her. She complained that 'no one treats me as a lady now'. Their uniform might set Norlanders apart from other nannies but in the eyes of other professions, it marked them out as someone's servant.

In the nursery, Maud missed the companionship of other women and wished dearly that her employer would 'feel a little tenderly' towards her and appreciate her efforts more:

> To me it is a strange thing that mothers and nurses are not the best of friends. If God had honoured me with the responsibility of a little soul to train for Him, I would search the world over till I found a woman to whom I could give all my love and confidence, and she who would use her life in the service of my child should be counted amongst my closest and dearest friends.

It was a sentiment that has had relevance throughout Norland's existence. Some Norlanders did enjoy a warm relationship with their employer, often chatting together as they put the children to bed, but the treatment of a children's nurse as an ordinary servant, as Maud described, had never been Mrs Ward's intention. From the beginning, Mrs Ward had set out to attract the very best clients to Norland and to educate for them the very nicest young women as nursery nurses. Yet, eradicating the misapprehension among employers that her nurses were average, untrained young girls was a tough mission.

As one employer explained to Mrs Ward, many believed that 'lady nurses' were nothing of the sort and only used that moniker in the hope of a better position or less menial work:

> One must also take into consideration the fact that a nurse's position is not a lady's position, and it is quite absurd for a nurse to expect to be treated like a visitor in the house where she lives, and except in exceptional cases, familiarity is apt to breed contempt.

This employer was also concerned about the cost to a nurse of wearing evening dress. If she were to be treated as a house-guest, then she would be expected to join the family at dinner and that required proper attire. Nurse Jessie Fox, Kate's sister, had deeper concerns. As she opined, an employer had friends with whom she could discuss her nanny, but a 'lady nurse' could neither talk to her employer nor turn to the servants for diversion. She reminded employers that 'because a lady becomes a nurse she does not cease to be a lady'.

At the time Jessie was on leave, having worked continually for fifteen months with a 'sweet, but very restless baby'. In the summer of 1902, Miss Sharman had enforced a three-month holiday in order for Jessie to recover her strength and it had given Jessie time to reflect on her comfortable background as the daughter of a gentleman and the isolated position in which she now found herself.

Despite Mrs Ward's lofty ambitions, being a children's nurse had become a lonely profession for many. Mrs Ward decided to close the discussion later that year, but by 1910 the subject had arisen again. A decade on, Norlanders had established an even more defined status. Miss Sharman laid down the rules on attending children's parties, at which she advised Norlanders they should not be expected to 'fend for themselves either in the servants' hall, bedrooms, or some other room in companionship with nurses not of her own class'. If a Norlander could not remain with her charge during a party, then the child should go unattended if old enough, in order not to put a Norlander in a difficult social predicament.

As Norland's reputation became cemented, hiring a Norland nurse could be a tricky endeavour, as rules were imposed on nurseries and often a Norlander requested at least two nursery maids to assist her. It was an expensive business, with experienced Norlanders commanding high salaries and newly qualified probationers asking £24 per annum. All Norlanders expected full board and private accommodation within their nurseries, ensuring that only the wealthiest families with the largest houses could afford to keep a Norlander in their home.

However, Mrs Ward had an idea that would mean a family might enjoy the benefits of having their children raised by Norland, without having to employ a nurse at home.

In the June 1902 *Quarterly*, she called her nurses' attention to a new feature of the magazine:

From henceforth we are starting paying advertisements, as we now print about 450 copies of each issue. I want all of you nurses to understand clearly why firms advertise their wares. They hope by so doing to increase their custom, so if you want to help to make the Quarterly *self-supporting, and in this way enable us to save money towards a "Norland Nursery", you must speak of advertisements and show them to your employers, their friends, and your own.*

For very proper reasons, Mrs Ward had succumbed to taking paid advertising. Her aim was to raise funds to set up a nursery at Pembridge Square to be staffed by trained Norlanders, in which student nurses could hone their skills with young children. Some nurses had attributed their failure to complete their probationary year to the fact that the course did not include adequate practical work with children; a short period on a children's hospital ward did not suffice.

The solution was for the Institute to open its own nursery:

For many years Miss Sharman and I have been aware that practical work in the nursery should follow on when the student had acquired some theoretical knowledge... But I had not funds at my command to enable me to risk more than one thing at a time.

In the past two years, finally the Institute had made a profit and Mrs Ward was able to buy the freehold of 7 Pembridge Square, two doors down from the Institute, which would house the nursery. However, the purchase and refurbishment had cost her £5,300 and she now appealed to her nurses and their employers for contributions, anything from 2s 6d for a nurse without private means to £1 for those on higher salaries.

Employers had already donated nursery furniture, but she asked for clothing too: 'Wealthy children also often have numbers of boots, winter coats, and other garments, out of which they grow long before they are worn out; these would be used to great advantage for the children of parents who can only pay our lowest fee.' Here was the acknowledgement that the Norland Nurseries were a cheaper option than employing a live-in nurse.

Numbers of children attending the nursery rose steadily, with some children staying for months at a time. Often, families posted to the colonies did not wish to take their children with them. While children of seven and upwards could be sent to boarding school, the youngsters would usually be lodged with a relation, but now they might attend Norland's nurseries where they would receive the very best care in their parents' absence.

Despite Mrs Ward's wish that her new facility should not be used as a dumping ground by parents unable to care for their own children, some couples used Norland's nursery when they wanted a holiday without their family or if their Norlander was on leave and they could not cope with their offspring without her. Charges were between £1 10s to £2 2s per week depending on the hours requested, and up to £100 per year for full-time care. Clothing and doctor's fees were extra.

In sad circumstances, the nurseries gave a home to infants whose mother had died in childbirth. Having met too late in life to start their own family, in the late 1890s Mr and Mrs Ward had adopted three orphaned children, among them a baby, but tragically the little girl died in the summer of 1900, aged three. Having spent all her adult life in the education of children and more recently the training of children's nurses, Mrs Ward launched herself into this new venture, taking personal control and frequently appearing in the nurseries to be with the children. When Nurse Ruth Dickie, a married Norlander, was widowed in 1910, Mrs Ward took Ruth and her daughter under her wing, employing her as nursery matron for the next twenty years, allowing Ruth to raise her daughter among the fee-paying children.

The nurseries became the perfect solution for families already considering employing a Norlander at home or those experiencing exceptional circumstances. After war broke out, the nurseries would become a haven for Belgian refugees and bereaved officers' families.

Norland offered other respite options for nurses and their charges. In 1894, Mrs Ward had built for herself a small country house in Bognor, Sussex, with a direct view to the sea. Three years later, in response to the proposed development of more houses, which would obscure her view, she purchased the land herself and built an estate of small cottages:

Knowing that our nurses often go to the sea to expensive lodgings and hotels, where the drainage is not all that could be desired, Mrs Ward mentions these small houses that are now being built... As they are being built by her own architect, the sanitary arrangements are perfect, and the houses fitted with every modern convenience.

Mrs Ward was an astute business woman. Now Norland nurses could holiday with their charges, surrounded by the trappings they were accustomed to at the Institute; Kate Fox took a four-month holiday in Bognor with the Greek princesses. Mrs Ward advertised her holiday homes every spring in the *Quarterly* in time for the nurses' summer breaks.

* * *

Living and working in London, as the majority of Norlanders did, they could not help but notice the parlous conditions in which much of the capital's working-classes lived. Church charities and other philanthropic organisations had long been struggling to cope with working-class poverty and sickness, and by the early 1900s, the government had finally decided to act.

The Edwardian era became a period of increasing state intervention in the health of the nation, the education of mothers in hygiene and nutrition, and the preparation of young girls for motherhood. As part of Norland's charitable works, many nurses felt they too had an obligation towards the city's poor and, in 1906 Nurses Jessie Smeeton and Rose Greenleaf founded the Norland Nurses' Mission Fund, 'to try to give a few poor children a better chance of becoming healthy'.

The Fund aimed to raise monies through subscriptions to pay for a Norland nurse to work in one of the new day nurseries established by charitable organisations and local councils, where infants from one month to five years were cared for while their mothers worked. This new position was not for the faint-hearted or those accustomed to luxury nurseries. Having raised sufficient money for a year's salary, Rose and Jessie advertised for their first 'Mission Nurse' to fill a post in Hammersmith. The description of the infants she would care for was enough to put off even the hardiest of Norlanders:

We must never forget that in addition to those infants who die under one year old, there are also many who survive the mal-nutrition and careless up-bringing of their infancy, though it is rare to find amongst these survivors many who could be called healthy specimens. Some of these die in childhood, others blessed with a larger amount of stamina, perhaps reach maturity, burdened with weakened bodies and enfeebled minds.

Undaunted by the prospect of being surrounded by such sickly babies and toddlers, or living among the working-classes, in 1907 Nurse Marion Rounthwaite became the Mission Fund's first nurse. She was a London girl, the daughter of an engineer from Wandsworth, who had completed her training in 1902. Her mission was to instil in the children in her care the inspiration to rise above their surroundings and background to become healthy, useful citizens; not to become, as the advertisement suggested, 'men and women dragging through life, wearied out with the struggle, not enjoying work or amusement'.

Later that year, Marion contracted typhoid and was forced to take several months off work. So far the Mission Fund had attracted Mrs Ward's and Miss Sharman's support from a distance, but at Christmas 1907 Miss Sharman wrote to her nurses, imploring one of them to replace Marion. It was an opportunity to gain extensive experience with babies and she hoped that someone might consider filling the role for one year, long enough to learn much but not too long to become exhausted.

A new day nursery at South Acton had been established by a women's charity and was opening imminently and Norland wanted to be represented conspicuously in this new facility. Nurse Maud Daviniere volunteered her services. Working from 8am to 9pm, Maud's day was a constant round of bathing, feeding and changing the babies of London's washerwomen, who toiled in the nearby laundries. Norland employers had funded eight out of the twelve cots at the nursery and provided furniture for Maud's private accommodation. It was not the life she may have envisaged when she entered Norland for training in 1895, but Maud found the work fulfilling and would remain at South Acton for several years.

Meanwhile, Norland's mission work had come to the notice of London society ladies who organised charitable works. Muriel, Viscountess Helmsley was a staunch advocate for day nurseries and at the *Daily Mail's* 1908 'Ideal Home Exhibition', she invited Miss Sharman to organise a crèche at Olympia during the two-week event. Every morning, working mothers brought their babies to the hastily-erected model nursery to be weighed, bathed and dressed in clothes donated by the Duchess of Marlborough, after which they ate three good meals, slept in perfect rows of cots and awaited collection in the early evening.

The stand was so popular that the Norlanders on duty had to 'enlist the aid of three stalwart policemen to move the crowd on'. The nurses involved were quizzed on how to bring up children, the best foods to offer, sleep times, development milestones, as well as the perennial maternal competition over teeth:

We explained the probable reasons why John, aged eight months, had no teeth, and in the next breath expressed our admiration that Mary, aged only four months, should already have cut her first without any trouble.

Appearing on the public stage, sponsored by titled ladies and demonstrating their expertise through benevolent work was the perfect arena for Mrs Ward's nurses. The Mission Fund founders Rose Greenleaf and Jessie Smeeton had their fingers on the pulse of childcare reform, and Norland was now leading on both private and public fronts.

As well-educated young Edwardian women with a nurturing spirit, it is not surprising that Norlanders could marry their personal ambition with a desire to do good. Living in the wealthiest households and often working for politicians' families, many were exposed to conversations ranging from the state of the nation to the day's proceedings at Westminster, and the growing campaign for universal suffrage. What they might have overheard and the discussions they had among themselves could not fail to produce a cohort of young women with strong and well-informed opinions.

Mrs Ward's personal ambition to introduce bright young women into the country's nurseries also stemmed from a desire to empower these women, to provide them with a career and consequent independence. She refrained from advocating her support openly for the expanding women's suffrage movement, but occasionally a hint of her endorsement seeped through in her letters published in the *Quarterly*.

During a Norland nurses' 'at home' evening at Pembridge Square on 31 January 1907, Miss Sharman had asked what those attending thought of women's suffrage. One nurse had responded that 'it was not in her line', while Rose Greenleaf, who was doing so much to alleviate the pain of poverty in the day nurseries, took umbrage at the thought and declared that women should certainly not win the vote.

On a visit to South Acton, a group of Norland probationers had reported:

> *Our quest led us through a region of fried-fish studios and reeking gas jets, we arrived cheerfully outside our destination, to be greeted with hoots and cries from a crowd of small boys "Suffragettes"! Some of us quickly denied this accusation, thus greatly astonishing them. They said, "we thought all women wanted a vote!"*

With so many prominent ladies supporting the women's suffrage movement, the association was not necessarily to be shunned. Some Norlanders strongly supported the cause and at the Hyde Park Procession held on 13 June 1908, Nurse Ruth Yates walked proudly with another nurse in full Norland uniform, along with her employer. They marched among thousands of women from all levels of society and Ruth noted the crowds cheering along Embankment and outside the Albert Hall. She was in high spirits, protesting peaceably for a right she considered she had earned.

At Kensington Gardens, Ruth's little girl charge and her father joined them. Obviously, they had had equally as good a time: 'Her face was decorated with chocolate, her white gloves were in deep mourning and from under her coat appeared an overall! The chocolate we partly effaced, but the gloves, which I hastily removed, have never recovered.'

Ruth was brought back to the reality of her era: that it was seen as a woman's duty to nurture the family while men went about their work and could not be relied upon to care for a small child for a few hours without mishap. However, with true Norland optimism, Ruth concluded: 'with smiling countenances we arrived at our destination, feeling we had well earned our tea and our vote'.

As the suffrage movement gathered momentum, increasingly Norlanders sympathetic to the cause cast aside caution and wrote freely on the topic of emancipation. Nurse Muriel Bois was an ardent supporter of the movement, selling the suffrage weekly paper *The Vote* in the marketplace in Shrewsbury, where she cared for a vicar's children. Muriel held strident views on women's ability to change society, once they were allowed to do so:

> *There is no sphere in life where woman's influence is not needed by the world, and the world will be all the better and sweeter for it... As for the political world, I think the influence of women will be a cleansing stream. That is the reason why some men do not want you in politics. [Men]* know *that once women do get the vote, the wrongs and injustices will have to be exposed before being set right.*

Muriel's opinions were warmly received by Mrs Ward and Miss Sharman. They both felt strongly about women's suffrage, but had declined to influence their nurses by offering their own thoughts on the matter. However, they now confessed that they too were avid readers of *The Vote*, which they bought weekly.

In 1911, the government's National Insurance Act became law and stirred up a hornet's nest at Norland. Every worker who earned less than £160 per annum was obliged to insure him or herself, at a cost of 4d per week, with their employer making a 3d contribution and the government a further 2d. This allowed workers to claim sick pay and also financed the beginnings of a national health service, providing the workforce with subsidised access to a doctor when necessary.

Six years previously, Nurse Marian Burgess had wished she had insurance against loss of wages through sickness when she suffered a bout of 'flu over Christmas 1904, forcing her to take five weeks away from her nursery. It had cost her dearly and she had proposed that Norland should buy an insurance policy into which nurses could pay an annual premium and enjoy the benefits if they fell ill whilst at work. Nannies were prone to infectious diseases due to the nature of their work with small children and Marian hoped that an insurance policy would alleviate a nurse's worries if she became ill.

With a further Act making provision for limited unemployment benefit, administration of the new laws caused a tremendous headache for Norlanders. Many received their wages direct from the Institute and they wished to know if Mrs Ward intended to stop their National Insurance contributions at source. Others, paid by their employers, were now in the unenviable position of requesting that their contributions be deducted, as well as ensuring that their employers' contributions were made. As with most new bills, not everyone was behind the new system and many employers either refused to adhere to the rules or failed to increase the monies they paid to the Institute to cover the extra expense.

Mrs Ward was far from pleased at the position in which she found herself and her argument against the new Acts was rooted firmly in women's rights:

> *Many of you are intensely "Anti", or against us women who wish to have a word in the making of the laws we are asked to obey, and you therefore will not see any injustice in blindly paying every tax imposed on your private earnings. But I do not see why I or any other Employer should be turned into an un-paid Tax Collector, for by law women are not eligible for the post.*

She advocated resistance to the new law until women won the vote, and in the meantime she ordered Norland's staff to desist from calculating the new payments or helping nurses with their queries. Eventually, the Institute yielded like every other employer but Mrs Ward had shown her colours, leaving her nurses fully apprised of her position on women's votes.

However, among supporters of the suffrage movement, resistance to laws enforced by men was not to be confused with socialist politics or the formation of an international sisterhood. Largely, the ladies of the Institute were supporters of the hierarchical society from which they benefited. Tradesman's daughter Nurse Cicely Colls was a lone voice promoting sisterhood and socialism, using the universal wearing of the pinafore among women as a metaphor for female equality. In Cicely's view, Socialists were not 'twentieth century iconoclasts' and neither were they 'impracticable Utopians, selfish brutes or a danger to their country', but 'eager workers for social reform'. To Cicely's mind, reform was needed mostly with regard to the condition of working women: 'can you watch the ignorance and drudgery of the women, in unhealthy, stuffy habitations, and not be a Socialist?'

In the early 1900s, Cicely had spent her career working mainly in the industrial north and Scotland, where unemployment and poverty were rife. The effect of both hit women and children hardest, and Cicely was convinced solidarity among women of all classes was the only way their futures might be improved. She received no replies to her letter.

In the first decade of the twentieth century, Norland had found its feet, with a loyal, enviable client list and a reputation for superb childcare. The Institute was now sufficiently well-established for its own traditions to take shape. Since 1897, some nurses had campaigned for a badge of recognition for faithful service. Nurse Florence Newman, an early student at Norland, wished to have a badge with a motto that she could wear at all times, even when not in uniform. Kate Fox was a firm supporter of the idea too, desiring a badge to be worn 'in such a conspicuous place that everyone may see it'.

Membership of the Norland sisterhood and recognition of their status was important to the nurses, and at last in 1902 a Norland Badge was introduced; it came with a set of rules. In return for five years' service, three of which to be with one employer, a nurse could earn her Norland Badge, a small silver and enamel item, designed without sharp edges that might injure young charges. The Badge would be a free gift from Norland to the nurse and, such was the prestige surrounding its award, that Mrs Ward hoped it 'should remain an heirloom in your family'.

At the first distribution of Badges in June 1902, Rose Greenleaf received hers for seven years' service in a single household; Ianthe Hodges was given one for five years with the Countess of Dudley; and Kate Fox and Maud Seppings were among those who had worked for three years for one employer. The ceremony was attended by the Earl and Countess of Dudley, among other eminent employers close to the Institute. At the end, Rose Greenleaf presented Mrs Ward with a silver salvo 'as a token of affection and gratitude from 250 nurses' and Miss Sharman received a gold badge from Mrs Ward for ten years' loyal devotion. If Norlanders were not distinctive enough around London's parks and British cities, now the upper echelons of the Institute could wear a badge by which all other Norlanders and employers could recognise them wherever in the world they travelled.

From the Institute's earliest days, Norlanders had found posts abroad and they were always keen to share their foreign experiences. One of Norland's most adventurous nannies spent 1897 in Java, caring for three children under seven. Their British nursery routine was turned upside down by the climate, which required twice-daily baths and outdoor activities at dawn and dusk. But the majority of Norlanders who ventured overseas in the first decade of the twentieth century, worked in Europe and the British colonies.

In 1900, Nurse Kate Fox had described her travels around Europe with the Ruspolis to her fellow nurses in the *Quarterly*. She led a busy and privileged life. Nurse Ada Bagenal's employers had left behind their quiet corner of England to spend four months over the winter in Dresden, Germany, enjoying sleigh rides in the snow and sight-seeing, something Ada would never otherwise have experienced. Ada's family was living in the centre of the city: 'Quite close to the Grosse Garten, which is the Hyde Park of Dresden; it contains a large Zoological Garden and there is a long avenue of trees, where one constantly meets the King and Queen taking a walk.'

As in London, Norlanders frequented the parks abroad, but Ada had advertised the greatest attraction Mrs Ward's Institute could offer – a chance to brush shoulders with the celebrities of the period and to see the world. This was precisely what Nurse Helen Braycocks was doing on a round-the-world trip. Helen had set off in mid-1899 with her employers for a three-year world tour. She described the 'moist suffocating heat' during her journey through the Red Sea and a terribly rough passage across the Indian Ocean. With everyone on board ill, the captain arranged for the ladies to sleep on deck on one side of the ship and Helen parked her baby charge's pram alongside her own deck-cot.

By October, Helen was in Yokohama, Japan, and she wrote describing agricultural methods with fields 'smaller than most of our allotment pieces' cultivated 'with exquisite care and neatness'. She was certainly an Edwardian woman abroad; her descriptions betray her thoroughly colonial attitude towards foreigners. Having visited a temple, she noted: 'it is a weird sight to see their figures prone on the ground, mumbling away' and the Japanese mode of dress reminded her of illustrations in a children's picture book: 'all the world like rag dolls decked out in rainbow colours'. Seeing a Japanese man wearing a European-style hat was 'too funny for words'.

After Japan, Helen and her family set off for Manila where she saw a fleet of American war ships in the harbour. Helen had arrived in the midst of the Philippines' struggle for independence from their American masters. A month later, disembarking at Sydney in January 1900, Helen was in time to see Australian troops departing for the Transvaal, colonial soldiers heading off to fight in the Boer War. At times Norlanders were eye-witnesses to great historical events.

However, life was hard for Helen, as she was constantly on the move and coping with a toddler, ants, cockroaches, mosquitoes and local food. In her letter to Mrs Ward, she confessed that travelling with small children was ill-advised, but she was 'making the most of it, and am extremely grateful at having had the offer, for both in respect of my work and the strange lands I have visited'. Apart from being a high-class lady's maid, there were few other careers for women that would offer travel, good pay and full board and keep.

Helen was still travelling at Christmas 1901, when the *Quarterly* published its list of Norlanders' whereabouts, but by the following year Helen was no longer on the employment register; instead she appeared in the marriages column, having wed Walter Edward Elward in Japan during that year. Their liaison had begun in 1900 during Helen's stop there en route to Australia and endured, despite the intervening years spent in Tasmania and Ceylon. In July 1904, Helen gave birth to a baby boy. The new family remained in Japan, but Helen did not lack for female company, as another Norlander was employed at the British embassy in Tokyo.

Nurse Martha Butterfield had cared for two little girls in England for a year before travelling to Japan to live with their parents. She had enjoyed the long sea passage, although she had found Port Said 'disappointing, so squalid, smelly and dusty'. She had passed through the Suez Canal at night and regretted not seeing the desert, but the small town of Suez at dawn had been dazzling. Like Helen, she had slept on deck, although she added a detail Helen had omitted: the Lascars washed down the decks every morning at 6am and if one was not up and dressed in time 'you may have a salt water bath without the trouble of preparing for it'. Martha too complained of the incompetence of native servants, the heat and difficulties of caring for children in alien circumstances. It was a thread that linked all the nurses' correspondence whether in strange lands, colonial territories or closer to home in Europe.

Writing to the *Quarterly*, one nurse shared tips for treatment of recurrent illness crossing the Atlantic on her way to Jamaica with a sickly baby, while another described the catastrophic earthquake that hit the island in 1907. In Tunis, Nurse Ethel Sadler had visited the Arab and Jewish quarters of the city, the Palace of the Bey and had even dropped in on the prison before departing for Malta. Travelling to California, Nurse Dorothy Candler described her arrival at New York, having her baggage checked and finding Cook's agent, the official who would provide her with her onward travelling arrangements by train. Dorothy remarked that she was tended in her Pullman berth by 'a black waiter', something that disquieted her, but it did not detract from her joy at seeing Niagara Falls and Lake Erie. She changed trains numerous times before arriving in Los Angeles.

At no point in her description did Dorothy mention experiencing any nervousness at being so far from home; nor did she hint at anxiety about missing a connection or travelling unchaperoned surrounded by strangers, or even trepidation at working with a new family whom she had never met.

Newly qualified Nurse Viola Josa was eager that her charges should have a firm grasp of world geography. With the tales the Norland nurses shared through their correspondence and the stories they carried with them from nursery to nursery, geography was a subject easily taught through their personal experience alone.

After twenty years of hard work, Norlanders had spread around the globe. However, the exploits of some nannies closer to home in Europe also caught everyone's attention. The opportunity to live in Europe and work with families whose customs were similar to British ones, had enticed many nurses. Nannies to royalty, Kate Fox and Marian Burgess worked at the furthest reaches of Europe, but in cities across France, Germany and Switzerland Norlanders could be found in small groups. They walked their charges in the parks; they met for tea and birthday parties; when given time off they dined together or spent a Saturday exploring the sights.

Mrs Ward could not have asked for a better result from the venture she had begun two decades previously. There had been times when she had feared for Norland's finances. In September 1901, she had written to the nurses:

> In no sense is this Institution a charity, and, during my lifetime, I am most anxious that it should be self-supporting. In order to establish ourselves here, a great responsibility fell on my shoulders, the weight of which we hope to remove if our numbers keep up during the next five years.

Within the five years stipulated, Mrs Ward had managed to recoup her investment and had put Norland into profit. She ploughed the monies back into her project improving the facilities and hiring more staff as the Institute expanded. By the twenty-first anniversary of the Institute in 1913, Norland had certainly come of age. Its rivals were barely able to compete. Mrs Ward attracted the very best candidates, trained them and was able to keep them in well remunerated employment through her multifarious network of titled ladies, the well-to-do and Norland's highly visible mission work in Acton and latterly Bethnal Green.

The September 1913 edition of the *Quarterly* was sub-titled 'the Souvenir Number', stretching to twenty-four pages detailing Norland's history and achievements. It also included anecdotes from the early days, such as when one nurse probationer had insisted upon being escorted from home by a maid, rather than risk being seen walking through London unchaperoned. These quaint stories proved to Mrs Ward's nurses working at the front line of childcare around the globe, that they were the stuff twentieth century Norland was made of: robust, authoritative, well-educated, independent young women facing whatever the world threw at them. Custard, tantrums, disobedient staff – nothing phased a Norland nurse decked out in her demure uniform, badge pinned neatly above her apron on her left shoulder, bonnet strings ironed and hair swept tightly into a bun at the nape of her neck. She was an impenetrable edifice, commanding respect wherever she travelled.

Yet, war was brewing in Europe, Norland's core for noble employment for its best nannies. When war was declared in August 1914, of over 500 qualified nurses, 54 Norlanders were working on mainland Europe. During the weeks of increasing diplomatic tension and in the months and years after, as the conflict flared into the horror of the Great War, Norlanders risked their lives, and in some cases those of their charges, to return safely home to British shores.

What they described of these hazardous journeys and their experiences throughout the conflict brought the war to Norland's doorstep. Often employed by enemy families, caring for children they loved deeply, they would be cut off from safe routes home often working within striking distance of the theatres of war. With their working lives and privileges threatened by the conflict, their collective wartime experience was unique, like that of no other group of young women in Britain at the time.

Chapter 2

Declaration of War

M rs Ward's desire to place her nannies in the best households and export British nursery culture overseas had been successful, but her achievements were about to have devastating repercussions for the very women she had trained. At Christmas 1913, the Norland *Quarterly* once again published its annual list of nannies, detailing their employers' addresses and grouping them according to length of service. Business was good; among the qualified nurses on the register, three held the coveted blue enamelled Badge awarded to those who had served for fifteen years in a single post. Including the probationers, total figures had swelled to nearly 700 nannies and trainees, of whom 102 were employed abroad.

The spring of 1914 saw a heat wave spread across Europe. Nurse Margaret Evans had recently returned to Paris from a Norland tea party organised at Easter in Saint Legier by two Norlanders working there. Margaret described how the party had started with a walk in picturesque surroundings on the lower slopes of the mountains: 'To our left the snow-capped peaks, to our right the lake of Geneva, gray, misty and peaceful.' Afterwards, they retired to view the nursery where one of the nannies worked: 'The white paint and polished floor and dainty paper appealing at once to some of us who live much in hotels.'

They were seven in total and had 'come from all parts of Europe', some crossing borders to get there. As single ladies of independent means, they had travelled first class by train, spending their few days off together and using the Norland network to base themselves in places where they could do some sight-seeing. They were professional women who certainly did not require a chaperone, and each one had taken a position on the Continent in order to see something of the world. At the time, it was usual for young unmarried English girls to travel in Europe accompanied by a relation, but to travel unescorted, to organise their own meeting place and entertainment was particularly adventurous. Before they dispersed, they made plans for further meetings throughout the capitals of Europe. However, the freedom these young women enjoyed to traverse the Continent was to be measured in weeks.

In Britain that April, the Children's Welfare Exhibition took place at Olympia and the Norland Institute had taken a stand at the show. Norlanders and prospective employers gathered round to view handicrafts and home-made toys and listen to probationer nannies reading the latest faerie stories to small groups of children sitting at their feet. Across London, the weather was dry and warm. Norland Nurses walked their charges in Hyde Park, swapping gossip and news on their daily constitutionals.

Working Norlanders lived an Edwardian 'Mary Poppins' existence bound by the confines of their nurseries and the proper upbringing of their charges. Their world revolved around the Norland mission, scrutinising the accounts of its fund, negotiating salaries with employers and discussing what books to read in the nursery. They worked hard, but the comfortable, secluded position of the ladies of the households in which they were employed rubbed off. There was no inkling that war was approaching within the pages of the Norland *Quarterly*.

In 1914, Norlanders could be found worldwide – Marian Burgess in Russia looked after the Kirill Imperial offspring; Kate Fox, Constance Sadler and Kathleen Wanstall cared for German royal children; Irene Collenette worked for the Infanta Beatrice in Spain; and many others were employed by lesser aristocrats and private wealthy families across Europe. There were Norlanders in all Britain's dominions too, a handful in Central and South America, with May Hasler and a growing circle of nurses in the United States.

Overseas positions were sought after, most particularly those with aristocratic families. To gain employment within such a household, a Norlander required several years' experience. The route to this most coveted appointment usually began with a position in a middle-class family, then perhaps a move to a titled household in London, before being recommended for overseas and aristocratic employment. The birth of a second royal baby would require another nurse, and a second Norlander would arrive to care for the newborn, staying until the child aspired to a tutor or governess. Some royal households had two or three Norlanders in their nurseries, working alongside nursery maids who served the Norlanders and carried out the more menial tasks. Their assistance allowed the nanny to be totally absorbed in raising her charge. Over the years, the child and their nurse formed a special bond, perhaps closer than their relationship with their royal parents.

When Britain declared war on Germany on 4 August 1914, the lives of Norland nurses working overseas were plunged into mayhem. These women were intensely loyal to their employers, but their situation in many families rapidly became untenable. The declaration of war forced a dilemma that Norlanders' training could never have prepared them for: stay and risk their lives, hoping their employers could protect them or leave the children they loved. For women with a strong maternal instinct and the physical and emotional care of young children at the forefront of their training, the wrench must have been excruciating.

Norlanders mature enough to gain the best overseas positions had no previous experience of war. They were not old enough to remember the Franco-Prussian War of 1870, and no Norland nurses were in South Africa during the Boer War. In 1914, fear of the unfolding conflict and the prospect of separation from their own families proved too strong for most Norlanders, who decided to return home. Worrying news from Germany and Austria filtered back to the Institute through letters forwarded from nurses working in neutral countries.

Miss Sharman attempted to calm increasingly alarmed Norlanders, writing in the Christmas 1914 *Quarterly*:

> *We have found out that they are "safe and well" – very bare news, but reassuring. For your comfort I can confidently say, that I believe every Englishwoman established in a good post in Germany or Austria when war broke out will be as safe with her Employers now as she was in peaceful times.*

Miss Sharman's sentiments were not shared by a large proportion of the British public, however. By Christmas 1914, any hope of the war drawing to a close had faded, and as casualty figures increased, so did hatred of all things German.

Many well positioned Londoners and employers of Norlanders had long-term friendships with prominent Germans living in the capital. Prime Minister Asquith and his wife were frequent guests at the household of naturalised German banker Sir Edgar Speyer in Grosvenor Street, and Margot Asquith, on hearing the declaration of war, hurried to the German embassy to offer a last gift to the departing ambassador. Miss Sharman was not alone in clinging to a notion of German friendship and a mutual cultural heritage, which she hoped would endure the dislocation of war:

> *I would like to say that the Germans have always shown themselves to be considerate, generous and just as Employers of our Norlanders, many of whom have spent several happy useful years in German homes.*

News of several nurses working on the Continent had already been received during autumn 1914. Nurse Mignon Miller, employed by the Hungarian Countess Apponyi in Brussels, had fled with the family to safety in Hungary. Mignon had been unwell but the letter forwarded by her father gave no further details, except that the journey had been terrible. Mignon was on the mend and was reported to be nursing wounded soldiers – presumably Hungarians.

However, other Norlanders whose employers had a better understanding of the increasing international tensions had been able to plan ahead. Nurse Grace Taylor, working for Countess de Borchgrave in Brussels, left her post early and returned to England safely, bringing with her one of her 'little charges' and caring for the child in her own home.

Nurse Grace Welch had only just begun a nine-week temporary post in a small seaside resort, Heiligendamm on the German Baltic coast, when her employer thought it best for her to leave. She started her journey home on 1 August, the day Germany declared war on Russia:

For a few days past there had been a feeling of uneasiness and anxiety, and the first signs of mobilisation, but everyone thought these were preparations of peace rather than the heralds of war. Nowhere did I see any signs of hostility towards English people.

Somehow, Grace mistook mobilisation for 'preparations for peace'. Her sheltered upbringing, coupled with her Norland training and Mrs Ward's fixation on placing her girls with high-profile German households may have distorted Grace's interpretation of events. However, Grace was in for a shock when she started her return trip, as the train from Heiligendamm to Hamburg was crowded with people 'hurrying back from their holidays'. Yet, the wording of Grace's letter gives no hint that her fellow travellers might have been dashing for home, possibly to foreign countries, getting out before the war began in earnest.

Her train was delayed and the connection from Hamburg to Flushing (now Vlissingen) gave her only forty minutes in which to engage a porter to transfer her baggage. Frustrated at sitting outside the station in an immobile train for half an hour watching precious minutes tick by, finally she alighted on to the platform, where she found the station in chaos with luggage and people everywhere and the station officials overwhelmed. Grace had been unable to book her passage all the way, and she had expected to find a Thomas Cook agent waiting for her with tickets for her onward journey, but in the mêlée Cook's man failed to meet her.

Unfortunately, Grace did not speak German and no one around her seemed to speak English. By chance she bumped into another English woman, 'Miss H', who had been travelling in Germany and could speak the language. They decided to 'worry through' together. With no trains available until 11.30pm, they made their way to a *pension* to eat, before returning to the station to hunt for their missing luggage. It was even more crowded and now Grace observed there were military personnel everywhere. They gave a 'large bribe' to a porter to help locate their baggage and he advised them to return the following day at 6am.

They rose early on Sunday morning and were at the station punctually, but there was no sign of the previous porter. They promised to pay in gold if another porter would help them locate their bags, but they had little success. Now Grace noticed that the soldiers were armed. While searching shed after shed for their bags, Grace's Norland uniform proved useful, as German officials allowed her access behind the barricades, believing her uniform to be that of a military nurse. After two days in Hamburg searching for luggage and trying to reserve seats on a train, the British Consul advised the two women to leave immediately, otherwise it would be a further ten days before he could secure them passage.

It was now 2 August and Germany had been at war with Russia for twenty-four hours. In Britain, the government was wavering but everything pointed strongly to their joining the combat in support of France and Russia. The British Consul in Hamburg was outwardly hopeful that civilian trains would continue to run, although for the meantime they were commandeered for military use, manoeuvring German troops into position for their impending march through Belgium.

Forced to abandon their luggage and travel with only the clothes they stood up in, Grace and Miss H boarded an extremely crowded train: 'Which became more so as we got nearer the frontier. It was interesting to notice the people in the various compartments, all sorts of nationalities.'

They would witness violence on the way home. Close to the Dutch border at Wesel, the railway crossed the Rhine by bridge. In the carriage next to Grace and Miss H, the authorities discovered seven men who had planned to blow up the train in order to disable the bridge: 'They were taken from the train at Wesel station, and were shot, I suppose. In consequence of this, we were delayed at Wesel some little time while the train was patched up.' Grace's chilling brevity in describing this intended act of violence and the perpetrators' summary punishment reflects her Edwardian indignation at the audacity of men she assumed were lower class, who had attempted to carry out an act of terrorism.

The onward journey only afforded the two ladies standing room in the corridor, with a group of Englishmen chivalrously arranging their luggage into makeshift seating for them. Between Hamburg and Flushing in Holland, soldiers with fixed bayonets patrolled the train, arresting suspicious individuals. There was no restaurant car and any food they might have expected at the stations was already earmarked for troop trains. Arriving in Flushing at 6am on Tuesday, 4 August, they had suffered thirty hungry hours, but soon they were safely on board a Dutch boat tucking in to poached eggs, bread and butter and tea. It was a glorious morning to cross the Channel, although very cold on deck where Grace found herself a chair: 'Much signalling took place before we were allowed to enter Queensboro' harbour. It was delightful to feel oneself safe on English soil once more!'

Grace took a train to London and arrived at 9pm, two hours before the British Government's ultimatum to Germany expired. By the time she went to bed, Britain was at war and Sir Winston Churchill had cabled the British fleet: 'Commence hostilities against Germany.'

Not far behind Grace, also heading for the Netherlands coast was Nurse Kate Fox. After her dismissal from the Greek royal family, Kate had been taking short engagements with titled employers. She had arrived in Germany at Baden-Baden from Paris on 24 July with her charges and their mother: 'On 25th we heard some talk of war with Russia, the waiters of the hotel where I was staying with one of my charges being very excited. Many of them had to leave.'

Earlier that day, Austria-Hungary had severed diplomatic links with Serbia, whose greatest ally was Russia. Immediately, the Imperial might of the Russian Army began to mobilise with the intention of intervening on Serbia's behalf. It was not yet open conflict, but Kate's hotel waiters, anticipating war, were heading home to fight for their mother country. Kate also witnessed early German preparations for war; horses were requisitioned and food for civilians was restricted.

She had been in Baden-Baden for ten days when her employer summoned her to the sanatorium where she was staying and instructed Kate to pack because they were leaving that night. Relieved to be allowed to depart, she packed hastily. They had planned a long stay at the spa at Baden-Baden and the family had not travelled light, but thanks to Kate's sensible Norland training she knew to take only items for their immediate needs. She envisaged returning for their belongings in a few weeks, unable to comprehend a war lasting any longer. Kate had barely finished packing when disappointment came with a telephone call from her employer: there was no more room on the last safe train out.

On Monday, 3 August, with no hope of imminent departure Kate and the family were forced to take refuge with the Red Cross, which had taken control of the sanatorium. News reached them two days later that Britain had declared war on Germany the previous evening. Horror stories filtered through of those who had tried, and failed, to escape. After a fortnight behind the walls of the sanatorium, the Grand Duchess of Baden used her influence and a Greek doctor arrived. He had obtained permission from the German authorities to escort a party of foreign 'invalids' out of the country.

They must have been a conspicuous party: an aristocratic lady, Kate in her nanny uniform, the two children and two South African ladies along with their maid accompanied by the Greek doctor, all looking distinctly healthier than invalids from a sanatorium. Kate's employer took her aside to explain the risks and offered her what she considered a safer alternative. If Kate tried to leave Germany, she believed that she risked being shot as a spy, so her employer offered to guarantee Kate's safety if she wished to stay in Baden-Baden. This was the start of the war and anything was conceivable, even the execution of an English children's nurse. Understandably, Kate chose to continue with the Greek doctor's party.

On Sunday, 16 August, in broad daylight the party of women and children climbed into two German chauffeured cars. They drove first to Heidelberg, where they stopped for lunch. Their German mechanic showed their official papers every time an armed soldier confronted them at a roadblock. Then they travelled 110 miles to Bad-Ems for the night. They were refused accommodation at the first hotel they tried, because a number of military men were already staying there and the hotelier did not want trouble.

A keen-eyed resident had immediately offered the doctor 12,000 marks to destroy their passports, thus preventing their departure. Scared, the doctor swiftly moved his party on, instructing the women to destroy all their papers and letters identifying their English nationality and affiliations. Kate became particularly anxious when her testimonial book, her precious record of all her employment positions, was posted off by the doctor. She had no idea whether or not she would see it again.

By 17 August, the German Army was fighting on two fronts. In Belgium, the Battle of the Frontiers had started and this was also the first day of the Battle of Stallupönen on the Russian front. In Dusseldorf, one of several German cities supplying material to both Eastern and Western fronts, Kate saw roads blocked with masses of troops and wagons carrying beds and bedding for the Red Cross as casualties mounted. She recalled gun carriages having to be drawn aside to allow her small party to pass and described 'a beehive' of soldiers only a few miles from the frontier.

While Grace, whose journey had started in Heiligendamm on the coast, had not experienced any hostility towards the English, in Dusseldorf Kate was directed by the Greek doctor not to speak for fear of giving away her nationality. Hatred towards the English was rife in the city and they could not afford to stay a moment longer than necessary. While the ladies rested, the Greek doctor tried to find them alternative transport. He had heard that the mob was firing on any English travellers who arrived at the frontier. To leave by car would be fraught with roadblocks, troops on the move and too many people who might ask probing questions.

Finally, the doctor bribed a Dutch boat captain to take them by river. They crossed at Wesel, but it was a very different experience from Grace's border crossing. Now a fortnight into the war, security was much tighter and customs officials were actively searching for British spies: 'The doctor turned to me and said "If we get through the next ten minutes we are lucky and I shall be surprised; whatever you do don't speak".'

The Customs House officials checked all passports and divided up the passengers – Americans to one end of the boat, who appeared jubilant 'as they knew they were perfectly safe'; the English, French and Russians – the enemy – to the other. Then military personnel boarded the boat. Kate watched silently as the soldiers arrested five Englishmen, one with a German wife and child, who were en route to England. The mother and child were turned back and the husband was taken ashore as a suspected spy. Another Englishman was also led away, with his distraught English wife and two children remaining on board.

To Kate, a children's nurse who had only days before suffered her own farewell parting in the nursery and whose memories of her departure from her beloved Greek princesses remained raw, her nerves were fraying and the cries of the two-year-old boy must have brought her close to betraying herself. Her Edwardian stiffness kept her emotions in check as she listened to the toddler weeping: "The soldiers have taken Daddy; I want Daddy."

At Nijmegen the boat pulled into port and they rushed to board a train to The Hague. It was 19 August and garbled reports of who had declared war on whom had finally reached Kate's little party. As they entered Holland, the travellers feared that the rumour of Britain's declaration of war on the Dutch might be true and they would have to endure another escape. Thankfully, the train journey to The Hague was uneventful, and Kate chatted with American travellers who had enjoyed 'the kindliness of the Germans' on board a special train from Berlin to Antwerp laid on by their embassy.

Once they arrived at The Hague, the threat of discovery was behind them, but there were further dangers before they could reach Britain in safety. Already the English Channel was booby-trapped with mines and from the little boat the party boarded next, Kate saw cruisers, submarines and torpedoes. Like Grace, Kate arrived in England with only the clothes on her back.

In Austria, Nurse Kathleen Wanstall had decided to stay. She cared for the children of the German diplomat, His Serene Highness Prince Friedrich Wilhelm of Stolberg-Wernigerode and his wife HSH Princess Elisabeth of Erbach-Schonberg, who were posted in Vienna when war broke out. Kathleen was evidently very attached to her charges Ludwig Christian and Anna Marie, so much so that she risked her life to remain with them. At Christmas 1914, two-year-old Anna Marie died suddenly. Their shared bereavement may have made Kathleen's bond with her employers stronger, because she remained with the Stolberg-Wernigerodes throughout the war, probably enjoying a degree of security due to her employer's diplomatic status.

After her initial letter to Norland at the start of the war, Kathleen Wanstall did not manage to send further letters. When she emerged from Vienna at Christmas 1918, she left the employ of the Stolberg-Wernigerode family, took some time off, and then headed for the Grimaldi royal family nursery in Monaco.

In Darmstadt in south-west Germany, Nurse Lilian Eadie was in charge of the Grand Duke of Hesse's nursery caring for the Grand Duke's two boys, Princes Georg Donatus and Ludwig. She had been with them since Prince Ludwig's birth in November 1908. The boys were great-grandsons of Queen Victoria, two of many royal relations spread across Europe. The princes adored Lilian and did not want her to leave, but finally their father was forced to submit to the Hesse Government's demand that she depart. The authorities did not want their royal children brought up by an enemy nanny, who taught them English nursery rhymes.

Lilian was allowed to stay for Prince Ludwig's sixth birthday, before she started her journey home in November 1914. The Hesse family organised everything. At Hannover railway station, she sent postcards to the Grand Duchess and Prince Ludwig, and another to Prince Georg from Flushing in Holland. The princes kept her postcards, which are now part of the Hesse State Archive in Darmstadt, and Lilian's close relationship with the children is obvious from her messages on the cards, signing off her note to the boys with the special kisses they used.

By 28 November 1914, Lilian was back amongst her family in Topsham, Devon, but she found it hard to settle into rural life surrounded by anti-German sentiments and people who did not understand 'her' German family. Evidently the war in Flanders was not going to be over soon, and in Topsham Lilian was surrounded by neighbours who had suffered the first casualties of the war. Local boy Henry Copland had been declared the joint first casualty of the war, after dying at sea on board HMS *Amphion* on 6 August 1914; his older brother had died on board HM Submarine *D5* just three weeks before Lilian arrived home.

Having first-hand experience of Germany, with an enduring love for her Hesse royals, Lilian agreed with Principal, Miss Sharman writing in the *Quarterly* at Christmas 1914:

We must attack this spirit of hatred, and I believe that we women can do much. We must work, and pray, too, for our victory, but don't let us take part in any ribald joke at the expense of the German nation or people.

Norland understanding of and benevolence towards the enemy was already being practised in a Westfalian village outside Osnabrück. Personal ties to Germany found Nurse Maud Seppings in Lengerich when war was declared. She was looking after an ex-Norlander's five-year-old son and three-month-old daughter by a German husband, while the parents enjoyed a holiday in Switzerland. Three servants and two non-German speaking English ladies were staying in the house too.

On the declaration of war, to Maud's alarm, barricades with armed sentries were hastily erected in most streets. The soldiers manning these checkpoints examined the documents of all passers-by:

One such was immediately opposite our door, and his vigorous "Halt" coming at an average of once a minute, day and night, gave us the safety of military guardianship tempered by the risk that in trying to stop spies he might shoot us!

Maud and her group 'risked stray shots and sat on the balcony to see life,' watching the locals come out to shoot at a French aeroplane on reconnaissance. She witnessed a captured spy driven away to Munster and 300 Belgian prisoners being marched through the town. The town club 'was fitted up as a hospital' and her own household watered seventy horses heading for the front. Like families at home in Britain, German wives were readying clothes and food parcels for their men, who were about to depart.

The ladies of the town had formed a committee to provide canteen meals for the soldiers heading to the front. A true Norlander, Maud approved of the efficiency displayed by the German women: 'This was very necessary, as the Government gave no rations until the men reached their appointed destination. I must say the way in which it was done roused my admiration.' The German women raised subscriptions and attended Lengerich Station round the clock, handing a hot meal to every soldier through the windows of the trains. The plates were handed back and a food parcel along with a supply of tobacco was thrust into their hands to last them until their next stop.

Apart from the French aeroplane and the Belgian prisoners, Maud might have been describing a scene from an English village. Maud was naturally a friend to her German employer and had no reason to hate the Germans she lived among. The first atrocities of the war against Belgian civilians and captured troops had yet to be reported.

Maud's employers returned early from their holiday, and the husband, Herr H immediately applied for passports for Maud and the other English ladies at the United States Consul (the Americans had assumed the business of the British Consul in his absence). He accompanied her to a string of interviews with German officials and military, in the hope of gaining permission for these foreign nationals to leave the country. During the numerous short train journeys this involved, while alighting at Schwerte Maud witnessed German peasant refugees fleeing from the war zone. After two days and nights on trains, Maud and her party had made it to Munster. At the hotel where they lodged overnight, the proprietress begged Maud to locate her son, a waiter in England. It was a tall order, but a task Maud successfully completed a few weeks after her return, sending word to the hotelier via Norlanders in neutral Holland.

Round after round of paperwork ensued, finally concluding with an interpreter for the commandant of the German 7th Army accompanying them to the station for their return trip to Lengerich. Bidding them farewell, he patted Maud on the arm assuring her that she would get home safely. After clicking his heels and saluting them, they set off. However, Maud had a close shave in Munster when she was overheard speaking English to her two companions. A crowd of angry tram drivers and ticket collectors surrounded her and two sword-bearing policemen were called, but before the situation turned truly ugly, Herr H came to the rescue, showing his German passport and diffusing the grim mood.

With the correct paperwork signed, they began the journey home. Another delay at Ibbenbüren Station brought Maud to the attention of a zealous spy-hunter, who loudly identified her as English. However, she had a lucky escape because the stationmaster did not want the bother and decided to 'let them go on to Reine, they will know how to deal with them there'. Herr H escorted the party all the way and waved them off at Beutheim on the Dutch border. Maud finally reached Flushing on 22

August. On the boat from Rotterdam, the sun smiled down on her and the tired group of passengers en route to Folkestone:

We had to prove our nationality before we were let off the boat, and the policeman by the officials' table was so pleased to see a Britisher among all that motley crowd that he clapped me vigorously on the back with a hearty "You're all right Miss", a salutation which in my then condition sent me reeling.

She took a final train to London and from Victoria Station Maud headed for safety proper: the warmth and baths at the Norland Institute in Pembridge Square.

There is a distinct 'derring-do' tone to Maud, Kate and Grace's accounts of their adventures. They were Edwardian women with a measure of the Norland dash that afforded them bravery, forbearance and a confidence in the face of threatening foreign officials, before whom many upper- and middle-class women of the period would have fainted. Their vicarious aristocratic credentials lent them authority, while the austere Norland uniform made grown men step aside, and no Norlander would admit to an attack of the vapours. All of them had wiped royal bottoms, disciplined royal tantrums and dealt with stubborn royal employers. War would not deter these ladies from attempting to reach home; however there must have been times when fear gave them pause, although they would never have given voice to such emotions, particularly in their letters to their *alma mater*.

Physical evidence of the war had now reached London too. Not only were front-line casualties arriving daily at the city's hospitals, but refugees, especially from Belgium were pouring into the capital. There were many appeals for clothing and money across the nation and naturally, young women in a caring profession felt compelled to join in. The more adventurous Norland nurses signed up for Voluntary Aid Detachment work (VAD) and the Red Cross.

Nurse Emma Holland had been one of a few Norlanders to take up Red Cross training before the war and she was also a fluent French speaker. By August 1914, Emma was a 'surgery nurse' tending the first surgical casualties returning from the Continent. Her French was invaluable when her former employer, Mrs Henrietta Strachey, set up her own auxiliary convalescent home in Guildford, Surrey, for Belgian soldiers. Emma remained there as a nurse until the end of the war.

Nurse Dorothy Latimer had also trained with the Red Cross and on the declaration of war, she left her employment to nurse in a hospital for wounded soldiers at Worsley New Hall in Lancashire, donated by the 4th Earl of Ellesmere. Dorothy nursed the broken men returning from the British retreat at Mons:

> *Some of the men we have in now were in the retreat from Mons, where they say they were marching for sixteen days and nights without rest. Many of our soldiers died of exhaustion, and those who had to fall out for rest were taken prisoners by the Germans. The pitiable state of their feet, even now, shows what the march must have been to them.*

One man she nursed was recommended for the Victoria Cross for carrying his wounded officer for a mile through the firing line, despite being wounded himself. He and his comrades were quiet on the subject of heroism, looking on it as 'an absurd fuss to make'.

In late August, the Battle of Mons became the first terrible defeat experienced by the British Expeditionary Force. They were pushed back to the River Marne with 1,600 soldiers killed, wounded, and missing. Most of Dorothy's soldiers did not want to return to the front, although they knew they would have to. For many, the noise, sudden explosions and the sights they had witnessed in battle and the villages through which they retreated were harder to bear than any personal hardships. For the Belgian soldiers in Dorothy's care, it was different:

> *Last week we admitted twenty-eight wounded Belgians who had come straight from the trenches. They have suffered a great deal, some had not had their clothes off for six weeks, others stood for three days and nights in water in the trenches, and some travelled for a week after being wounded, in a cattle truck on a French railway.*

These men would return to the front the moment they were patched up. There was nowhere else for them to go, they possessed nothing but their uniforms and had no idea whether or not their families were still alive. In the British press, reports of the German Army's behaviour from the Mons and Malines district were filled with stories of rapes, shootings and the killing of priests and nuns. These reports were in part propaganda, intended to fuel hatred of 'the Hun' in Britain. Dorothy praised her Belgians' courage and listened to the weeping that filled the ward after lights out.

Writing from The Hague in November 1914, Gladys Pinson had witnessed the first great battles and advance of German troops into Belgium. In late August, she experienced two Zeppelins dropping bombs on Antwerp, followed by a day and a half of constant bombardment:

We had gone to bed on the ground floor, but I could not sleep as I could hear the sound of cannon getting nearer and nearer, and then at 11.30 the first shrapnel passed within 20ft of my room! I was out of bed like a shot and carried baby, cradle and all, into the lower regions where we were joined by the rest of the family.

Gladys and her employer's family hid in the cellar all night with the family doctor:

About 9 o'clock the first batch of English passed, in retreat, with ammunition etc.; about 10 or 12 motor 'buses and motors. I gave some of them tea, for which they were very grateful. One poor man had been wounded and I fear many more after, for there was an aeroplane directing the firing overhead and they were trying to hit them. Next came the Belgian cavalry and the doctor and I gave them something to eat and drink... As soon as it was dark, the English marines went past; it was terrible to see them go.

Gladys suffered the 'terrible shriek of shells' for the next thirty-six hours, as houses around them were hit and their own windows were blown in. When the bombardment stopped the following morning, Gladys woke up to German troops approaching down the street. She was living on the Chaussée de Malines outside Antwerp, the main road to Malines: 'The first contingent were anything but at their ease and had their guns ready to fire, and the officers their revolvers in hand!' They anticipated an ambush from straggling British soldiers or brave villagers, but strangely the soldiers were 'all decorated with flowers' and 'one officer had a pot of geraniums in each saddle bag'. The Germans wished to give the impression that they came in peace and were relieved that they had managed to conquer this village with little resistance.

Gladys understood that she was behind enemy lines, employed by a family whose king had refused the Germans passage through his country. But in true Norland style, Gladys ventured out and nipped upstairs to bake some scones, since the family had been without bread for nearly three days.

Like many Belgians, Gladys' family found their way to Holland and the refugee camps. Her employer, Doctor van Emden, hoped to be able to continue his medical practice in England, but fear of mines in the Channel stopped him from leaving Holland, and as a citizen of a combatant nation Gladys was not allowed to leave the refugee camp. The family was well-off, but they experienced the privations of war despite their privileged position. Gladys was forced to feed her baby charge condensed milk, which upset her stomach but was all that was available.

The mayhem of the first months of the war in Europe was felt by the wealthy, titled and well-educated alike. The ladies from Norland, who had taken up the best positions on the Continent suffered the same deprivations and fears as their employers. No one came away entirely unscathed, although money could buy comfort. After a brief stay in a Dutch refugee camp, the van Emden family took a house in The Hague, where Gladys continued to work for them.

As 1915 approached, casualties and refugees in Holland and Britain became a pressing concern for both governments. Relief funds were hurriedly set up, clothing depots organised and as ever, Norlanders were more than prepared to play their part.

Chapter 3

Relief and Refugees

Norland nurses' propensity to make do, make the best of things
and organise in the face of chaos was honed in the nursery.
Yet, from the first days of the war these abilities were being
employed by Norlanders caught across Europe and at the Institute by
students and staff. Among the combatant nations on both sides of the
war, society ladies were rapidly setting up hospital and clothing charities,
while existing charitable networks such as the Red Cross were rushing
into action to cope with the crowds of wandering refugees displaced in
the first weeks of the conflict.

In Britain, the impact of the war was not immediately felt by most
of the population. Those Norlanders in employment continued their
daily routines, and if the lady of the house happened to be engaged in
charitable events their children's nurse might be asked to join in. In the
years prior to the war, some Norlanders had attended weekly first aid
training with their employers, preparing for the day when war might occur.
However, with the first trickle of casualties arriving back in England,
Norlanders with first aid and nursing skills were not yet required for war
service. Trained military nurses were the only women allowed to treat
British soldiers in these first days of war and they had already travelled
to Flanders. Despite their keenness to offer assistance, the majority of
Norlanders had to continue with their everyday employment.

The 'war machine' of administrators, medics and recruitment officers
had yet to roll into action; these weeks were the lull before the storm, but
already the first wave of refugees had reached British shores – Belgian
families fleeing from the advancing German Army. Hastily established
relief committees met the refugees as they flooded into Southampton and
Dover, and organised onward transport for them to the cities. Norland's

founder Mrs Emily Ward opened the doors to her private home on the South Coast, encouraging Norlanders by her own example to do their bit for the war effort.

Twenty-two years after the establishment of the Norland Institute, the success of the Wards' business venture had helped to fund their recent purchase of Little Hallands, a part oak-beamed Tudor house, with later eighteenth century extensions, set in the midst of a large estate ten miles outside Lewes, near Brighton. Mrs Ward wrote to the Institute describing her rural idyll with chickens, little black pigs and a pair of nanny goats. It was the perfect setting for what she now had in mind.

Every Tuesday, Mrs Ward drove from her new home on the Sussex Downs up to London in her Daimler to ensure Norland was running like clockwork. In the city, surrounded by news hawkers and heightened talk of the war, Mrs Ward's attention was caught by announcements of the latest atrocities. From 4 August 1914 onwards, the first written descriptions reporting the war in the press came from neutral Belgium, with reports of the German Army taking first Liege and then marching across country towards Antwerp; the Belgian Army hindering, but failing to halt their advance.

As the conflict progressed, the focus turned from soldiers and ordnance to refugees fleeing to safety within Belgium and abroad. The Belgians were the first mass civilian casualties and dislocated people of the war on the Western Front. Some Belgians fled their homes before the bombardments started; others, like Norlander Gladys Pinson and her Belgian employer, stuck it out in Antwerp as the shells started to fall. As well as defending the city, the British were using it as a collection point for casualties and Gladys had offered her services to the wounded: 'I went to the English ambulance every day until we were bombarded, and then the wounded were all sent to England.'

Once the Germans had overrun the cities, many Belgian civilians scattered to avoid further violence, some to Holland and others to Britain. The news overwhelmed Mrs Ward and her husband, and they decided to take practical steps to offer assistance.

Hurriedly set up in early August 1914 by a handful of titled and well-connected ladies, the War Refugees Committee had established its headquarters at General Buildings, Aldwych in London. The Wards asked a close friend to make a representation to the Committee offering Little Hallands and the estate for the Committee's use, but it was turned down. Undeterred, their representative walked straight from Aldwych to the Belgian Consul, who immediately despatched nineteen refugees, newly arrived from the Belgian war zone near Malines, by train to Little Hallands.

Mrs Ward's group of Belgians had escaped the horrors of battle but they had been homeless refugees for over a week. Still in shock and carrying few personal possessions, they were all from the same town and most were related. The Wards collected the group at Seaford Station, amidst a friendly crowd eager to see the spectacle of real-life 'plucky little Belgians'. A friendly doctor passing by hailed Mrs Ward as she waited at the station: 'I'll doctor your Belgians free whenever you want me.' It was an offer that all too soon Mrs Ward would have to call upon.

Despite being unable to communicate with her guests in either their native French or Flemish, Mrs Ward supplied a supper of milk, coffee, bread, cheese, and jam to make them feel more at home. Describing the arrangements in her Christmas letter to the Institute, Mrs Ward said she had 'thoughtfully provided tobacco for the men and sewing materials for the women'.

Word quickly spread around Lewes that Little Hallands had taken in Belgian refugees and Mrs Ward was overwhelmed with applications for the Belgian women to go out to work as domestic servants. Many were wives of well-off men and had never had to work before, but they were desperate and grateful for the offers. With very few possessions and no money, the men and women were compelled to try to support themselves. In Belgium, the men had been diamond cutters and brass workers, but there was little call for those trades in Lewes, so they turned their practical skills to carpentry and farm work.

Among the first party of refugees taken in by the Wards were twelve children. One boy named Ferdinand developed scarlet fever three days after his arrival. Scarlet fever is a highly contagious disease, especially in close confines, but one that early twentieth century families and children's nurses were used to dealing with themselves unless complications developed.

Ferdinand's mother cheerfully remarked to Mrs Ward: "Madame, we will shut him up in a room for four days, keep the windows closed, and give him only water to drink. When the eruption is gone we will give him a bath, and it is all finished."

Over the next few days, all the children succumbed to the illness, yet all survived. At a time when scarlet fever killed one in twenty and there was no known cure, Mrs Ward's Belgians had proved more resilient than expected.

The refugees had arrived in England in their best clothes, with spares wrapped in bundles, but they were not well equipped and winter was looming. War charities were trying to help by requesting cast-off clothing donations. Mrs Ward organised a clothes collection for her refugees from the local neighbourhood, as well as receiving additional items from the relief committees in London.

Norlanders were eager contributors to the clothing depots, gathering up out-grown children's clothes from their nurseries. During one of her London visits, Mrs Ward went with Miss Sharman, to a relief committee collection centre in Warwick Square, where they commented on the efficiency of the women working there. Mrs Ward was able to ask for 'a coat for a short fat man' or 'a petticoat for a child of six' and was immediately handed each of good quality. However, she was concerned that the Belgian ladies would find it hard to grow accustomed to the narrow British skirts then in fashion, when they were used to wearing wider skirts. There were cultural differences in the kitchen too. The Belgians did not like English tea and so a supply of cocoa was provided.

Relations of some of Mrs Ward's group of Belgians had arrived in London a month later, and were hoping to join the first batch of refugees. However, the Government had passed a new regulation forbidding Belgians from residing on the coast for security reasons, and despite appeals to the local chief constable, Mrs Ward was allowed to keep her Belgians, but not to welcome their relations.

In late September, news arrived of the destruction of Malines and Mrs Ward's refugees realised that they would have to remain in Britain for the duration of the war, reassured by the announcement made by Prime Minister Herbert Asquith, that Belgium 'may count on our wholehearted and unfailing support to the end'. Mrs Ward's hospitality was one of hundreds of small gestures shown to Belgian refugees by Britons during the course of the war. When the war ended, over a quarter of a million Belgians had sought refuge in Britain and accepted the assistance of wealthy individuals in a position to help.

However, circumstances were different for Mrs Ward's Norland nurses. In London, Miss Sharman attempted to curb the rush of emotions felt by ordinary Norlanders in the first months of the war and inject a sense of proportion. Not everyone had the financial resources of the Wards and, in spite of their caring profession, the nurses had to look to themselves.

Perhaps Miss Sharman had the foresight to realise that the war would not be 'over by Christmas'. Her letter in the Christmas 1914 *Quarterly* shows a practical and thoughtful approach in response to an appeal for £1 per Norlander to be donated to the Belgian Relief Fund from Nurse Marian Burgess, who cared for Her Imperial Highness Grand Duchess Kirill's family in the comfort of the royal palaces in Russia:

> *The reason that such an appeal has not been sent to you sooner from the Institute itself is that we knew the war would press heavily on the resources of our Norlanders; and we felt that they could help more effectively by work than by money. The calls upon our Norlanders have been numerous, some have had to give extra financial help at home; some have lost their positions; some have had salaries curtailed.*

Marian had witnessed the Russian gentry's speed in raising funds to send a hospital train to the Eastern Front within ten days of the outbreak of war and she felt that Norlanders, with their excellent organisational abilities, could manage to arrange something equally impressive. Her first idea was to open up to Belgian refugee children the Fieldhouse Flats at Mrs Ward's Bognor Regis retreat. Any Norland nurses not currently in employment, who could afford not to take paid work for a few months, might volunteer their services to manage this impromptu holiday-home crèche. However, this was scuppered by the authorities' decision to restrict Belgians from living on the coast.

Alternatively, Marian felt that a £1 donation from all 600 nurses and probationers could raise the sizeable sum of £600 in a matter of days, which she suggested be offered to the Belgian Relief Fund, specifically for the relief of babies. Marian was convinced of winning support from her colleagues and felt everyone could spare the money, but if not: 'Of course, if anyone honestly cannot, then let her give 10s., but I feel sure all will give £1.'

Two months later, Nurse Jessie Fox made a second appeal, this time for the Institute's Foundation Fund, which she hoped the Norlanders would not forget in the crush of charities being established:

> *We women cannot give ourselves, as our brave troops are doing so nobly. No doubt much is being given for the soldiers and refugees; but I expect we all realise that our usual charities should not be allowed to suffer, and that most of them need greater help than usual.*

Jessie was struggling to attract subscriptions for the Foundation Fund. She was eager to offer training to a girl less fortunate than most Norlanders, who might have need of a career and an income during the war.

Requests for charitable donations, either in the form of cash or goods, were being advertised throughout the country. By June 1915, Norlanders had collected £38 11s 4d (worth around £2,800 today) in response to Marian's appeal. They sent the donation to the Belgian Relief Fund with a special request. Maud Seppings had seen a letter in the *Morning Post* claiming that 700 quarts of milk were required daily by the children and infants in Malines, a Belgian city now in German occupied territory. Dedicated to the care of children, the Norland Institute expressly asked for its monies to be put towards 'milk for Malines'. A further £3 5s collected in response to *The Telegraph's* Shilling Fund was sent with it.

These were sizeable sums of money collected from young women who earned, on average, an annual salary of between £30 and £70. The unskilled women in domestic service with whom Norlanders rubbed shoulders in the servants' quarters of their employers' homes and who also enjoyed board and lodging, were paid approximately £12 to £28 per year. Norlanders' training and their unique position, neither upstairs nor down, attracted a good wage. In comparison, women and girls employed in the new munitions factories were paid £1 per week.

The Institute also funded a bed in the King George Hospital in London at a cost of £25. This hospital was an emergency wartime facility, which treated over 70,000 troops between 1915 and 1919. In December 1914 when the hospital was established, a general call had gone out for public subscriptions. Within a fortnight all 1,650 beds had been funded by the public, with each one named for its benefactor. Norlanders had been quick off the mark to raise a subscription and unsurprisingly called their bed 'Norland Institute'. In the early months of the war, Norlanders chose charities that resonated directly with their personal experience, either through their commitment to children or through connections with privileged households. The Institute's financial support of a bed at King George's is typical of the latter, as the first bed was subscribed by Queen Alexandra, the King's mother. Mrs Ward's rush to fund a Norland bed placed the Institute firmly within the society circles she had always courted.

Accounts published in the June 1915 *Quarterly* note Norland's 'relief financial statement' as having donated £106 2s 9d to Belgian relief funds, the Red Cross and the bed at King George's. Despite their generosity, Marian Burgess was disappointed to discover that Norlanders were not prepared to give up an additional £1 each for her Belgian appeal, and she felt that the £100 total eventually raised among 600 nurses was paltry.

Many families were now feeling the cost of war in their personal finances, even the more well-off. Titled families could still draw on the traditional income from their estates, but when wartime restrictions were tightened on overseas financial investments, this affected many households where Norlanders worked. The situation was often compounded if the man of the house had already departed for Flanders. In many households, with no one left who was sufficiently qualified to run the family's financial portfolio, it was an unforeseen blow, especially to many middle-class families who relied on the head of the house's salary, as well as investments.

For some Norland nurses, the straitening of household finances meant the loss of their job, as nurseries were handed over to cheaper nursery maids and ordinary servants. For recently qualified Norlanders working towards the prestigious Badge, requiring three years' continuous employment with a single family, this was devastating. The Badge was their entry to employment in the best households, but for many this promotion would have to wait until the war was over.

Some Norlanders wanted to do more than give donations, yet with nursing still barred to those trained outside the military, there were few opportunities to head to the Continent to offer hands-on help. One Norlander, however, had found a way not only to travel to war-torn Europe, but to offer her services to the numerous refugees there.

Since 1911, Nurse Margaret Evans had worked for Madame Dusendschon in Paris; she had holidayed at Easter 1914 with other Norlanders in Saint Legier, but by Christmas 1914, the Dusendschon family had removed themselves to the safety of London. Margaret had travelled from one comfortable home to another with a family who offered her a stable career, but she felt drawn towards doing more for the war effort. The numbers of women flocking to work in the munitions factories had yet to accelerate, and the Women's Land Army would not be formed for another two years.

As she came from a caring profession and was a practising Christian, Margaret decided on a particular path into voluntary aid work. The Quakers' Friends' War Victim Relief Committee was re-constituted in October 1914 to help relieve non-combatants in areas devastated by the violence. As a Quaker herself, this was an obvious organisation for Margaret to join and, after giving her employer notice, in the spring of 1915 she joined the Friends in Holland.

Between the initial German invasion and the fall of Antwerp, almost a million Belgians out of a total population of 7.6 million escaped to Holland. By 12 October 1914, the Dutch Government was in negotiation with the German occupation authorities for the repatriation of civilian refugees. Also an estimated 40,000 British military refugees, servicemen who had dashed to Holland to avoid being captured as prisoners of war, were to be disarmed and interned for the duration of hostilities under international law. Gradually, over the winter of 1914 to 1915, thousands of Belgians returned home, yet 105,000 refugees remained according to Dutch records.

Unwilling to return to continue life in German occupied Belgium, or too frightened of further violence, these were the people amongst whom Margaret worked. The refugees were separated into three distinct groups: Group A included 'dangerous, criminal and unwanted individuals'; Group B consisted of the 'less unwanted'; and Group C was designated for the 'respectably needy'. Even in desperate straits, the strict class segregation of 'nice people' from the 'unwanted' had to be upheld.

Margaret worked at Ede Vluchtoord, a camp set up by the Dutch Government, which was intended for C category families. In reality, the class groupings were not strictly adhered to, except where the undesirables of Group A were concerned.

Ede was designed to hold 10,000, but never housed more than 5,400 people, mainly old men, women and children. Margaret was enchanted by the location, but felt pained by its recent transformation:

Imagine beautiful moorland — apparently limitless moorland — interspersed with dense beech and pine forests and traversed by magnificent avenues of beech trees extending eight or ten miles. On to this beautiful moor have been dumped 5,000 homeless human beings — and wooden accommodation has been hastily built for them.

In March 1915, the Danish Government donated 325,000 Dutch florins to their Dutch neighbours to assist with the cost of sustaining the refugees and some of the money went towards 'demontable' wooden houses. In Ede, 160 of these wooden buildings were constructed, 'superintended by a delightful Belgian foreman'. The huts were used as workrooms and others as living quarters, as Margaret described:

The people sleep in long wooden barracks or zaals, painted white, with tarred black roofs; each zaal contains just over 60 cabines and each cabine averages 5 people; roughly speaking we will say a zaal holds 250–300 persons. Straw mattresses and blankets and covers are provided; these are placed side by side on the floor, and during the day are piled one upon another. Large families are given two cabines and sort themselves as they please.

The camp was divided into four villages or 'dorps'. Each village had a church with up to six schools clustered around it. Margaret counted thirty Belgian school-masters and mistresses working in the refugee schools, and noted that these paid professionals received better food and housing than the other refugees. Each village also had a crèche and kindergarten run by religious sisters and young refugee girls who worked as 'pupil teachers'. Boys over school age were trained for a trade at a technical school situated on the outskirts of the camp. Dutch doctors and nurses ran a small adult hospital with maternity and children's wards, and an isolation unit attached.

Each dorp had a laundry and a central kitchen, with communal dining rooms arranged round it and sleeping barracks positioned further out. Three meals a day were provided: coffee, bread and butter at 7.30am and 5.30pm, and a bowl of vegetables and soup at midday; meat was an infrequent addition. Occasionally milk, eggs and white bread were given to nursing mothers and invalids. It was a monotonous diet, but sufficient to survive on.

Everywhere she looked, Margaret was astounded at the industry, commitment and organisation that had been achieved amidst the chaos of the war. The Dutch had erected a system of fully functioning small communities with services and employment. However, she had also picked up a hint of resentment among the Dutch: 'The Dutch are a kindly nation, and have shown their kindness efficiently, but there is much innate antagonism between Belgian and Dutchman.' As a neutral country Holland did not participate in the war, but proximity to Belgium forced Holland to take in its neighbours' refugees. From the Belgian point of view, they were forced into accepting Dutch charity when their own country was in enemy hands and they were powerless to recover it. This naturally caused simmering tensions, which were suppressed by outward politeness and gratitude.

Alongside other English ladies running a knitting group, Margaret and her travelling companion immediately set to organising work for young Belgian girls. They taught them how to make wool rugs for the cabines, to embroider handkerchiefs and underlinens, and how to repair old clothes and make Christmas toys for the little ones. The girls were paid 1s 8d a week by the Society of Friends. They gave the girls 9d each, banking the remaining 9d for them. No one knew what they would face when the war was over, and the Friends were helping them to invest for an unknowable future.

The younger children in the camp were enjoying the freedom war had brought them in which children of all classes intermingled, as Margaret noted: 'Two thirds of the population come from Antwerp or its neighbourhood, and slum children are having the time of their lives in healthy air, with regular feeding and excellent instruction.'

Margaret found the work strenuous, but interesting. She spoke no Flemish and a little French, but despite the language barrier she was succeeding in her goal to 'help them live clean lives': 'The idea that "Engelochen Damen" have left their own country to help them pleases them and raises them; a cheerful face helps them to rise above the indifference that creeps over them.' Margaret's distinctly hands-on account of her volunteering experiences is quite unusual, especially so early in the war. When Mrs Ward published it in the March 1916 *Quarterly*, Margaret's letter was a powerful advertisement to rally Norlanders' efforts.

Also still on the Continent, Gladys Pinson had left the refugee camps in Holland with the van Emden family and now gave her employer's address as Kermont, Petit Saccones, Geneva. The van Emdens were well-heeled and able to fund a new life in neutral Switzerland after their brief stay in the Dutch camps. Previously confined to the camp in Holland, Gladys was now free to travel. She had had enough of her first-hand experience of war, and the *Quarterly* records that she was 'home for Christmas 1915', catching up with family for the first time in eighteen months.

As the British and French armies struggled to maintain the Western Front, and refugees fled from the advancing German forces, relief work had become a new civilian industry. Volunteers continued their efforts to meet the needs of the increasing numbers of displaced families.

Miss Ethel Ashby, a former Norland Nurse and a Quaker like Margaret, worked in the Friends' London warehouse receiving and distributing clothes and stores to 'all fields of work'. Ethel was the twenty-fourth student nanny to train at the Institute, gaining her Norland Certificate in 1894. Her first engagement had been with a family in Lincolnshire, but she disappears from the Norland employment register before the end of the nineteenth century, and it is likely that she took a full-time position with the Friends on leaving her nannying career.

Ethel wrote to the *Quarterly* from the Friends' London offices using the pages of the June 1916 issue to reach like-minded young women willing to work in the refugee camps. Her appeal requests 'someone to take charge of a creche at Amersford', a voluntary position unless 'a small salary were much needed'. Two years into the war, recruiting for a post with a Norlander who might still have some savings left to support herself was a difficult task and the *Quarterly* does not mention anyone having filled the post.

Organisations like the Friends had been working in northern Europe since the first weeks of the war. As the numbers of displaced persons increased, so did their need for volunteers, but it was a hard life. The Friends' volunteers lived in similar quarters to the refugees, ate the same food and suffered the vagaries of the northern European climate. The Friends' 'Fourth Report' details the severity of the 1915-16 winter and how their volunteers endured the perishing cold in huts, where the temperature remained below zero throughout the day and plummeted at night.

The 'Fourth Report' also mentions Margaret Evans, who was now volunteering at Sermaize les Bains, 65 miles east of Reims and perilously close to the front-line in the Marne Valley. That winter had seen thirty-five cases succumb to pneumonia in the small Friends' hospital at Sermaize les Bains. Margaret described the refugees' dire circumstances in the *Quarterly*. She had previously been working in the crèche and in the embroidery rooms in Holland, which she had described as 'relief of the mind' for the refugees. Two years on, she was now working with the French peasantry and was horrified by the state in which she found them. In France, Margaret's work was 'relief of the body', which consisted of helping to distribute seeds, chickens and rabbits for the remaining inhabitants to sow and raise for food. Situated only a few miles from the front, she lived in perpetual fear: 'At night, the constant rumbling of the guns and sweeping of searchlights make it impossible to forget the horrors of war so close at hand.'

Real-life stories from the war zone told by one of their own spurred Norlanders on to keep up their donations, and stood out among the many letters sent to Norland from titled ladies running charities and small hospitals. In March 1916, Constance Gwladys Robinson, Marchioness of Ripon had received £7 16s from Norland in response to an additional appeal from the King George Hospital. The Marchioness was one of fourteen prominent society ladies who had signed a 'declaration of war on luxury' in September 1915. They also formed the 'Women's War Economy League' and promised to eschew expenditure on imported goods; to buy as few items of luxury clothing as possible and not to introduce new fashions; not to use 'automobiles' unless for charitable reasons and not to employ male servants eligible for public service.

To Norlanders frantically saving their pennies and sewing garments for refugees late into the evenings, sitting alone in nurseries up and down the country, the Marchioness must have seemed a role model. They worked for ladies like her and could sympathise with the economies she vowed to make. The Marchioness's letter expressing 'how deeply their kindness is appreciated' was sure to render funds for the next collection at King George's.

The length of the country, women and young girls formed sewing circles and knitting groups, busily making comforts for the soldiers at the front and their straitened families at home. Two nannies had organised weekly sewing meetings at Norland Institute and had soon completed nineteen outfits for children aged two to eight. They were donated to the 'Officers' Families Fund' set up by Lady Lansdowne. This fund supported officers' families experiencing hardship due to the war. Families, whose menfolk came from the professional classes and had given up their jobs to enlist, were now struggling to live on an officer's pay. The fund was specifically for their benefit, financing house rentals and removals, and children's education. The needs of families like this must have resonated deeply with Norlanders, some of whom came from similar backgrounds.

The same sewing meetings produced outfits for the babies and toddlers residing in Norland's own nurseries. Pearl Woodruffe had arrived at the nurseries aged just four weeks in August 1914. The 'Committee for the Relief of Distress amongst the Professional Classes' had sent this newborn to Norland's nurseries in Pembridge Square to be cared for by the nurses and she was still there at Christmas six months later.

In the nursery with Pearl was Silvere van Molle, an 11-month-old Belgian refugee baby from Alost, whose parents had left him at Norland while they sought proper accommodation. Just weeks later, his two-month-old infant brother also arrived at Pembridge Square. Little Albert George Raymond Nicholas, named for all four leaders of the Allied nations (Belgium, Britain, France and Russia), was a delicate baby who needed the extra care of a dedicated children's nurse.

The boys stayed at Norland throughout 1915 and Madame van Molle's letter of thanks for the kindness shown to her family was published by Mrs Ward in the June 1916 *Quarterly*. According to his mother, Albert had become the perfect Edwardian baby: 'He is the sweetest little boy I have known; he quite surprises me, he is very happy, and his Papa has not heard a cry yet.'

It was not only refugees who benefited from the charity of Norland's regiment of caring young women. Nurse Maud Daviniere worked at The George Yard Mission Creche in Whitechapel, London which looked after youngsters while their mothers worked in the East End munitions factories or went out charring in middle- and upper-class homes. The mission crèches run by Norlanders frequently sent out requests for clothing, boots and stockings, but Maud's appeal was specifically for toys to place under a Christmas tree for the children: 'And though naturally our thoughts are with the brave soldiers and sailors and what we can do for them, we must not forget their children this Christmas, many of whom have lost a father in the war.'

Maud's was one of several appeals to appear in the *Quarterly* at Christmas 1915, and Mrs Ward's response reflects how the war a year further on had changed attitudes. No longer were she or principal Miss Sharman so careful of their nurses' purses. They had read the news reports of the carnage at Gallipoli, Ypres and all along the Western Front; they had seen the casualties on their visits to their sponsored bed at the King George Hospital, and had realised that Britain would be in this war for the long haul: 'Amongst the many appeals there is choice and scope for the tastes of all, and we women can help our country by *giving* [sic], though we are unable to fight!'

Norland's make-do and mend attitude produced an international factory of nannies all knitting, sewing and mending, and sending their handiwork back to the Institute for delivery to the charitable committees. One nurse produced 'a dressing-gown cleverly made out of an old blanket, prettily embroidered'. There were petticoats and lavender bags, a tea cosy made from 'silk cigarette flags' all sewn together. Someone had cut up a pair of white kid gloves and turned them into a set of gnome and pixie finger puppets. Nurse Beatrice Moxon, who had worked on continental Africa since her probationary post in Algiers in 1909, sent a parcel of clothes from her new position in Rondebosch, South Africa. She had been hard at work since the beginning of the war and Mrs Ward thought her handiwork formed 'a most attractive exhibition of Norland ingenuity'.

Mrs Ward sold some of the hand-made items at her Christmas Thrift Stall, raising £19 11s 3d. She divided the money between Serbian mothers and babies, the most recent group of refugees to hit the news, and Margaret Evans working with the Quaker Friends in France, who decided to use it specifically for the relief of the children.

Displaced persons continued to flow back and forth across Europe, while new cohorts of fleeing people appeared occasionally, as fresh theatres and battlefields opened up. However, one group of men who had been in northern Europe since the outset, and were still there in summer 1916, were neither prisoners of war nor refugees. They were the British Expeditionary Force's first troops to fight in Flanders.

Sent straight to Belgium to halt the advancing German Army, their forces had been routed in the Battle of Mons. Forced to retreat, some had marched day and night back to France injured, bootless and weary. These were the men Nurse Dorothy Latimer nursed at Worsley, Lancashire, and whom Gladys Pinson witnessed in retreat. However, others had fled in the opposite direction. The First Royal Naval Brigade had been cut off and their commanding officer, determined they would not become prisoners of war, headed for the Dutch border.

Since they wore military uniform, they could not be classed as refugees, neither could they be treated as prisoners. Therefore, according to international law, they were interned. The Dutch Army barracks at Rabenhaupt in Groningen were hastily prepared to accept 1,500 bearded, hungry soldiers and sailors, while their officers were billeted in hotels in the city, having given their word of honour they would not try to escape. All the men were interned for the duration of hostilities.

In spring 1916, Nurse Madge Gribbon arrived at Groningen to visit the troops. Madge was another Norland volunteer working in Holland with refugees and her trip to Groningen was a day out from the rigours of her own camp. A sailor acquaintance showed Madge and a friend round the wooden encampment, which the troops had nicknamed 'Timbertown'. In contrast to the efficiently run civilian camps, here the soldiers and sailors had largely had to shift for themselves once installed in the bare barracks. Madge listed the facilities now available:

> *Everything that is wanted is to be found here – post office, savings bank, printing press, carpenters' shop where they make the most wonderful boxes. Tennis courts laid out by the men themselves; the barber, the cobbler, the tailor, not to forget the photographer are all there.*

The soldiers here were bored. They had planted kitchen gardens around the camp and they were industriously occupied in workshops, but this did not sufficiently distract them. After some escapes, the British Government negotiated with the Dutch for leave passes allowing the internees to take days out around Groningen and they were employed in the shipyards and factories, and trusted to return at night to the camp. Eventually, a furlough was negotiated and the lucky few went on leave to England on a promise that they would return.

But it remained a tedious existence and to fill the time, sixteen men had formed a theatre troupe called 'the Follies', which Madge saw in rehearsal: 'They give a variety entertainment on the same lines as Pelissier did a few years ago in London, and they have indeed taken Holland by storm.' Madge refers to H G Pelissier, an English-born theatrical producer who toured with 'Pelissier's Follies' and had previously given royal command performances to King George. The soldier 'Follies' at Groningen had persuaded the Dutch authorities to let them tour around Holland, and their seventy performances meant 'there are few who do not know them, for they have surely won their laurels'.

The stranded soldiers and sailors also won Dutch hearts:

They have in Groningen, what is called the "English Fever", and it is very amusing to see a sailor with a Dutch girl on his arm... One sees the little children slip their hands into those of the sailors and run along beside them.

With English yet to become a global language, Madge remarked on the limited conversation between the sweethearts. She heard two words frequently spoken, 'dag', which she wrote as 'da-ag' to emphasise the strange pronunciation and 'goodbye', which was 'considered more modish than the Dutch word'.

As a neutral nation, Holland was not attacked, but receiving large numbers of refugees and interned troops put a strain on the Dutch economy. Other nations donated money and the Red Cross distributed relief, also helping internees to maintain contact with home by forwarding letters. However, on a local scale, having troops from one participating nation stationed in town for the duration provided entertainment and previously unimagined relationships were forged. When Armistice was declared in November 1918, several Dutch and British marriages took place in Groningen.

Margaret's letters from Ede Vluchtoord and Sermaize les Bains place her at the heart of the relief effort on the Continent. Newspapers reported from the front and described German atrocities in an effort to whip up support for the war, which clearly was not going to be over by Christmas 1914, but the personal descriptions offered by Margaret, Madge and their colleagues are written without any agenda beyond their desire to raise funds for their missions. Despite the horrors they witnessed, they were doing what Norlanders did best: organising and caring.

Their letters were among the first to reach Britain describing the war effort overseas and they provoked a constant stream of donations: cash and clothes to the charitable committees and funds. The 695 Norland nurses and probationers listed in the Christmas 1914 *Quarterly* were concertedly doing their bit for King and country. This was their first attempt at war work, something they would come to be very good at.

Chapter 4

War Work

After a busy autumn settling in her cohort of Belgian refugees at Little Hallands in Lewes, Mrs Ward declared her intentions for the rest of the war to all readers of the Norland *Quarterly*:

I am able to serve my country down here by daily personal service. You know how firmly I believe in personal sacrifice, in personal service ... Now we all have the winter to face, living on from day to day with Patience, Courage, Hope and Humility.

Patience, courage, hope and humility were attributes that British society of the time expected of its womenfolk, but they were especially applicable to the Edwardian Norland nurse. Norlanders required patience in their work with children; they needed courage to travel overseas unaccompanied; and many had already shown their mettle by escaping Germany in the first weeks of the war. Humility was essential to every children's nurse working in upper-class homes where they had to toe the line to keep their jobs.

Before the war, middle- and upper-class women who enjoyed financial stability had been expected to remain at home, supported by their husbands or fathers, to care for their families. These women occupied themselves with rounds of tea parties, organising the household servants and charity work. Married working-class women might take in piece-work, sewing or laundry, usually something that could be undertaken whilst keeping half an eye on the children, cooking meals and doing housework. Some worked in factories, with older daughters toiling alongside them. It was a class-ridden society in which people knew their place and did not anticipate social elevation or relegation.

Somewhere between the lower- and upper-classes in the social strata came the Norland Nurse. She needed sufficient polish to rub shoulders with women from all strata of society and that was all part of the pre-war training at the Norland Institute. Apart from tuition in the latest childcare education methods, nursery management and practical skills such as care of sick children, the course fees included tuition in etiquette – how to behave towards employers as well as domestic servants.

Mrs Ward considered her girls a class apart, but to afford the fees, many prospective Norlanders from humbler backgrounds had worked prior to their entry to the Institute. Often, they had been employed as music teachers, seamstresses or hospital auxiliaries, some as nursery maids, saving their wages whilst living at home. Norlanders were certainly working women, but they had been specially trained for their profession, and their uniform set them apart. Well-disciplined and with a few months' hospital training under their belt, Emily Ward's spirited girls were perfect candidates for war work.

As the first casualties of the war were transported back to England, Norlanders keen to join the war effort offered their basic nursing skills to the numerous hospitals hastily being established all over the country. Before the war, Mrs Ward had encouraged Norlanders to volunteer for the Red Cross and in March 1912 she, along with Principal Miss Sharman, had launched a Norland branch. This was to include nurses and their employers, who would train together to prepare for 'voluntary aid in time of war'. The branch had folded before the war began, but a few Norlanders up and down the country had chosen to train at their local Red Cross branches.

The Red Cross was an international organisation, which had only been established in Britain since 1870. Working on the basis that developing skills during peacetime was the best way to be prepared when war came, the Red Cross and St John's Ambulance had trained thousands of women volunteers in basic first aid and nursing. They were known as VADs, the Voluntary Aid Detachment, mainly recruited from middle- and upper-class circles. Now, Mrs Ward attempted to form her own corps from independently Red Cross-trained Norlanders, but there were insufficient nannies available. Those Norlanders already trained had been snapped up by their own VAD divisions, such as Nurses Emma Holland and Dorothy Latimer, who were engaged in Red Cross work on home shores as early as October 1914.

Ever resourceful and determined to have Norland involved in the first wave of wartime nursing, Mrs Ward offered her nurses' services to the hospitals in which they had received their probationers' paediatric training. She managed to place Norland nurses with 'grateful matrons' at hospitals in Salisbury, Darlington and Middlesex among others. Some stayed for several weeks and Nurse Rosalind Blott, who had only recently completed her probationary period, went straight back to Brondesbury, near London, for six months. The hospital matrons used Mrs Ward's children's nurses to assist their trained medical nurses in routine tasks – cleaning, laundry and feeding patients. Essentially, they were filling the gaps left by nurses heading to the front. Mrs Ward was disappointed that so few hospitals had taken up her offer, but the War Office had declared that only trained, certificated and experienced nurses would be accepted for war work.

However, if they persevered, volunteer auxiliary nurses might succeed through other avenues. Nurse Emma Holland had initially trained as a medical nurse but, as hospitals were not equipped with lifts in the late 1880s, she declared that the constant climbing of stairs had 'broken her down' and so she entered Norland training instead. Given her nursing training, Emma had been encouraged to join her local Voluntary Aid Detachment in 1909, which was run by her employer. She had achieved her first aid and 'home nursing' certificates, and had gained 'considerable practice on Boy Scouts and Girl Guides'.

When war was declared, Emma wrote to the VAD Headquarters offering her services. Ten days later, she was sent instructions to rendezvous with another four VAD probationers at Victoria Station, where they took a train to their specified hospital. Her letter to the Institute, written in November 1914, obeys the strict censorship laws hurriedly enacted at the start of the war, and Emma declines to name the hospital or even the town she travelled to. She was thrilled with her first placement as 'surgery probationer on the women's side', watching and learning until she was allowed to do the simpler surgical dressings. Then she passed practical tests in bed-making, sweeping, dusting, polishing and bath-cleaning, before graduating to 'the men's side', where she worked nights alongside a nursing sister.

Her four companions only lasted a fortnight, but Emma excelled and was kept on for six weeks. She received a glowing report and when they no longer needed her, she went straight to 'Red Cross Hospital ----------', where at last she was really allowed to nurse, 'and soldiers who had been wounded at the front too'. Her description of 4.30am dawn starts with blanket baths, temperatures and pulses to be taken for thirty wounded, and the ward tidied – all before 7.15am – would not have enticed the faint-hearted among her Norland readers. This was hard graft, but Emma loved it. Eventually, her employer set up her own convalescent home and Emma went to work with her there for the rest of the war.

Another Red Cross-trained volunteer, Nurse Dorothy Latimer was tending Belgian soldiers who had come straight from the retreat from Mons. Working alongside civilian-trained nurses on night-shift at the Earl of Ellesmere's hospital, Dorothy felt she learned more about nursing than if she had been on day duty. There were fewer nurses around and she was allowed to do more medical tasks, rather than simply mopping up and emptying bed-pans.

The soldiers filling the 135 beds were convalescent cases, who had been transferred from Manchester. They had been back in England for a few weeks, but the terrors of the trenches had not left them. The sounds of their nightmares pierced the quiet during Dorothy's night rounds: 'They call out in the night, warning us to be careful of the shells, which they imagine are bursting all round us. One poor man even sings "It's a long way to Tipperary" in his sleep.'

Dorothy nursed the sole remaining member of a trench of fifteen men, whose fellow soldiers had been wiped out by a single shell. The men rarely discussed with the nurses what they had seen, but they did complain about the rations. Concentrated beef made up into hard cakes resembling dog-biscuits were all they had had to eat for weeks. Water had been scarce too during those first weeks of battle, while the British Army figured out how to organise supply chains to the front lines and there was little surplus for softening their rations. Once the men had been discharged from hospital, Dorothy commented that they received only ten days' furlough before they were sent back to the firing line. Only one man whom she nursed said he 'really wanted to go back'.

The British soldiers were respectful of their Belgian comrades, with whom they had fled Mons, and understood their loss. They tried to teach the Belgians English, and offered them cigarettes and tobacco. Dorothy heard one Tommy say that he had been so hard-pressed for tobacco in a French hospital that he had smoked tea leaves rolled up in a letter from home and he did not want any Belgian to have to do the same.

While the men were on her ward, Dorothy noticed the change in their spirits. Some amputees with only one leg hopped around the ward, helping to make beds or sweep the floor. Dorothy was quietly pleased that they recognised her experience and thought her a fully-trained nurse. She heard a joke exchanged between two Scottish patients:

"Have ye heard of them Voluntary Aid Detachments, Jock? Turning out inexperienced girls to nurse us wounded Tommies? I wouldn't be nursed by none of them, would you?"

"Certainly not," the other replied. "I'm no' having any o' them near me."

While the War Office continued to impose narrow restrictions on the qualifications required for women to hold a hospital post, many Norlanders remained ineligible for this first and most obvious wave of war work. While their employers started charities, held committee meetings and volunteered as VADs, busy working Norlanders running their nurseries had not been able to take a few hours off every week to complete their VAD training. It was a frustrating situation for many nannies, who dearly wished to do their bit. Mrs Ward arrived at the conclusion that Norlanders were probably best able to serve their country by continuing to work diligently at their calling and adapt to the altered circumstances of their employers.

For some Norlanders, even continuing in their current careers became untenable. Already by Christmas 1914, some nannies had been dismissed from their positions because their employers were already suffering the financial strictures of the war. Mrs Ward went to some pains to explain in the *Quarterly* that their dismissal was: 'Through circumstances caused by the war and entirely beyond the control of the individual nurse.'

In the first year of the war, Norlanders found other opportunities through which to contribute to the war effort. Only recently qualified, Nurse Mildred St George was working for Lady Cowdray in Midhurst in Sussex on the outbreak of war. Anticipating that the farm's dairyman would soon wish to 'be set free to go to the Front', she found herself learning how to be a dairymaid. Likewise, Nurse Vera Toyne, still a probationer, had put her Norland training on hold and was 'training herself to undertake a man's duties' in the stables. Being fond of horses and realising employers were short of grooms and coachmen, Vera was in her element and learning new skills.

Nurse Frances Wellman had assumed the role of assistant quartermaster in Lord Frederic Fitzroy's private hospital in Balcombe, Sussex. Lord Frederic, a 91-year-old Crimean War hero, staffed his hospital with Red Cross and St John's Ambulance VADs and opened it to the wounded for convalescence. Frances was in charge of cooking, washing linens, and 'mending and marking the men's clothes', employing her former nursery skills.

By Christmas 1915, the Institute recognised that many Norlanders 'have given up their special career during the war' and had followed in Florence Nightingale's footsteps. Mrs Ward expressed her understanding of their need to help: 'One cannot but feel sympathy with those who are so anxious to show their gratitude in a practical way to the men who have gone through such terrible ordeals suffer for the sake of their country.' Mrs Ward was naturally proud of her girls' achievements, but there is no mention of women's rights in her Christmas message. Mrs Ward wanted Norlanders to explore every opportunity their professional education afforded them, but whilst the country was fighting for survival any thought for women's political futures was put on hold.

While Emma and Dorothy wrote to the Institute describing their VAD work at home in the first months of the war, as hostilities progressed and a shortage of nurses was experienced in the war zone, an increasing handful of Norland VADs made it overseas to work alongside medical nurses in Red Cross units. Nurses Kathleen Park and Violet Reilly were posted to a British military hospital in Malta, while Nurse Violet Gray was nursing in Eastbourne but hoping to be transferred to France. Nurse Elsie Borthwick was working as an orderly in a women's hospital in Troyes, south-east of Paris and extremely close to the front line. At some point during 1917, Elsie moved to Hong Kong and took up paid employment with a banking family there. Perhaps her nerves could no longer take the sound of shells falling close by, or her savings had run out, forcing her to take a paid position.

Nurse Constance Hunt, a seasoned Norlander who had previously worked in St Petersburg for a titled family, had been employed by an American family living in Paris since 1912. At the start of the war, she moved further away from the fighting to Houlgate, on the French coast near Caen, where she helped to nurse in a hospital run by American ladies. She was in a safe zone, remaining there for ten months before returning to Britain to work as a VAD in Newton Abbot gaining the extra skills she needed to take her back to Europe where she continued to work as a VAD for the rest of the war.

Despite hostilities and the rapid advance of the German Army into France, many Norlanders remained in Paris, ever watchful of the proximity of the war to their nurseries. Since 1913, Nurse Elizabeth Anderson had worked for the Duchess of Dampierre in Rome, and when the Duchess decided to visit her Paris home, Elizabeth accompanied her and the children. In this city, where the constant pounding of the guns and explosions continued day and night, several other Norlanders were living on the same avenue. It was a small comfort to Elizabeth to be able to discuss the news with other independent young British women, and to debate how they might escape if the German Army advanced too close. They had all read the newspapers and accounts of escape in the *Quarterly*, and they knew what to expect.

Other Norlanders were closer still to the fighting in Orleans, while Nurse Gertrude Carlisle was nannying in Grenoble. Given the rapid incursions into France made by the Germans during 1915, there was no knowing for how long they might remain safe. However, unlike Norlanders working in Germany on the declaration of war, these nannies were employed by

Britain's allies and, although if it all became too much to bear they might ask to leave their position, no self-respecting Norlander would desert her nursery while her employers' children needed her.

Having been forced to leave her royal charges behind when escaping Germany in late August 1914, Nurse Kate Fox wrote to the Institute in November 1915 extolling her new-found vocation. Since returning to Britain, she had completed midwifery training with the Salvation Army at The Mothers' Hospital in London, where she now worked. This hospital had opened in 1913 as an extension of the Salvation Army's obstetric hospital, Ivy House, and it followed the same principles, acting as a place of refuge and medical help for unmarried pregnant women.

In 1902, Parliament had passed the Midwives Act to regulate the profession and ensure that all practitioners were certified. Mrs Ward had encouraged Norlanders to add midwifery to their training if they found themselves between jobs and Kate was not the first to find this newly-recognised profession a satisfying addition to her nannying skills.

The Mothers' Hospital had 48 beds and aimed to cope with 600 births every year. However, as the war created more widows and destitute mothers, the hospital started to accept married working-class women whose husbands were away fighting or had died. These women could not afford a stay in one of the women's hospitals or to pay a midwife to attend them at home.

Kate had been working at the Mothers' Hospital since February 1915. She was keen to praise the work of the Salvation Army Sisters and rally more Norlanders to her crusade to save their fallen female patients:

They have given up everything for the sake of saving lives and souls, and nobly they carry on the work in a most unobtrusive way... I should so like any Norlander who is interested in babies (and is there one who is not?) to pay us a visit.

As an older Norlander used to royal families, Kate may have found ordinary nursery work mundane, considering it somewhat beneath her, but training to be a midwife was a natural extension of her Norland experience and allowed her to help those less fortunate. Given the tone of her letter, however, being an unmarried mother in her care may have been quite a trial.

Kate's work exposed her to a way of life she had never previously experienced, and her charitable fervour came to the fore: 'I know at this time all are doing their utmost to help the soldiers of today, but I feel I must ask that the soldiers of the future shall not be forgotten. Surely infant life now is more important than ever!' Kate requested clothes, rags and material scraps to be sent to her. She saw herself as raising Kitchener's future army and urged Norlanders to assist her:

> *I think it is a great pity so many* [Norland] *nurses have given up this work to take up war work. Those who have done so could surely not have fully appreciated their privilege in undertaking such important work as saving and caring for the lives that are so precious to the Empire at this present moment.*

Kate felt strongly that every Norlander must contribute to the war effort within the sphere of her training. Since Norland nurses were trained to work with children, in Kate's opinion Norlanders should find family-oriented war work. She had started a debate that would rumble on until the Armistice.

Kate would have approved of Nurse Edith Sperling's choice of alternative wartime employment as head matron at Cordwalles School in Maidenhead, where she had moved shortly after the war began. Cordwalles was a boys' preparatory school in the Berkshire countryside. Her charges were aged between seven and thirteen, and she found the work was quite different from a nursery. 'Getting into the ways of school life' had been more difficult than Edith anticipated, especially when it came to discipline: 'One was apt to be too lenient with the boys, and they were quick enough to take advantage of it.'

Already the headmaster had advised her to be stricter with the boys, but one area of her work was not dissimilar from running a nursery – the regular routine. The maid called Edith at 6.15am, when she dressed and went to the dormitories to check all the boys were well. While the older ones dressed themselves, she helped the younger boys and ensured 'all are properly groomed, as I am responsible for their appearance'. Then chapel, breakfast and school unless anyone required 'doctoring, such as ears, eyes, nose trouble'. Once school had started, Edith supervised the servants to make the boys' beds, and prepare elevenses and lunch. There were laundry baskets to empty and sort, returning each boy's linens to his locker, and Edith liked to fit in an hour's walk every morning before she was required to attend the boys' sporting activities: 'I am not supposed to go off the premises in the afternoon, in case there should be an accident in the football or cricket field.'

Her pitch-side first aid kit included boric acid lotion, bandages and strapping wool. Once games were finished, the boys had tea and then returned to classes, while Edith prepared her 'medicine tray ready for the night'. She enjoyed reading to the smaller boys during supper and chose a group of five for a bath every evening. The rush occurred when the older boys came up to bed and everyone with an injury or sickness had to be ministered to before the headmaster put the lights out at 9pm.

Her duties were the same as running a nursery, but on a far greater scale, which became most apparent when there was a measles epidemic. Twenty-two boys succumbed simultaneously and Edith still had seven in the sanatorium with other ailments. She worked day and night nursing them through their fevers, only to discharge her last patient and then be confronted with tonsillitis rampaging throughout the school.

Nearby, Nurses Dorothy Waters and Marie Middlemass were working for families at prestigious Eton College. Dorothy worked for the Bookers family in Cotton Hall House, caring for the housemaster's own children, while Marie lived in Coleridge House, running Housemaster de Montmorency's nursery. Living with these families on the school premises, both Dorothy and Marie would have been acutely aware of the numbers of officers being killed, as the roll call of Eton's dead was announced at morning prayers.

Nurse A May Hamilton-Smith worked for Eton's biggest rival, as matron for West Acre boarding house at Harrow School. May had worked here since 1903, and had cared for many Harrovians, including some young men now fighting. Over their years at school, the matron spent more time with them than their parents, creating a strong bond, and it was natural they should stay in touch with her:

> *The letters I receive from old boys, and particularly at this time from those at the Front, show me that they remember the old days when they were here... Some, too, have died for their country in this war. As to the future it is difficult to say what will happen; the older ones must go, and we must keep up the supply of young ones to "follow up".*

May's letter has a resigned air, but her sentiment was the same as Kate's: their task was to raise men for the Empire and war at whatever cost. While May was responsible for future officers, Kate delivered the babies who would man their battalions.

Many Norlanders had yet to suffer a personal loss to the war; instead they wished to share their joy when one of their former charges was distinguished for his bravery, like Nurse Lydia Dawson in Glasgow. Lydia had worked with the Mann family since 1903 when she was still a probationer. She had now moved on to another family, but her contact with the Manns continued and she was extremely proud of her soldier charge: 'My boy, Ian Mann, has gained the Military Cross. I wish you would put a list in the Quarterly of all 'Norland Babies' who are or who have been serving in the Army or Navy. We are *so* [sic] proud of our boys.'

Lieutenant John (Ian) Anderson Mann had joined the army in 1913 while studying at Trinity College, Cambridge. He was in the Cameronians, 5th Scottish Rifles Territorial Force and had landed with his regiment in France in November 1914. For eighteen months, he had led his troops without sustaining any personal injury before being seconded to the 25th Squadron, Royal Flying Corps in March 1916.

On 23 June 1916, the *London Gazette* announced the award of the Military Cross to:

> *Second Lieutenant (temp. Lt). John Ian Anderson Mann for consistent gallantry and skill. In the course of seven days, 2nd Lts. Mann as pilot and Reid as observer attacked no less than eight enemy aeroplanes.*

They drove down four, three of which were seriously damaged. The
remainder were driven off, one escaping by getting into a cloud.

Ian had gone from soldier to pilot to hero in a few exhilaratingly and
hectic, short months.

Lydia had wanted to share her pride with her Norland colleagues in
the June 1916 *Quarterly* and her letter to Mrs Ward reached the Institute
with barely time to spare before publication. But the lifespan of a Great
War pilot was short and two months later Ian was dead, killed in action
on 9 August 1916, along with fellow crew member Captain Hart, whilst
flying on patrol duty over German lines. Like women all over the country,
Lydia was plunged from joy to despair. Mrs Ward never published a list
of Norland charges and their war achievements. It would have been too
sobering to witness the demise of so many officers they had raised.

Despite the grief many nurses were experiencing for their lost charges
and family members, Norland's war work had to go on. While Miss
Sharman praised all those who had left their posts in favour of VAD
and other types of work, she was equally keen to assuage the guilt
experienced by those Norlanders who had not been released from their
nurseries:

Circumstances have made it impossible for you to take up any work
directly connected with the War and your own work may seem to you
in comparison to be insignificant and ineffective – and you feel to be
resting in a pleasant backwater of life. This is an unjust appreciation
of your work; there are enormous possibilities of good work for our
King and Country in your hands, you have only to realise it and to
use your opportunity.

She too believed that Norlanders were perfectly placed to raise the next
generation of officers and nurture their families while the men were at
the front. She illustrated her argument by quoting the latest testimonial
from one nurse's employer, from which she had redacted the names to
avoid unnecessary embarrassment:

I can only repeat how much attached we all are to Nurse --------, and what a valuable friend and helper she is to us all. Major ------- told her when he went to France to the War, it is a great comfort to him to feel that she is with me and with the children in these anxious times.

Removing the burden of anxiety about how wives might cope without their officer husbands had become the latest Norland attribute. Along with it, Miss Sharman exhorted them to think to the future in their nurseries and a time when the war might be over: 'We can and we must work for greater trust and sympathy between the different nations of the world. This is our work in the present crisis.'

However, for some Norlanders, their war work became the supply of munitions to avoid crises at the front. After the failure of the British offensive at the battle of Neuve Chapelle in March 1915, it became apparent that the British Army was using up shells faster than the factories could produce them. As the 'shell scandal' became public knowledge, the Liberal government was held responsible and was forced into a coalition, with David Lloyd George heading the newly formed Ministry of Munitions. Immediately, shell factories began to recruit huge numbers of women to this latest form of war work.

Norlanders chose posts suitable for professional working-women. Nurse Catherine Hambly had given up her nursery position in Maida Vale to become an inspector of munitions at a shell factory and Nurse Helen Luke worked at the War Trade Department in Westminster 'putting in 42 hours a week with a certain amount of overtime as well'. Compared with her colleagues employed in nurseries and public schools, these were comfortable hours and the overtime ensured that munitions could be well-paid.

Keen to maintain numbers on the employment register when the war ended, Mrs Ward offered a contrary view:

War work is not easy, nor well paid, nor comfortable, and those who in some humble sphere are doing their bit may come back to us purged from the faults of which they were conscious, and become in the deeper sense of the word true educators.

In her opinion, munitions work was a penance to be endured, during which a wayward Norlander might improve herself. The new principal, Miss Jessie Dawber, agreed that Norlanders' responsibility was 'strengthening the characters of the next generation, and inspiring noble aims and high ideals in the future citizens of the world'. Norlanders formed a new class of respected professionals trained to educate the nation's children; they were not nursery maids who fetched and carried food trays and laundry. Norlanders were educated women and Miss Dawber felt their work was in the nursery, but she insisted that those who wished to take a more active role in 'England's struggle' would gain experience 'of great value to them when the time comes for them to join the Norland ranks again – or to pass on to another sphere of useful work'. Such opposing views of a Norlander's role did not bode well for Miss Dawber's tenure under Mrs Ward.

Jessie Dawber took over from Isabel Sharman after the latter's death in January 1917. Miss Sharman's loss was keenly felt by all the Norlanders. Nurses' letters flooded into the Institute and filled the February 1917 *Quarterly* – a memorial number with all articles and letters dedicated to Miss Sharman's memory. Like so many personal losses during the war, Miss Sharman's death went unheeded by the world outside the Norland Institute and her family.

The war moved on relentlessly, as new theatres of horror opened up all over Europe. In June 1915, Mrs Ward had already made an appeal for the latest casualties of war: 'Next Winter in both Belgium and Serbia actual poverty and starvation will be the lot of many; in fact, the whole of Europe will feel the effects of war, pestilence, and famine far more than it does at present!' It is strong oratory from someone only wishing to attract further donations of clothes, but the war was then starting its third year and it had become a true world war, with Eastern and Western Fronts, and the Balkans Front in the Near East.

As ever, Norlanders had taken the opportunity to travel and were to be found on all fronts. Nurse Ursula Jaques was now stationed in the Balkans at Salonika, while Nurse Margaret Kennedy was also in the Mediterranean, working as an orderly with the Scottish Women's Hospital. Ursula was a member of the Queen Alexandra's Imperial Military Nursing Service

Reserve. After she had completed her Norland certificate in 1903, she had trained as a medical nurse in the years leading up to the war. Since arriving in France late in 1914, she had spent a year setting up numerous military field hospitals, before being redeployed to Salonika in November 1915 during the British Army's protracted retreat from Gallipoli.

Conditions were appalling in Salonika, with few medical facilities, an impoverished and starving people, and displaced Serbian refugees flooding in. There was a massive influx of casualties, as British troops headed west through the Mediterranean after the disaster at Gallipoli during the summer of 1915. Ursula was there with British military support and supplies, whereas Margaret had travelled to Salonika with the Scottish Women's Hospital, which lacked a designated military escort.

Established in August 1914, the Scottish Women's Hospital (SWH) was the innovation of Dr Elsie Maud Inglis, a Scottish surgeon who had overcome every obstacle of the male establishment to become a top surgeon, setting up a women's hospice in Edinburgh and pioneering anaesthetics for women in childbirth. She was a force to be reckoned with, although the War Office had curtly dismissed her offer of medical assistance at the start of the conflict. Determined not to let her skills be wasted by blinkered government ministers, she offered her services to France and Serbia. Both countries welcomed her warmly.

In Serbia, the SWH organised field dressing stations, fever and surgical hospitals in disused schools, railway stations and in remote tents, funded by the American Red Cross and huge donations collected in Britain. Although the SWH received a staggering £450,000 from British donations alone during the four years of the war, its staff was unpaid and Margaret Kennedy worked as a volunteer.

Margaret was thirty-two and had been a Norlander for over a decade before the war. Her work as an orderly required self-determination, Edwardian mettle and a large dollop of elbow grease. An orderly's job was to clean constantly, which in Salonika included wounded soldiers, civilians and dusty compounds where dressing stations would be hastily erected. One minute Margaret would be consoling a patient or helping to feed him, the next hauling laden baskets of soiled bandages and amputated limbs to the incinerator.

Every time a hospital or dressing station had to move because the enemy was approaching, if they had time and space, all the equipment and furniture had to be packed up, carted on ox wagons and re-erected at a safe distance. Each time there was a unit move, Margaret's job was to clean the chosen building, scrubbing it as close to sterile as possible, making up beds and settling the wounded into their new abode. It was monotonous, hard physical work exacerbated by the weather, which alternated between baking hot and dry, to freezing cold with snow.

By Christmas 1917, Margaret had returned to Britain, where she took up the role of matron at Dun Holme, one of the boarding houses at Sherborne Girls' School in Dorset. With exceptionally grim conditions in Salonika, Margaret had completed her stint of voluntary work and had returned home to a paid job, doing what Norlanders were primarily trained for – caring for children. At Sherborne, Margaret settled into her role of assisting the housemistress with the girls' daily routine, somewhat akin to Edith's role at Cordwalles School. She had private rooms in the boarding house where she tended the girls' ailments, organised their laundry and activities, and took them on visiting parties to nearby Sherborne Castle which had been turned over to the Red Cross as a hospital for the duration.

Nurse Agnes Howie had gained her Norland Certificate in June 1913, aged twenty-one, and was working in London at the outbreak of war. At once, she volunteered as a VAD and between November 1915 and June 1919, she worked as a nurse, first in England and then travelling overseas to Egypt and Palestine. In her testimonial book, her first employer on her return to Britain noted that Agnes had been awarded the Victory Medal Ribbon and the War Medal Ribbon. To qualify for these medals and ribbons, the recipient must have served in a theatre of war during the conflict. Over six million were awarded to British citizens in recognition for their personal sacrifice during the war years.

Agnes never wrote personally to Norland describing her experiences. Nursing in the dust of the Middle East with casualties arriving by ship from recently evacuated Gallipoli would have left little time to put pen to paper. After Gallipoli the casualties did not stop, as more flooded in from Macedonia, then Sinai and Gaza. During Agnes' three and a half years in the Middle East, she and her comrades faced an unrelenting stream of wounded soldiers, often presenting with diseases such as dysentery along with their battle wounds. Agnes had travelled a long way from the comforts of her father's farm in Fife and her medal ribbons were hard won.

Norlanders based in Europe experienced the war in diverse ways. Some opted for hands-on war work, while others maintained their nurseries, but their invariable stoicism in the face of so much suffering, death and struggling with interminable war regulations sets them apart. Many Norlanders must have lost family members during the war, but this was not mentioned in their letters to the Institute. Instead, they chose to share their achievements and pass on their news, enduring personal grief in silence.

In November 1918, Mrs Ward wrote in the *Quarterly* that 'since 1914 over 200 nurses have taken up war work'. With an average of 700 nurses on their books in every year of the war, nearly a third had volunteered or worked for the war effort. It was a significant contribution from a cohort of nicely brought-up ladies, who had hoped to enjoy careers in London townhouses, châteaux and palaces. Instead, the war proved to be a professional hiatus, which saw Norlanders working in tents within earshot of the front line; emptying endless bedpans in hurriedly converted stately home hospitals; and caring for young boys suffering their private griefs in dormitories after lights out.

Kate Fox was especially encouraging of younger Norland nurses who decided to remain within the world of childcare:

Norland Nurses will realise that by doing their work whole-heartedly and faithfully they are doing the noblest of all war work in caring for the future generation, and in training the children to be good and faithful citizens of our Empire.

When the war was over, however, the transition was going to be a brutal shock for royal Norland Nurse Kate Fox.

Chapter 5

War in the Nursery

By summer 1915, living with the war had become routine for many Britons. The public could only absorb so much news from the front before becoming mired in despair. Detailed daily reports were now to be found on the inside pages of newspapers and only the most important stories made the front page.

On the whole, Britons had settled into this new way of life. The first rush of volunteers had begun to dwindle, but conscription was not yet an option and family men who had not signed up in the first year of the war remained at home. Working women continued to manage their families and their jobs, while a few joined their daughters working in the munitions factories. Boy Scouts and Girl Guides assisted at first aid training sessions; they collected clothes and food parcels for servicemen and refugees, and worked alongside the explosion of charities across the country. From the youngest to the oldest, nearly everyone became involved in some way with the war effort.

In London, Nurse Hilda Chater, who had qualified in 1893, had arrived at a temporary appointment. She was caring for a six-week-old infant whose mother was ill. The parents had left the capital for a short holiday in the country only to return on 29 September, the day of a Zeppelin air attack. Shortly afterwards, the mother wrote in Hilda's testimonial book: 'It was wonderful how quickly she got the children down to the basement and the day following she took the children away to the country.' For this family and other Britons on the home front, taking an air raid in their stride had become an everyday affair and, as long as no one was hurt and property remained undamaged, physical contact with the war could be exciting.

Apart from those killed and injured by successful Zeppelin and submarine attacks on the mainland, the immediate pain of war still remained a relatively distant affair for most people. However, as casualties were shipped home to Britain and then returned to civilian life, the evidence of what war did to men became plain for all to see. Young men walked British streets with empty sleeves and trouser legs or were pushed in wheelchairs. For some, this was proof that war was wrong and a small but increasing number of citizens began to question the morality of the war. The sinking of RMS *Lusitania* in May 1915, with only 761 survivors among the 2,000 passengers on board, had cemented in most Britons' minds the belief that this was a righteous war against a heinous aggressor, who had to be stopped at all costs. The few public voices that questioned the war were stifled for the moment.

Behind closed doors at the Norland Institute, this weighty debate had become a matter of great concern among Mrs Ward's opinionated nannies. Letters to the Norland *Quarterly* trickled in before a written skirmish broke out, requiring its own subtitle in the correspondence pages. With an unusual touch of humour, Mrs Ward published the correspondence under the banner heading 'War in the Nursery', unwittingly fuelling the debate with her customary letter on the *Quarterly's* first page: 'We women in lovely, smiling and peaceful England hardly realise half the terror of all that is going on across the seas, and in our deep blue waters, protected as we are by our brave soldiers and sailors.'

The 'terror' she described was the Germans, portrayed in the British press as 'Huns' or 'Boche'; thoroughly nasty characters capable of the worst atrocities against soldiers and civilians alike. In the first months of the war, the British press had been full of reports of indiscriminate bayoneting and summary collective punishments by the occupying German troops in Belgium, but it was the most lurid stories of rape and child mutilation that fuelled hatred. Some reports were true, but with a population struggling to understand why the assassination of an archduke in Serbia could lead them into war, these accounts from the front line quickly provided justification for taking up arms. Equally, the Germans believed themselves threatened by British imperial might and their press portrayed Britain as the aggressor, as many Norlanders had discovered whilst living in Germany.

In the early months of the war, the hostility displayed between the two nations had greatly distressed Miss Sharman, who felt compelled to quell any such emotions among her Norlanders:

> *The terrible spirit of enmity which exists in Germany towards England is to me the most terrible part of the war. With that between us peace, a lasting beneficial peace, will be almost impossible. I am sure we ought each one to do what we can to stem the flood of hate. We say we do not hate the Germans, but every time we turn a joke against them or give voice to our wishes for their humiliation, we fan the fire and increase the spirit of hatred.*

Miss Sharman's incredulity that the situation had deteriorated so quickly did not extend to the nursery and she hastened to quote from a conversation with a nurse who had returned from her German employer in the weeks before the war: 'Her little charges were constantly playing soldiers and battles, but "they never fought the English".' Cushioned from the increasingly tense political situation, clearly this nurse believed that in German nurseries run by British nannies, the special relationship between the two nations that had existed since Queen Victoria's reign would guarantee that hostilities would soon peter out.

Keeping the war out of the nursery was a sentiment that the Norland principal was eager to promote, as she believed vehemently that children must remain innocent of such xenophobic hatred:

> *The older children will [sic] play their war games; but we can lead their thoughts to understand that war can only be justified because righteousness must come before peace, and above all things we must not allow them to grow up to love war for war's sake.*

Having declared their personal views, Mrs Ward and Miss Sharman watched as the pages of the *Quarterly* began to fill up with nurses' letters continuing the debate: were they fighting a just war or not?

Nurse Cicely Colls launched straight in with a lengthy letter at Christmas 1915. Like Miss Sharman, she was determined to keep war out of her nursery:

Nowadays everyone speaks, thinks and dreams of "battle, murder and sudden death," and the echo of these cries has penetrated to all the nurseries of Europe... and now the spirit of hatred, which no normal child knows, casts its shadow around!

Cicely had trained in 1896 and she had enjoyed full-time employment in England since gaining her Norland Certificate. Surrounded by Britons excited by the war and loathing the enemy, Cicely's opinions were distinctly out of step with the majority of her fellow citizens. In a society where the establishment was at pains to describe Britain's involvement in a 'just' war, Cicely had spotted the ultimate outcome of this new type of conflict – total war:

Let us at least emphasise that war is evil, and that courage can be shown in many ways. Giving one's life for any believed-in cause is noble, but do we clearly realise that as we each hope that those dearest to us may safely return, and each man hopes he will be lucky, yet the practical effect is to take as many lives as possible?

It was now the end of 1915 and during the second year of the war, Britain had lost tens of thousands at Gallipoli and in the massive offensive at Loos in Flanders among many other military actions. Poison gas had been used for the first time by both sides, and as the war consumed men, conscription was looming in the near future. Before the next generation of Norland-raised children might fuel the war, Cicely hoped to intervene with an argument for which she felt children's nurses were perfectly suited:

Fellow workers, between us at the present time, we must have about 2,000 young children in our care! Now, if these are taught the things that make for Peace, and we each ask other nurses that we meet, and

other nursing institutions to join us, there is already a small nucleus of
"Hope" in the next generation and the glorious days yet to be.

Those 'glorious days' meant British victory, but unmistakeably Cicely alluded also to a workers' union of nurses bent on preaching pacifism. She was way ahead of her time.

Despite the increasing threat of marauding German submarines, at this stage of the war, the *Quarterly* was still getting through to North America, where Nurse Hilda Hiley read Cicely's letter. Her response began a personal war of words for the next two years.

Hilda had grown up in Bristol and, after qualifying at Norland in 1905, she had worked in New York since 1913. Although she had not returned to England during her latest employment, she had kept in touch with public opinion back home, in fact like many expatriates she had become staunchly British while surrounded by neutral Americans. However, Hilda recognised the luxury of contrary opinion that her position afforded her so distant from the war: 'Perhaps, had I come into closer contact with the ghastly sufferings which have come to so many, or personally suffered a great loss, I could not write as I do now.'

Like Cicely, she did not desire unnecessary hatred of the enemy in her nursery and she recognised that children were 'ready to see good in all men', but she was prepared to guide their consciences:

The thought creeps into their loving hearts that on both sides children, perhaps small cousins, are praying to the same God to let their [sic] *side win. When that thought perplexes them I think they are old enough to grasp the idea that we can and should all pray that truth and right and justice may win the day wherever they be found.*

Hilda's charges were Americans, but they had French relations on their father's side and Austrian cousins through their mother's line. Naturally, Hilda supported the British in the war, but in a multi-national household she was more aware than most of the complicated nature of the war in Europe and she felt her responsibility keenly: 'I have found American children very quick to respond to the influence of the English governesses and nurses who care for them, and I think it is our duty towards those children that they should see the war impartially.'

Living on East 60th Street within yards of Central Park, where British nursery nurses congregated with their charges, and surrounded by a large community of opinionated expatriate Britons, Hilda was honest enough to write that 'here in the States the air is full of controversy over the war'. Hilda was also exposed to the conflicting opinions of educated Germans living in the cities of the Eastern Seaboard, when she attended children's parties with her charges. It was a confusing time for anyone with European allegiances, but at least the war could be discussed openly in America without fear of reprisals if one was overheard.

In alluding to reports of atrocities against civilians in Belgium in the early months of the war, Hilda felt sufficiently free to be able to discuss with her charges the traditional soldier's code of honour:

What they must learn to hate are the deeds which dishonour any true soldier, and the lack of self-control which causes that dishonour. All brave soldiers, when they fight, hope to meet foemen "worthy of their steel" and are ready to acknowledge bravery and heroism on which ever side it is found... but as far as we can tell now terrible deeds of savagery, wilful cruelty and injustice have disgraced one side more than the other.

Deeds of kindness and acts of bravery by combatants on both sides had filtered back to Britain through official and unofficial routes, and the Christmas Truce which 'broke out' in places up and down the Western Front, often against commanding officers' wishes, had been reported. Yet, what was being described at home fuelled a new war, one based on shock and hatred, aimed at winning recruits to Kitchener's New Army.

Keeping her insight into the current crisis centred on the children in her nurses' care, Miss Sharman tried to maintain a sense of balance, reminding Norlanders that before the war, many of Norland's 'best' employers had been German royals: 'May I suggest a few points, which can be emphasised in the nursery even now? "Daddy is a brave soldier, and of course loves his children, and wishes them to be brave. And so do the German daddies".'

Immense tact was required of nannies, who knelt nightly in the nursery with their charges to say their prayers. All fathers were brave in the eyes of their children, and equally, God was on their side. Cicely quoted a particularly thorny conversation with one of her charges prior to the war: 'Some years ago, an English child of eight, said: "Nursie, if the Germans come and fight us, and ask God to make them win, and we ask God to let us win – what will God do?' It was the kind of question to make most Edwardian parents blench, but Cicely was equal to the task. 'Truth, Right and Justice' was her answer to God's conundrum, but despite Cicely's efforts to remain impartial and guide her charges along a Christian path, inevitably the war had still sneaked into her nursery: 'I heard a little girl praying very simply and seriously, "Please God, kill the Kaiser somehow!"'

To a child hearing all sorts of discussions in her parents' sitting-room and below stairs among the servants, it was a perfectly natural request, but Cicely could not bear such murderous thoughts and instantly corrected the child:

> *"How would you like the little German girls to ask God to kill our King?" Wide, open-eyed surprise. "Oh, but they wouldn't."*
> *"Then they are kinder than you, for most of them like their King, and they don't all think him wicked."*

Prayers were being offered up in homes and churches all over Europe, for the nation, the men at the front and an end to hostilities. As ever more nurseries and families were affected by the loss of a father or close male relation, Cicely's pacifism and Miss Sharman's selfless views grew increasingly hard to maintain. Addressing her nurses in the March 1916 *Quarterly*, Mrs Ward added a stark note of reality: 'If the wishes and prayers of the women and children of the world could stop this awful war it would cease to-morrow.'

Cicely and Hilda did not know one another personally; they had trained at Norland a decade apart and it would have been considered impolite to seek each other out through the employment address lists at the rear of the *Quarterly* to continue this debate through private correspondence. As a result, their letters printed in the spring 1916 edition had crossed. They were no longer arguing against each other, but using the *Quarterly's* pages to air the confusing emotions most Norlanders must have struggled with during these uncertain years of the war.

Hilda asked the readership to consider the death toll so far and how women might respond to the sacrifice made by their men: 'Our duty is to make our lives better in return for the gift of all the splendid young lives which the war has claimed.' Cicely compared the concept of self-sacrifice to pacifist principles, in tune with the limited but growing number of conscientious objectors, men of fighting age who had refused on principle or religious faith to put on a soldier's uniform once conscription had been brought in: 'It is grand to "give" one's life, but never fine to "take" it from any human being; then in a few generations war may pass away, and life will be more gay and interesting and varied.'

To Norlanders surrounded by total war for nearly two years, there appeared to be no end in sight, although Miss Sharman envisaged a solution if generations to come could forget their enmity: 'We must look to the fact that the babies in the nursery today will, we hope, be friends with the present German babies.' Mrs Ward closed the debate for now, lauding Cicely's call to keep the war out of the nursery. She made no comment as to which side she personally favoured:

Nurse Cicely reminds us that it is not for little children to criticise or condemn [the war]. *She begs us to reserve judgement before them, and implores us to keep before the children the wickedness of jealousy and the beauty of pity and forgiveness.*

The Norland *Quarterly* was sent to Norlanders and their employers. The opinions aired within it throughout these middle years of the war were often contrary to wider public opinion and the guiding hand of a government desperate to maintain the momentum of the conflict. The nurses' letters to the Institute were not subject to the official censor and Mrs Ward did not know what hands her publication might fall in to. That she allowed such forthright views to be printed when the continued employment of her nurses depended on their being seen as upright members of society is testament to her dedication to women's education and healthy debate about the war.

As the war dragged on – with Lloyd George's Ministry of Munitions commandeering factories for war work, requisitioning raw materials and labour throughout the country – no one could have foreseen the impact that the 'shell crisis' of 1915 would have on Norland. U-boats had been targeting merchant ships and food shortages had been felt for some time in Britain, although many working nannies would not have noticed this, cushioned by the resources of their wealthy employers. The impact on the Norland Institute was seen instead in less obvious forms: their distinguished uniform and finances. Norland's German-manufactured source of apron material suddenly dried up on the outbreak of war. An English factory took on the order for the cloth, but with so many factories now requisitioned for government use, Norland admitted defeat. Mrs Ward bemoaned that apron fabric could not even be 'procured from Switzerland'.

The material used for Norland cloaks had also become expensive, now costing 9s 6d a yard (in 1910 the same material had cost 3s 9d), and 'owing to the requirements of the Government will soon be unobtainable'. Norland cloaks used up large quantities of cloth, of similar material to those worn by the military, and the shortage forced Mrs Ward into an economy that would have been unthinkable before the war. Norlanders would be compelled to adopt the latest fashion in overcoats, wearing a woollen garment similar to the VAD coat – an ankle-length untailored and over-sized topcoat. Whereas the traditional Norland cape had a tendency to blow over a nanny's head like an umbrella turning inside-out in windy weather, 'this [new design] would suit all figures and be very practical.' It was the first of several grudging compromises for Mrs Ward.

By Christmas 1917, the proposed new coat had still not materialised, as wool had now been commandeered by the government for military uniforms and any surplus was terribly expensive. Mrs Ward declared that existing stocks of the old brown cloth would only last if nurses economised.

The rise in the cost of living imposed by the war was having an impact on far more than the wardrobes of the Institute's nurses, however. Norland Place School, established forty years ago by Mrs Ward, now changed ownership and was bought-out by four Norland-trained teachers employed there. Mrs Ward's *Quarterly* letter at Christmas 1915 extolled the success of her 'model institution', but beneath her effusiveness for the school's future lay the need for money.

The Norland Club, which had been established in 1913 at 7 Pembridge Square to provide accommodation to nurses visiting the Institute, was sub-let to war workers, but the toughest blow to the Institute's finances was a lack of fee-paying students. As increasing numbers of middle-class young women were entering relatively well-paid jobs in munitions factories or undertaking supervisory and clerical work in the War Office, foregoing professional training while the war lasted, the numbers of new students at the Norland Institute dwindled.

Mrs Ward did not wish to ask her working nurses for subscriptions to avoid falling into debt; instead she asked the Norland *Quarterly's* global circulation of 800 to bring the need for 'fourteen probationers for July, and sixteen for October' to the attention of any young women they thought suitable to train at Norland. The Institute's staff was already making 'petty economies', but Mrs Ward could not countenance cutting corners in training or the service she provided to her clients. Norlanders and their employers expected the Institute to 'maintain our usual high standard', even when the rest of the country was retrenching.

However, Mrs Ward did economise in one area; with paper becoming more costly, it pained her to announce that 1916 would see the publication of only three *Quarterlies*. This was not quite the blow to nurses that the curtailment of social gatherings at the Institute had been. Since the early days of Norland, nurses had been encouraged to return to the Institute, bringing tales of their exploits to inspire the student nurses, allowing Mrs Ward to catch up on their news and to hear lectures by visiting speakers. Norland was their second home; somewhere friends could socialise and swap advice on nursery topics, since they were rarely allowed visitors to their nurseries. During the winter of 1914, London-based nurses had gathered for Mrs Ward's 'at homes' to sew and knit, making garments for the various refugee charities they supported. This was war work they could all become involved with and the social evenings had been well attended.

So far, the physical ravages of the war had barely touched Norlanders. They were doing their bit, as far as they were allowed, and they were making small personal economies. Nevertheless, despite submarine and aerial attacks on the East Coast, they had yet to experience war on the home front through personal loss or air-raid. However, with the onslaught of Zeppelin airship attacks on the capital from May 1915, the government had imposed a 'blackout' on cities up and down the country to confuse the airships' navigators.

With London's streets swaddled in darkness, finally the war began to disrupt the Institute's daily routine. No one could predict when the next air raid might be and Mrs Ward felt she 'could not ask any nurses to come out at night'. Early air-raids had often taken place during daylight in order for the bombers to spot their targets, risking retaliatory fire from the ground, but as the war progressed night raids became the norm.

By autumn 1917, the Germans were increasingly using the new Gotha aeroplanes to harass London, and they carried out a devastating and consistent wave of attacks during the first week of September. With the capital deep in darkness, the nightly raids had been planned to coincide with the bright glow of the harvest moon. Their main targets were the London Docks in the East End where, earlier that summer, they had killed 162 people in a single raid in Poplar, 18 of whom were children at a primary school.

Nurse Helen Bell had only recently completed her Norland training and was working with a family living on the edge of Greenwich Park in Blackheath, barely a mile from the Port of London. It was a smart part of the city; a far remove from her childhood on a farm outside a rural Lincolnshire market town.

On 4 September, Helen experienced first-hand one of the 'harvest moon raids'. She remembered a clear and calm starlit night, with the family 'on the watch for signs of a raid'. She had put the two little boys to bed, on the third storey of the house where she occupied a neighbouring room. They noticed nothing unusual until the adults prepared for bed at 11pm:

I looked out of my bedroom window and saw that the searchlights were very busy, then listening very intently I heard the hum of a German machine. We know their sound very well, as it is different from that of our own 'planes, theirs being a lower note in another key altogether.

Helen dashed to wake the maids and the family's older daughter also on her landing as 'a syren [sic] gave a long call of warning'. While she grabbed seven-year-old Michael, his mother gathered up five-year-old Stephen, and wrapped in eiderdowns, they all went to the drawing-room. Like many children across Britain, the boys slumbered on during this first upheaval:

We had not been down three minutes before we heard five loud bangs which shook the house, wakened the boys, and gave us all a shock, especially my employer, who received a sudden puff of air in the face as she happened to be gazing out of a window. The next morning these five bangs proved to be bombs, or aerial torpedoes, very near to us, but two fell in gardens and three in a field.

Helen's understatement and desire not to be alarmist – essential traits for a children's nurse – concealed the true horror of what she and the family had endured. The 'puff' was the blast felt from an exploding shell, something many soldiers in the trenches had experienced and which had sent numerous casualties straight to the Regimental Aid Post. Possibly protected by the walls of the house or distance from the centre of the explosion, none of the family or servants were injured. However, the following day, the War Office reported that the attack, comprising 11 Gotha aeroplanes, had killed 152 Londoners. The shock was enough to spur Helen into action.

In preparation for another raid, the next day they furnished the cellar with carpets and curtains, stocking it with fruit, as well as playing cards and sewing for entertainment. Helen and the family spent several nights listening to the muted sounds of gunfire in their underground 'dug out'. In order not to disturb the boys' sleep, Helen arranged two dining-table leaves on bricks so that their bedtime now started in the cellar, with no need to transfer them during the night. Helen had obviously made the family quite comfortable and received high praise from one of the boys: "If yer knows of a better 'ole yer can go to it, but I'm going to stay here."

On 24 September, Helen noted another clear and calm night; perfect bombing conditions. She spotted 'star shells' put up by the London battery to illuminate the sky and assist spotting of enemy aircraft. Descending to safety, Helen and the family took their supper 'downstairs' because: 'The sound of the gun firing was deadened in the cellar, but not so much that we could not hear the whistle of the shells as they went over our house.' There were benefits to such discomfort, even when they were forced to eat lunch in the cellar too: 'Personally, I find I get a great deal of sewing done on raid nights, and the Germans would be very surprised could they see our jocular faces and spirits.'

Helen enjoyed a long period of employment with her Blackheath family, staying with them throughout 1917, before disappearing from the Norland register. Yet, increasingly nurses moved from nursery to nursery as work became more fragmented. Families could no longer afford their services; others had departed for the country and, with the man of the house away at the war, there were fewer newborns whose mothers required a maternity nurse. Hiring Norlanders for short periods to see them through a family difficulty or simply to alleviate the mother's tiredness became an increasing trend. The size of middle- and upper-class families had been falling since the turn of the century, but they were still larger than most modern ones, and with domestic staff also becoming harder to retain, the care of the children fell to the mother, sometimes the least maternally experienced woman in the home.

The nurses' correspondence addresses listed in the register changed more frequently and it became obvious to them all that yet another facet of Norland was being altered by the war. Of course, this sparked a fresh debate, which saw the Institute divide again into two groups as described by Cicely Colls:

The experienced, capable and adaptable nurses who are equal to any emergency, and the young probationers for whom things have been more or less arranged and who work directly under the supervision of the mother or another Norland nurse.

The older, experienced nurses who wore their green and blue bars for twenty and fifteen years' service in a single household attached to their Norland Badge, had started work long before the war. Those still to gain the service bar had trained in the years immediately prior to the war and were now suffering the knock-on effects of wartime economies in formerly wealthy households, forced to take up short-term and temporary work. However, this suited some Norlanders, like Nurse Mabel Lister who relished the importance she felt in each new post: 'I must confess I rather delight in being wired for to go to a post where things are in a muddle! It is such a chance to show what Norlanders can do!'

Since 1911, Mabel had taken stints of temporary work and particularly enjoyed substituting for a Norlander taking a holiday. Assuming temporary responsibility of a well-run Norlander's nursery meant 'very little difficulty' when it came to domestic arrangements, since all the nurses had been taught to organise a nursery in exactly the same manner:

Of course to go from a well-ordered nursery with two Norlanders and a nursery-maid to an employer who is perhaps in a hotel and has never seen a Norland nurse, whose experience of nurses has been an Indian ayah, presents a test to one's powers of adaptability.

Nurse Annie Avery's first posting had been for a month, filling in for a Norlander who was going on leave. On arrival at the house, she finally realised what her expensive training had been about:

The first things that struck me were the extreme neatness and tidiness of the cupboards and the order and method by which everything was arranged. It made a lasting impression, and I made up my mind that when I had a permanent post my nurseries must be as tidy and as methodically managed as this nurse's were.

For Cicely, such realisation had been acquired through painful experience. She admitted that in her early years in the 1890s, as a probationer working with families who had no knowledge of Norland, she had lost two jobs due to 'unfamiliarity with the nursery details which some parents consider "essentials".' The third job she took was a six-week engagement with a frightful family of five 'badly-trained and unmanageable children'. The nursery-maid was older than Cicely and only came downstairs at 8.30am and would not 'be told anything'. The seven-year-old could not put on her own boots; another she called 'a nervous "difficile" sleep-walking child of six', with a 'young pickle of four, a croupy ex-baby, and a coughing baby!' They were a tough family to manage by any standards and when offered a permanent position, Cicely headed for the nursery door.

She believed that temporary posts, which from personal experience could be very trying, were only for the 'capables' and had not ventured back into temporary work until gaining many years' experience in permanent posts. Cicely considered she was giving a little back to the Institute 'by helping it out of a difficulty' by replacing a nurse who had been dismissed, taken ill or simply needed a break and she basked in the importance of 'being wired for', although that too could be inconvenient:

> *I had only just returned from a temporary post and was going out to do some necessary shopping (I really had no suitable clothes), when I met the telegraph boy on the doorstep with a telegram saying "Please go at once to _____".*

The answer to the problem, she advised nurses intent on taking temporary work, was that they should have their bags packed 'for different circumstances, as well-known newspaper reporters are said to have'.

On the whole, Cicely favoured permanent work where the children grew to love her; she formed a strong understanding with her employers; life was comfortable if monotonous; and the salary was regular, often supplemented by 'little gifts as tokens of appreciation and good will'.

However, 22-year-old Nurse Dorothy Sanders was heavily in favour of temporary work, especially for young nurses whom she felt needed to gain varied experience as quickly as possible, as she had done:

One month I was with two very small boys, whose one delight was hand-made toys, so I was busy making toys. Directly I left these two boys, I bustled immediately to three small boys; but the youngest of these was a fast crawling baby, so handwork had to be put aside, and baby knowledge had to come to the front. The same day that I left these boys, I departed to three girls.

Dorothy agreed heartily that having separate bags packed for different types of nursery was essential, but she rued the fact that all her efforts over her four years as a nanny did not accrue a service record that would earn her a green or blue bar for her Badge. Temporary work did not count towards the bars, for reasons that Mrs Ward declined to explain. Given her ambition to see Norland nurses employed by all the best families and in royal households, in which loyalty and long-term service were valued, perhaps temporary postings were too akin to casual work carried out by many working-class women, and thus deemed to be beneath her highly trained nannies. However, as the war emptied the purses of the middle-classes, increasing requests for temporary nannies were made, which suited some Norlanders perfectly.

On the whole, Mabel's temporary employments had been happy with one exception: a little boy whose only experience of childcare had been an Indian ayah, 'whom he slapped if she did not please him!' Norlanders have always operated a policy of complete discretion in declining to name the individual children they work with, which was just as well if this boy's mother hoped to engage another Norlander in the future.

Yet, whatever nanny-magic Mabel used on her charge seemed to work, because after a few days they were 'firm friends'. She was undeterred by the experience and particularly enjoyed the prestige that accompanied setting-up a nursery system, so that on her departure the mother might continue the regime with the help of just a nursery maid. In the Norland register, Mabel always gave her home address because, with her rapid flitting from job to job, the postman could not keep up.

Old-timer Nurse Ianthe Hodges supported Mabel's wish to gain a varied experience from working with different families. In 1915, Ianthe was one of only three nurses sporting a blue bar for more than fifteen years' service. She had been in the employ of the Countess of Dudley since 1899. As one of Norland's high-status nannies, surprisingly she took a balanced outlook on the work of young Norlanders like Mabel:

Watch and listen as you go along. Nothing is too small to do and nothing is "beneath you" to do. Common sense, alertness, adaptability to people and surroundings and love, is the whole secret of nursery work.

Ianthe declared that if she were given her twenty-three years of nannying again, she would do exactly the same and take a permanent post, but the new world required a different kind of nurse, and temporary work was to be embraced.

After such enthusiasm for temporary work, nanny to the royals Kate Fox stepped in to argue that temporary work for newly-qualified nurses would not help them to learn proper practice and they 'would get more than ever infected with the restless spirit of the age'. Kate preferred young Norlanders to serve their early years under the wing of an older, more experienced nanny like herself. She did not anticipate a Norlander enjoying a personal life or wishing for time off, unless it was 'quite convenient to her employer'.

Length of service was a subject that continued to exercise Nurse Annie Avery, who recognised as early as 1917 that there were few families 'large enough to permit of keeping a nursery for fifteen years'. Family sizes among the upper-classes had been falling since the 1890s, and the nanny as 'family retainer' was an increasingly rare engagement. Annie felt that if you could stay for five years, then five or ten more would not be much effort, having already got everything running like clockwork. With temporary work in the ascendancy, Annie argued that the latter should count towards a bar, particularly if the nurse gained consistently excellent testimonials. Nurse Kate Viall agreed, suggesting that nurses who stayed in a position solely in the hope of gaining a bar were staying for the wrong reasons and might be filling a post better suited to another nurse.

In her editorial, Mrs Ward ignored the growing unrest about the bar system. The general atmosphere of emancipation among women spawned by the war had afforded her nurses a voice they had previously not dared to use within the hallowed halls of Norland. Mrs Ward supported women's suffrage, but she remained deaf to dissent among her nannies. Instead, she deftly turned the subject back to temporary versus permanent work: 'It must be remembered that the opinions of Badge nurses carry weight. One of our younger nurses writes: "I have always looked up to any Badge nurse with respect and admiration, not to say awe, as one looks up to a soldier who has won the V.C."' She implored the younger nurses not to feel hurt if those of more mature years had earned 'the right to be dogmatic'.

The debates on the war and working patterns remained strictly within the walls of the Institute and the pages of the *Quarterly*, while outwardly the nurses remained spotless representatives of the world's first nanny training college. Mrs Ward was increasingly cognisant of the competition on the streets of London, with her nannies surrounded by so many men and women dressed in smart uniforms denoting their regiment or nursing organisation, and she wanted her children's nurses to take equal pride in their allegiance to the Institute. Once employed, Norlanders could decide whether to wear their uniform or their own clothes, and an array of badges and broaches depicting the Norland Institute's 'NI' had proliferated.

Mrs Ward was determined that her nurses would look as smart as any VAD and would be as instantly recognisable. In March 1916, she introduced the Norland monogram, a silver badge with holes at either end so that it could be sewn on to a cloak, lying flat and avoiding the need for a pin, which might catch in a baby's shawl or scratch a child. It was a hard-earned badge of achievement worn by some to signify their own form of war work in raising the next generation. It cost 2s 6d and had to be returned to the Institute, along with a nurse's uniform, if she broke her connection with Norland. With war-straitened families dismissing their Norlander in favour of untrained nursery-maids, Mrs Ward felt compelled to enforce this latest regulation in order to avoid dilution of the Norland brand.

Little by little, the war chipped away at Norland in unforeseen ways. Mrs Ward also came under pressure to organise a Norland war savings association from which nurses could buy bonds, helping to alleviate the government's war deficit. The sale of War Bonds was a national movement,

Nurse Kate Fox with Their Royal Highnesses, Princesses Olga, Elisabeth and Marina 'Baby' of Greece, c. 1910. Kate was at the height of her popularity in the Greek Royal household. (Norland College archive)

Mrs Emily Ward, founder of the Norland Institute, with Miss Isabel Sharman, the first principal, 1893. (Norland College archive)

Nurse 19 wearing the Norland Institute's earliest nanny uniform. (Norland College archive)

Norland's outdoor uniform 1892–1900. (Norland College archive)

Norland Badge, first introduced in 1902 with silver, blue and green bars for 10, 15 and 20 years service respectively. By Christmas 1919, only two nurses had gained a green bar; one of them Nurse Ianthe Hodges. (Author's own collection)

Postcard from Nurse Kate Fox to the Norland Institute whilst travelling in Europe with the Ruspoli family, summer 1903. Kate's note mentions the nursery suite she occupied in the castle during her stay. (Norland College archive)

Nurse Kate Fox with Their Royal Highnesses, Princesses Olga and Elisabeth of Greece, c. 1905. (Norland College archive)

The first Norland Institute probationers pose for their class photograph, September 1892. (Norland College archive)

Sitting-room for nurses visiting the Norland Institute for Mrs Ward's 'at homes' and other social gatherings, 10 Pembridge Square, early 1900s. (Norland College archive)

Nurse Beatrice Todd's charges: Princes Sigismund, Waldemar and Heinrich of Prussia. (Norland College archive)

Nurse Beatrice Todd sending greetings to Miss Sharman from her royal employer's home in Kiel, Germany, 1904. (Norland College archive)

Postcard from Nurse Kate Fox from the Chateau Royal á Decelie, Athens. Kate left the Ruspoli family in order to take up employment with Her Royal and Imperial Highness Princess Nicholas of Greece, Christmas 1903. (Norland College archive)

Mrs Emily Ward, founder of the Norland Institute. (Norland College archive)

Nurse Beatrice Todd, Norland's first 'royal nanny', with her German charges, early 1900s. (Norland College archive)

Probationer nurses in nursery uniform at the end of the War, 1918. (Norland College archive)

with children investing their three pence pieces weekly in local school associations. Norland had to be seen to join in and consequently the Norland Nurses' War Savings Association was established.

The employment of staff at the Institute had remained unaffected, unlike that of the nannies, but their hopes for the future were also thwarted by the war. The blockade of the English Channel by German submarines made it extremely risky for anything but essential shipping and the dangers to vessels passing through the Suez Canal had prevented Miss Burke, who had worked on the Institute's staff for five years, from leaving England to be married in the Far East. She would have to stay a further five months until the USA joined the Allies before she could find safe passage by ship, via Canada, to Shanghai. Likewise, parents stationed in India and the Near East whose children boarded in Norland's nurseries, could not return to England to fetch them and there were nurses still overseas in non-combatant countries, who wished to come home.

By 1917, they had endured the war and its privations for three years, and Norlanders celebrated, even the smallest victories in Mrs Ward's words: 'Let us hope that the war conditions next year will be so improved that they may be allowed to travel overseas, and that by this time next year many happy reunions will have taken place.'

However, one novel entertainment, described in the penultimate *Quarterly* of 1917, had emerged from the occasional British successes on the Western Front. While taking their afternoon perambulations around London with their charges, Norlanders could now visit the latest attraction. If the zoo no longer held their children's attention; if tea in Kew Gardens was too far to traipse before returning in time for the 'blackout' and interest in watching the hospital trains pulling into Charing Cross had waned, then the Edwardian child could enjoy the delights of a visit to the captured German guns on display at Hyde Park. The *Quarterly* editorial described it as the perfect distraction for Norland's children. While the nurses had argued about whether or not to expose their charges to the war, the war had directly entered the cosy sphere of nanny's afternoon walks.

Even the most cosseted nursery could no longer avoid the conflict and Norland's 'war in the nursery' would strike up once again in the months before the Armistice.

Chapter 6

Missions and Mothercraft

An advertisement placed in the *Quarterly* in June 1915 sums up the effect of the war on one Norlander and many other women facing similar circumstances. A married ex-Norlander was advertising for a position to which her seven-year-old son could accompany her. Prior to the war, this would have been unthinkable. When a Norlander married, she automatically had to leave her employment because Mrs Ward ruled that marriage and working as a children's nurse were incompatible. A woman's husband would support her and the wife's duty lay with her anticipated new family. However, the war forced Mrs Ward to be more lenient in special circumstances.

This particular Norlander's husband was 'serving for the duration of the war' and as a soldier's pay was more limited than her husband's usual salary, she felt compelled to return to work. She was prepared to undertake any duties, 'preferably in a nursery where there would be the companionship of other boys about the same age'. Employers were directed to contact Miss Sharman, protecting the woman from the shame of being forced to return to work in such circumstances.

Buried in the Sussex countryside surrounded by her Belgian refugees, Mrs Ward was hugely sympathetic to the continued misery caused by the war, especially among Britain's foreign allies: 'The Christian nations throughout the world are mourning for homes, friends and dear ones, and they are suffering privations and sorrows innumerable.'

Within weeks of the outbreak of war, Mrs Ward had been in the thick of things organising, networking and exercising Norland's influence, but a year on she appears to have lost her earlier grasp of the domestic impact of the war. Her understanding of the situation on the British home front was contrary to that of her nurses working in London:

Here we live in England in comfort and ease as is evidenced by the reduction in the number of the inhabitants of our workhouses and prisons, while the wives and children of our fighting forces are living in comfort and contentment on their separation allowances.

The workhouses and gaols were emptier than previous years because the men had been recruited into the army, and their families were far from living in the state of blissful well-being Mrs Ward envisaged. Separation allowances paid by the military to families whose men were at the front were not generous and many, like the anonymous Norlander and her son, lived in reduced circumstances, for some the deepest poverty they had yet experienced. Also a woman's allowance could be withdrawn by the War Office if her behaviour was deemed immoral, for instance turning to drink in her loneliness or seeking comfort in another man.

During the decade prior to the war, the Norland Nurses' Mission Fund had supported two children's crèches, one in Acton in West London and another in Bethnal Green in the East End. After war was declared and men began to join the forces, Norland's workload rocketed in both missions as more mothers sought employment to supplement their income. It was while working here that a handful of Mrs Ward's nurses witnessed the true extent of poverty in the capital.

At the beginning of the twentieth century, 145 of every 1,000 babies born in Britain died in the first year of life. By 1913 those figures had improved marginally to a loss of 109 babies per 1,000 live births, but the situation remained dire in the Victorian rookeries that continued to exist in pockets around the city. This was the period of the Eugenics movement, with politicians and philanthropists concerned for the quality of the race, particularly as the threat of war loomed. The state launched an intense phase of government interference in the health of the working-classes. The 1908 National Insurance Act targeted education and the general welfare of the population. It established unemployment and maternity benefits, with 30 shillings paid to each pregnant woman towards her confinement, but the provision of free school meals was a step too far.

A Royal Commission recognised that free school dinners would physically enhance the condition of the state's future adult citizens, but concluded that this might remove parental responsibility and families on the bread-line might give up feeding their children, expecting them to survive on their daily free school meal. Full of good intentions, although limited by the political economy of the day and age-old working-class traditions, the Act was the beginning of the Welfare State, but given the extent of the problem, such legislation was merely a sticking-plaster. This was the environment in which Norlanders at the crèches worked, confronting these issues with as much tact and empathy as they could muster.

Nurse Marguerite Cole gave an eyewitness account of her visit to a London elementary school at Christmas 1914: 'The children were so bright and happy, but oh! *so* [sic] poor. I noticed one small girl in the front row was wearing a slipper on one foot and a sand-shoe on the other, both women's size!' This was in winter, but during the summer the children went barefoot. The sixty little girls, aged six to eight, were perfectly well-behaved for their teacher. Marguerite noticed that she kept a 'birthday box' containing toys and clothes of all kinds and sizes, from which she gave every girl a present on her birthday, providing luxuries the children's own families could not afford.

Norlanders were not trained to teach; they could only observe and comment on the poverty in state primary schools, while their own privately-run Norland School attracted a more privileged set of pupils. Only through their mission work did Norlanders experience this kind of deprivation.

In October 1915, the Cooperative Women's Guild published *Maternity*, a collection of 400 personal accounts from women describing childbirth, domestic arrangements and standards of living, compiled by the Guild's leader Margaret Llewelyn Davies. Shocked and enthralled by its detail, the book sold out going to a second edition within a month. The children described in *Maternity* were the very babies that Nurses Marion Rounthwaite, Maud Daviniere, Inez Lucas and Eleanor Farmer cared for in Norland's missions during the war.

In June 1912, Nurse Inez Lucas, who had previously worked for a family in Dublin, returned to London and took up the role of matron at Norland's Acton mission crèche. Inez hailed from leafy Crouch End in North London, where her father was a solicitor, and Acton in West London, although just 12 miles distant, might have been a different world. It was the capital's laundry, where married women toiled fourteen-hour days enveloped in steam, their arms plunged in boiling water. While they worked, they left their babies with Inez at the crèche. It cost sixpence a day and included food, bottles and a wash administered with 'much love and care'. With no free state childcare, the alternative was leaving the infant in the care of an older sibling or a local woman who took in babies.

Inez was surrounded by poverty, but she marvelled at the ingenuity of the mothers for whom she worked: 'Many of our babes come to us bare-footed: one original mother lined her small boy's boot with linoleum, the sole having quite gone, and some have rags for socks!'

Within Inez's descriptions of her work, there is no hint of disgust at the squalor she witnessed; instead she is full of delight at the children's antics, her accounts of events at the crèche always followed by a plea for funds and donations. At Christmas 1914, Inez wrote to the *Quarterly* asking for clothes, babies' bottles, safety-pins and any old linens and toys for her charges. This Christmas her request fought to be heard amongst the refugee relief efforts, but the Norland Nurses' Mission Fund had had a good year, realising an unexpected £30 from their Summer Bazaar.

However, the Norland Nurses' Mission Fund required an annual income of £100 to support the crèches and their staff. Inez asked all nurses who paid regular subscriptions to be timely with their next payments, adding a polite reminder for those who might have forgotten to forward their last donation. Inez signed off noting that 'most of our babies have relatives serving their country' and that the crèche was 'so much more needed just now than it has ever been before'. The crèche was then at capacity with forty cots and Inez noted that recently she had been forced to turn away fourteen babies in one week. Attendance accounts for 1914 record 6,057 individual 'baby days', up by 1,600 from the previous year.

The increased demand reflected the flood of London's mothers into war work. Consequently, Inez was working flat-out. She was assisted by a nursery-maid, a cook and occasional help from Norlanders with spare time, yet Inez worked longer hours than the mothers who left their babies with her. She was up early to prepare the crèche before their arrival, with hours of cleaning to do after their departure. Her predecessor Nurse Maud Daviniere had managed a little over four years before succumbing to typhoid, which had forced her to take a lengthy period of rest. By June 1915, Inez too had 'broken down', according to Miss Sharman, who announced Inez's resignation in the *Quarterly*.

Inez was exhausted and Miss Sharman recognised that the three years Inez had given to the mission crèche was the maximum a nurse should expect to give, although 'two years were sufficient'. In order to prepare any Norlanders wishing to take up the role of matron at Acton, Miss Sharman advised attendance at lectures on 'Infant care, First Aid and home nursing', as well as some acquaintance with 'the women of the working-classes'. The difference in standards of health, education and general behaviour between traditional Norland employers and working-class families was obviously something for which the new matron would have to prepare herself. Having described the more intimidating details, the most important characteristic that Miss Sharman sought in Inez's replacement was that the nurse should be 'zealous in her wish and endeavour to serve and minister to the poor'.

During Inez's tenure at the crèche, she had introduced lectures in 'mothercraft' for local schoolgirls, who invariably took temporary care of their siblings while their mothers worked and might become mothers themselves some day. The Norland Nurses' Mission Fund treasurer, Marion Rounthwaite, praised Inez's work particularly with her 'regulars', the babies who attended five days a week:

One could always pick out the regular ones by their sturdy appearance and rosy faces; and we know that the mothers appreciated her work, for six children have been at the Nursery since they were three or four weeks old, and they are now three years or over.

The Factory Act of 1891 had made it illegal to employ a woman within four weeks of the end of her confinement, but many were forced to return to work sooner.

The doctor had prescribed Inez 'a good holiday' and the Fund forwarded her a month's salary and £5 'to help towards the expenses'. Compared with the gifts received by nannies working for royalty, this was small-pickings, but it was considerably more generous than anything the mothers at the crèche could expect from their employers, despite working a seventy-hour week for less than 20 shillings.

In the interim, a non-Norlander was taking over, but the Institute hoped that a Norland-trained matron might be found very soon. By August 1915, Nurse Eleanor Farmer had taken up the role and she came highly recommended as Inez's successor. Eleanor had previously gained her midwifery certificate along with courses in physiology, hygiene and sanitary training, all of which qualified her for further training as a health visitor and school nurse. She was highly experienced and had spent the last year in the post of superintendent at the Leeds and Stockton Babies' Welcome, an educational society aimed at teaching young mothers how to take care of themselves and their infants.

Eleanor described her work at the Welcome, with baby weighing on Thursdays and a doctor on hand for medical advice. Mothers were given tea and a biscuit, cocoa if they were expecting, while they listened to a lecture on infant welfare. At the close of the lecture, Eleanor noted that 'a box for voluntary contributions is put in a conspicuous place' in the hope that mothers with a few pennies to spare might make a donation to supplement the Welcome's funds. Babies were visited once a month at home and more frequently if ill.

Organisations like the Welcome society supplemented the limited work done by the state. Before the war, qualified health visitors were sorely over-stretched, with only 600 to cover the entire UK in 1914. There were only 650 state and volunteer-run welfare centres, and attendance was also voluntary. Eleanor expressed frustration with the basic lack of knowledge displayed by mothers on everything from hygiene to feeding to nursing sick infants, the latter an area in which superstition frequently competed with medicine. Eleanor sounded the perfect candidate to continue Inez's programme of 'mothercraft' skills for mothers and young girls.

She was assisted by two Norland probationers, which was twice the help Inez had had, but Eleanor had expanded her role into the wider community, checking on families at home whenever time allowed. She realised that it was an uphill battle to educate mothers in the proper care of infants if they could not afford to implement her lessons during the days they spent at home: 'However well a baby is fed and looked after on four days a week, if it is neglected or mismanaged on the other three days, it makes very slow progress.'

When the factories re-opened after the weekend and the babies were returned to Eleanor's care, she suspected that some had probably not had a proper meal since they left her, nor a change of clothing. The arduous routine of bathing, dressing and feeding started again and in some instances, the process of de-lousing as well. While the babies took their afternoon nap, any spare time left after washing and cleaning the crèche was spent in teaching the toddlers their alphabet and numbers on a blackboard donated by students at the Institute.

While Eleanor was making a big difference to children in Acton, across the city, after four years recovering from her illness, Nurse Maud Daviniere had returned to work, this time at the George Yard Mission crèche in Bethnal Green. Many inhabitants of London's East End from the previous century would have recognised Maud's directions to any Norlanders wishing to visit her:

Guided by the words "George Mission Yard" painted on a window in the Whitechapel High Street one turns into a darksome passage bounded by high walls and grimy houses such as Dickens describes, and mounting many stairs one arrives at the Day Nursery.

It consisted of a long, narrow room, which, until Maud took over, had been an insanitary and dingy infant school. Maud had painted the walls, erected cupboards and installed lavatories and wash stands for children. Above the baby room was another room containing a 'battered rocking-horse' for older children to play in. The rooftop was flat and, in true Norland tradition, the babies were put out here to sleep in warmer weather irrespective of the smoke and soot from neighbouring factories. She noted that her children looked 'more like country children than little East-End ones', but once again they were the few within the morass of undernourished, poorly clothed and under-educated youngsters who roamed London's streets.

With two crèches receiving Norland grants to support their work, the Norland Nurses' Mission Fund found itself over-stretched. Nurses' subscriptions continued to arrive annually, but few new subscriptions had been opened. It was decided that monies received during 1916 would be donated to Acton at Christmas, after which all subscriptions would be directed solely towards the Bethnal Green crèche. The Fund committee considered the Acton nursery as a 'fledgling and urged that the time had come to give it its final push from the nest in order that it might realise that it could fly alone'. With Acton subsisting only on state help and local charitable donations, Eleanor resigned and returned to the north to work as a health visitor.

Bethnal Green benefited greatly from the committee's decision. Maud's nursery moved out of the George Yard Mission and took up residence at Somerford Street School, the former premises being lent by London County Council. The 1914 *Report on the Sanitary Condition and Vital Statistics for Bethnal Green* calculated the mortality rate for children under five years as 48.3 per cent. This was the age group Maud cared for.

The Somerford Street premises were an improvement on the George Yard Mission. Maud described the amenities within her new rooms. The 'receiving and bathroom' had a large porcelain sink, a bath, a 'tortoise' stove with hot water tank and airing cupboard: 'The children are received, undressed, weighed, bathed and put into nursery clothes in this room; later in the day, the nursing mothers come there to feed their babies.' These women dashed to the crèche in their lunch break in order to breast-feed their infants. Breast-feeding had been going out of fashion among all classes, but wartime shortages of food-stuffs had driven many working-class women back to breast-milk. It was free and nutritious, but breast-feeding did require the mother to be in tip-top health, which many of the women Maud met were not.

Maud's second room was full of toddlers playing with second-hand toys, and her third room provided sleeping quarters for the babies, with rows of cots and a 'pound' to keep them safe while Maud and her assistant prepared the infants for their nap. The fourth room was a staff-room, although there was little time to relax. Maud even had a refrigerator and 'the apparatus for the bottle fed infants'. In 1915, making up bottles and sterilising them was a time-consuming job.

Through their annual subscriptions, Norlanders had donated £100 in Maud's first year at the new crèche, but Maud was in desperate need of further monies for day-to-day running costs and she made a personal plea for extra funds: 'You who live in pretty, cosy nurseries with a bright and cheerful outlook, please send your kind thought and a shilling for two nurses who care for 20 babies every day and live in one of the dreariest parts of London.'

Maud and her assistant Norlander lived in a three-room flat nearby. It was clean, but spartan and a far cry from the comfortable quarters Norlanders enjoyed. Marion Rounthwaite, in her treasurer's role, appealed for money to buy Maud and her under-nurse an oilcloth to cover their bare floorboards. Mission work was certainly not for the career Norlander; it required other qualities, including the ability to endure the latest dangers inflicted on their charges by the war.

Some of the children in Maud's care had already lost fathers to the war, and the mothers who sent their children to Maud had experienced the air-raids in the docklands, but at Christmas 1917, Nurse Edith Sperling, after a visit to the crèche, reminded all Norlanders of their duty to support Maud and the mission, which was 'in danger of eclipse' by war charities. She requested money and toys, but particularly rag dolls for Bethnal Green:

> *Think of the surroundings of our own nursery children and their many possessions – and then let your imaginary sight wander over a scene that I saw just after a German aeroplane had dropped a bomb in East London and had succeeded in reducing half of a small street to ruins.*

Walking through London's East End after a bombing raid, Edith had witnessed a small girl sitting on a pile of rubbish and debris amidst shattered buildings. She was hugging a piece of wood, on which someone had drawn two eyes and tied a rag around for a dress. Edith asked the child what had happened: "'Daddy was killed wiv a bomb, but I got my baby" and she went on hugging her dirty bit of wood … That child had probably a kinder mother than most, and had made the doll for the child as best she could.' Edith's attitude may have been superior, but her intentions were charitable. Edith offered a pattern for a rag doll made from stockings and buttons for eyes, but her final petition to her sister nurses drew on a social concern she knew they would all recognise:

Nothing is stronger than the maternal instinct or more fruitful in the result for the benefit of the race, and anything that can encourage the growth of this in the appalling moral atmosphere which surrounds these children of the slums needs no apology.

Raising the standard of health among children was paramount, not only to Maud in her mission crèche and to all Norlanders, but the newspapers had also picked up the theme, couching their headlines in demands for better food and 'homes fit for heroes'. Never before had working-class men or their children enjoyed such attention from the state and philanthropists, and it would be the role of working women, like Norlanders, to put government programmes into practice.

Just because there was a war on, standards of childcare at Norland and what the Institute stood for would not be adjusted. With many nurses believing they had a responsibility to raise the next generation of British soldiers, child discipline was perceived as particularly important. Mrs Ward had received complaints from three employers about Norlanders slapping their children since the start of the war. Since its establishment, physical rebukes of any sort had been forbidden by the Institute, leaving 'physical punishment… to be administered to the children by the parents, never by the nurse under any provocation whatsoever'. Mrs Ward warned her nurses that at Great Ormond Street Children's Hospital, slapping a child meant instant dismissal and she remained 'determined that other methods shall be adopted where love fails'.

In a society increasingly full of frustration, fear and militarism, the Norland Institute continued to be the great innovator abiding by Froebel and Montessori childcare practice in Edwardian Britain. There was no room for corporal punishment in Norland's practice and Mrs Ward's stern words sparked a flurry of letters from nurses eager to offer their advice and personal experiences.

From her nursery in Liverpool, an experienced older Norlander, Nurse Margaret Knowles shared her thoughts on 'leading versus driving'. Her great secret in managing her nursery was never to be 'hurried'. She wrote that 'many bad days are started by nurse being late or hurried' and not being sympathetic in her actions towards the children. When receiving a hungry and tired child home to the nursery after a walk, she advised not ordering him upstairs to wash for dinner which would make him cross and likely to refuse, but to take him by the hand, chatting about his excursion and turn the chore into a game by offering to 'see if we can both be ready *before* [sic] the gong goes for dinner'.

Margaret's approach was supported by Nurse Annie Avery, who had learned through years of experience that 'nannie's commands are not paid much attention to' if the nurse made commands as a habit and once orders were issued, there was little more a nurse could do short of handing out threats. A nurse must be 'just in one's dealings with children', only offering strict instructions when absolutely necessary, so that the child would instinctively know that a command must be obeyed.

This was *avant garde* thinking, but Margaret and Annie were expounding the fundamentals of Mrs Ward's 25-year-old approach to childcare. It was contrary to the behaviour of most parents with whom Norlanders worked. In many homes, the father of the household was expected to mete out discipline and no matter how strict he might be, nanny could never intervene.

However, nanny ruled in the nursery where she implemented the latest thinking on childcare. Weaning was first on nanny's agenda. With breast-feeding becoming more of a necessity and continuing for longer, particularly among the less well-off, Jessie Smeaton, now working on Norland's lecturing staff, reminded her nurses that babies were to be weaned at nine months: 'the age when independence is desirable, because the digestive powers are such that additional feeding is both desirable and necessary for the child's welfare'. The transfer from breast to bottle was to be gradual and cow's milk to be introduced 'never stronger than half and half' mixed with water until baby could tolerate undiluted cow's milk. The process had caused one nurse considerable upset during hours of nursing a sick child.

Nurse Constance Harper had cared for a toddler since his first year and the transfer from breast to cow's milk had gone smoothly until the baby developed pains, which at first she attributed to teething. After sleepless nights administering the remedy of 'albumen water', watered-down egg white, she gave up and called the doctor. 'Careful experiments with Horlick, Glaxo, Albulactin and Nestle's milk', all powdered milk substitutes, were tried before the doctor declared a diagnosis of milk intolerance. The doctor ordered rectal 'injections of strong Castile soap and water twice a day' to combat the baby's constipation, while Constance had to feed him castor oil 'in liberal quantities night and day'. All milk was forbidden and the one-year-old was put on a diet of 'beef tea, minced butcher's meat, fish, and eggs'. Every time the child suffered a flare-up, Constance was ordered to 'irrigate the bowel every three days'. It was a punishing regime for baby and nurse, and Constance sought advice from other nannies who might have cared for a child with the same condition.

The hours of care Constance had invested in her charge were matched by Nurse Jacoba Watson's efforts to save her charge's life. The 14-month-old had succumbed to influenza and for five days suffered a temperature raging at 104°F. Jacoba nursed him day and night for five days, 'during three of those days I had him in my arms the whole time, and had to eat all my meals with one hand when I could manage to get them'. She considered it a privilege to care for a sick child in this way and in her letter she hoped that her sister nurses would take courage from her example when faced with ailing and grieving children who 'cannot bear nurse out of their sight for a minute'.

Unable to attend Mrs Ward's 'at homes' to swap gossip and nursery advice, the *Quarterly* rapidly filled up with letters discussing lesser ailments, particularly from younger nannies or those unable to meet their colleagues in London's parks. Nurse Linda Kemp in Plymouth offered remedies for that 'tiresome nursery complaint' – warts. She had dealt with them using acetic acid, celandine and even silver nitrate. Rubbing with a piece of stolen beef, which was then buried in the garden, had failed, but 'applications of castor oil several times a day after washing' had proved effective.

Other nurses offered their thoughts on table manners; one recommended *The Middle Class Cookbook* for healthy nursery fare, and Nurse Dora Tanner had suggestions for Christmas gifts during wartime. After trying to buy paper for origami only to learn that the shop had run out due to shortages, Dora had gone to a wallpaper shop where the sales assistant offered her old patterns from the back room, which she usually gave to the town's poor to decorate their homes. Dora spent the following months decorating rooms for a doll's house with her charges, making 'boxes, photo-frames, and blotters as Christmas gifts' for their family.

The war demanded imagination and resourcefulness from Norland's nurses. When toys broke, there was little on offer to replace them, but Nurse Kate Viall put her faith in 'war-time pets' to amuse her charges. The Institute had always recommended the keeping of pets, as it engendered in children the responsibility of caring for another animal and now they could be a great source of comfort too in homes affected by the war.

Kate was busy maintaining a menagerie for her children with varying degrees of success. She fed tortoises on a range of vegetable scraps and the children took them outside in the sunshine. She had 'water-tortoises' in a tank in the nursery, which were manageable, but the budgerigars had given her the most trouble. They were fussy eaters and sensitive to the British climate. Her advice: 'if a budgerigar dies, replace it immediately, or its mate will die too' and the children would be terribly upset.

From her nursery in Broadstairs, Nurse Harriet Harvey Laity recommended a pet that would not only provide a good companion for children, but which would also generate food and a wartime income. Harriet's little charge kept hens. Confined to a bath-chair, the child had previously owned rabbits and doves, as he could pet these animals in his chair, but after buying a cock and hen at a Red Cross sale, Harriet and her charge had gone into egg production. They now had 'seven laying hens and several well-grown chicks', which had laid 700 eggs in seven months 'and have been a greater delight than the rabbits'. Harriet kept a careful account of the eggs, with 'their market value paid to the child in War Savings Certificates'. Even pets could do their bit for the war.

Being inventive, finding ways to make the new world work for them and their charges, offering solace to others, always putting themselves second and being perfectly unflappable was gradually setting Norlanders apart from the society that was crumbling around them. Repression of the emotional strain the war was inflicting on them was expected from women of their class and profession, but the physical isolation of their role was something they could discuss among themselves.

Nurse Margaret Bodington struck a chord when she described the solitude of the wartime nurse. Probationer nurses training at the Institute in London had moved away from home to attend the course and any homesickness they felt was understandable, but she noted that trained Norlanders were feeling isolated too. Working all day with few adults around them, unable to meet as regularly, many felt separated from normal life and the new strains of dealing with a household in which often the husband had left for the war were taking a toll. Others, increasingly employed in temporary work, felt the wrench every time they left a nursery having learned to love a new set of children. With the war creating dislocation among the entire nation, it was eroding Norlanders' usually effervescent morale.

Drawing on her own early career experiences, 40-year-old Nurse May Hasler wrote from her nursery in New York City to pep everyone up. After completing her training in 1899, May had spent the first ten years of her Norland service working with a country family, four miles from the nearest town, consequently leading 'a more or less isolated life', with few entertainments: 'My only relaxations were political meetings in the village to which I trudged a lonely mile bearing a lantern and feeling sure that behind every gate post was a lurking ruffian.'

May did not wish this style of life on any nanny and now highly recommended that to 'be good citizens as well as nurses' they should ask for regular time off and fill their free hours with the latest entertainment: 'Hear lectures; see the best plays, hear good music, and if you like dancing, dance ... You should make a better not poorer nurse because for a few hours a week you meet men and women and lead a different life.'

It was not the traditional approach Mrs Ward would normally have encouraged, but these were changed times and her nurses were becoming modern young women. May's advice to the younger cohort represented *carte blanche* for them to take the new opportunities the war might offer. They saw the girls from the munitions factories able to afford new clothes and enjoying music hall visits on their increased wages, and some Norlanders desired the same freedom from the limitations of the Institute's Edwardian ethos of service.

They served the wealthy, supporting wives and children through the war. Some worked alongside the poor, living in meagre conditions, keeping long and arduous hours, risking aerial bombing in London's East End. Their mission was to do their duty to all the people they served and to promote proper 'mothercraft', but the war was knocking the stuffing out of Mrs Ward's nurses. Two years in, no one knew how much longer they would have to keep going and morale among Norlanders in Britain was waning.

As reported by the *Quarterly's* editor in 1917, one three-and-a-half-year-old boy attending the Norland Nursery had stood by the window watching the snow melt in an unseasonal spot of winter sunshine. 'He gazed at it for some time, and then said reproachfully, "What a waste in war time!" Throughout Europe, many must have felt that all the beauty in their lives and their hard work was being erased by the punishing strictures of living with war.

The little boy had summed up Norland's mood perfectly.

Chapter 7

Further Afield

S ince the early days of the Institute, Norland nurses had dispersed to the four corners of the British Empire and beyond. Not only children's nurses to aristocracy around the world, they worked for middle-class families too and several had settled into life in foreign climes, never to return.

When war broke out, Norlanders trapped in combatant countries within Europe, like Nurse Kate Fox, attempted to return home, but those living outside Europe had little notion of the increasing suffering at the front. None of them witnessed the human detritus of war on British streets, and the newspaper photographs of the conditions in the trenches and the misery of refugees were too far removed. The reality was so horrific that it was beyond the ken of many living in non-combatant nations.

The letters to the Institute that Mrs Ward chose to publish had often arrived on her desk weeks before and once published, were further delayed while the *Quarterly* wormed its way through the overseas mail service. For those living abroad, news filtered through via English-language newspapers, already out-of-date by the time of their arrival. Among them were a handful of Norlanders still on the Continent, but geographically on the periphery of the conflict. They were able to continue their employment in neutral countries neighbouring those at war. They were blissfully unaware of the life their sister nurses were leading at home and at the front; Nurse Mary Faulconer was a prime example.

Mary was living in Oporto, Portugal. Mr H W Jennings, for whom Mary worked, had been employed by the George G Sandeman port company since 1898 and had moved to Oporto in 1903, becoming company manager seven years later. Mr Jennings was a life member of the British Overseas Club, an association of many tens of thousands of expatriate

Britons scattered around the world. The Club rules required adherence to the Crown and promotion of all things British in whatever corner of the globe members found themselves, as well as annual subscriptions and donations to the war fund. Mary was living in an enthusiastically patriotic household, but as yet with no immediate experience of the war.

Mary had worked with the Jennings family since 1912, when she had been a probationer. Her first charge was one-year-old Marion Gwyn Jennings, born in January 1911. After a brief family holiday with the Jennings in St Albans during the summer of 1914, Mary returned to Oporto where a second daughter, Ruth Rosemary Gwyn, was born in June 1915. The Jennings family was held in high regard in Oporto and Mary enjoyed the lawn tennis club and Sunday services at the Anglican church. This was an English village-style community in a bustling Portuguese town, where the climate was a distinct improvement to that of her father's farm in Sussex.

Mary wrote to Mrs Ward in early summer 1915, describing a journey along the Portuguese Atlantic coast to Albergoria Nova with her charge, Marion, now four years old, for a brief stay at the family's weekend retreat. The Portuguese coast was patrolled by German U-boats, then blockading British shipping and hampering Portugal's trade with Britain. The vessels could be seen from the coast, but the war was not on Mary's radar as she accompanied her charge on a day excursion to the nearby wood pulp estate. Mary described the pulping process in great detail and declared that she 'found it most interesting, watching the different processes, and I hope this account will be interesting to you'. Mary did not mention if the wood pulp was being produced for war manufacturing elsewhere; it was simply a fascinating experience to share with other nannies.

In an edition of the *Quarterly* full of nurses' news about the London mission crèches, statements of account for various war funds and Miss Sharman's lengthy letter extolling the nannies to continue in their efforts to support the war, Mary's letter stands out in the midst of organised chaos seeping through the pages. Mary was living a charmed life on the margins of the conflict in one of few European countries yet to become officially embroiled in the war.

The Germans and Portuguese had, so far, respected each other's sovereignty except in Portuguese Angola, where German troops had made incursions into Portugal's colonial territory since late 1914. In March 1916, with the situation along the coast and the disruption to trade with Britain, the insult could not be tolerated any longer and Portugal entered the war on the side of the Allies. Mary's family could no longer keep the war at arm's length. Sandeman's continued to trade and the Jennings family stayed in Oporto, where they had two more children after the war, but Mary returned to Britain in time for Christmas 1917, to take up temporary employment. Being in a country at war had changed everything for Mary. Portugal was no longer a neutral state and if she were going to have to witness the war first-hand, then she preferred to do so from the safety of home.

There were others living in countries already involved in the conflict, but so far removed from the trenches that life seemed to continue with little interruption. Nurse Beatrice Moxon had been in Africa since 1909. The daughter of an Excise officer, Beatrice had trained at Norland in 1908 at the age of thirty-two, which was quite old for a Norland student of the period. After her probationary posting to a family in Algiers – an unusual move – since the summer of 1913 Beatrice had worked for Mrs Lucy Molteno at the Molteno family estate, Sandown, in Rondebosch, a suburb of Cape Town.

The Moltenos were politicians with huge farm holdings in the Karoo. The family had a long and eminent history in the Cape Colony, with the grandfather of Beatrice's charges, Sir John Charles Molteno, becoming the first prime minister of the colony. John Charles Molteno Jr, Beatrice's employer, was a member of parliament who had opposed the Cape's involvement in the Boer War in 1899. Having once been a business associate of Cecil Rhodes, he broke off their relationship after Rhodes's attempts to discriminate against black South Africans. Beatrice was living in a highly politicised and privileged household, prominent in Cape society and outspoken in their views.

However, once Britain declared war with Germany, the South African government automatically supported the mother country and the Molteno family's previous reticence in following Britain blindly into war disappeared.

Beatrice was surrounded by the town's inhabitants, who were mobilising for war in neighbouring German South West Africa (now Namibia) as well as tackling a rebellion at home. The South African population was divided between those loyal to Britain and those newly-made Afrikaaner Britons, who had been defeated in the Boer War and who were now asked to fight for the 'king and country' they had considered their foes barely a decade ago.

It was a full and busy household with a liveried coachman decked out in silver buttons, top boots and gauntlet gloves; three maids; a cowman and several gardeners; and Mrs Molteno's five children: Lucy aged thirteen; Carol, twelve; John Charles and Peter, eight and six; and the baby, Virginia born in 1911. Beatrice had her hands full, particularly with young Peter, whom she described in a poem shared in the Christmas 1915 *Quarterly*:

> *He has a crop of curly hair, 'tis golden brown in hue, with quite a small tip-tilted nose, and eyes of deepest blue.*
> *With agile speed he climbs a tree, and from the dizzy height, his roguish face peeps forth with glee, just like a woodland sprite.*

Her penultimate verse showed that life with a family in the South African bush was a far cry from daily walks in Hyde Park: 'The roof-top is a promenade, of which he is very fond, but that of course is not allowed, or he might go beyond!'

Peter's outdoor antics were to become a fraught matter between Beatrice and the children's eccentric aunt, Betty Molteno. Betty loved the great outdoors and held progressive views on the raising of children. With her lifelong partner, Alice Greene, Betty had already taken care of the children in 1912, while visiting the Molteno's holiday property, and had been appalled at their wayward behaviour. Betty described them as 'spoilt, untidy and unable to entertain themselves'. When Lucy Molteno's health deteriorated in 1913, Betty and Alice moved into Sandown to help and to teach the older girls. Immersed in all the latest educational thinking, they taught the girls in the mornings, and indulged in games and outdoor play during the afternoons. It was exactly what Beatrice had been taught, however, she and the ladies struggled to agree over discipline.

Beatrice, an older single woman, with a nursery to run along strict Norland lines, might have formed a friendship with Betty and Alice, but the boundaries of staff and close family relations could not be crossed. What is more, Betty and Beatrice approached childcare from opposing camps. When John fell out of a tree cutting his foot on a rusty nail, a tree Beatrice had expressly forbidden the boys to climb, the ladies returned to Sandown to find Beatrice extremely cross with the boy. A doctor was called, but his instructions of frequent poulticing and keeping the limb raised had been ignored by Beatrice after the first few days and John was up and about, putting weight on his injured foot. The ensuing row caused Betty to retire to her room with heart palpitations.

It was a noisy, boisterous household with guests coming and going, and the children enjoying the freedom of the South African veldt. With only a half-day off every week and few other Norlanders within travelling distance, it was also a lonely existence and it was likely that Beatrice, older and perhaps set in her ways, had gone too far. However, Beatrice would not be reprimanded for her actions because Betty was unlikely to report the event to her sister-in-law Lucy Molteno, whom she also thought unable to raise the children in the correct manner.

During the autumn of 1915, Mrs Molteno gave Beatrice a much-needed day off from the tumult of life at Sandown, so from Rondebosch she travelled into Cape Town to meet fellow Nurse Geraldine Dobbie. Geraldine was employed with a family in Wynberg, just a few miles south of the Molteno estate and she had been in Cape Town since Christmas 1912. With similarly restrictive leave arrangements, this was their third attempt to scale the Table Mountain in eighteen months and they were determined to succeed, although their start time of 9am was decidedly leisurely compared with today's recommendations.

There was a late autumn nip in the air, which made the ladies walk briskly to Platte Klip Gorge, the starting point for their hike. Beatrice noticed snow in the crevices as they climbed, but it was hot and they quenched their thirst in a mountain stream. They reached the top without mishap and Beatrice declared: 'The view of the peninsula was magnificent, with the Atlantic and Indian Ocean on either side and the snow-capped Drakenstein Range in the distance. I crawled to the edge and looked down a sheer drop of 5,000ft.'

Afterwards, they walked for an hour across the top of the Table to Maclear's Beacon, the highest point, experiencing an unseasonal snowstorm as they walked. They followed tradition by laying stones on the Beacon and carrying away a small one as a souvenir. They had a map and a compass, and navigated their return route, sometimes wading through the waters in Skeleton Gorge, which they had previously experienced as a stream and now was a torrent. The day was finished off with 'tea at Kirstenbosch sitting on a rustic bench under spreading oaks'. It was certainly an achievement for two Edwardian women in full skirts with no safety equipment or supplies, and Beatrice was very proud that 'two Norlanders had climbed Table Mountain *alone* [sic], for we did not meet a soul from start to finish'.

Mrs Ward in her 'editorial notes' praised Beatrice and Geraldine, and hoped her readers would find the account 'interesting'. It was so much more than that – a real victory of mettle and determination over Edwardian attire and female status. However, Beatrice was simply writing to describe the unusual adventures of two children's nurses enjoying a period of employment in a far-flung corner of the Empire.

Evidence of the war and local rebellion surrounded Beatrice and Geraldine, who lived close to the Wynberg military camp and hospital, but after their excursion, Beatrice returned to Sandown to settle into knitting and stitching clothing to be sent back to the Institute for the Belgian refugees. Apart from this involvement in war work at a distance, the hostilities had not touched Beatrice despite South Africa being one of Britain's closest allies and pivotal to the Allied forces' conflict in Africa.

By the first anniversary of the war, even in countries closely allied to Britain, there remained pockets of peace where Norlanders could continue their pre-war existence. Nurse Gwendoline Malim had worked in Inverness in 1913, but during 1914 when the Norland register gives no employment address for her, aged thirty-one, she fell in love with the Reverend Charles Russell Canham, eventually marrying him in Moose Jaw, Canada on 12 August 1915. She was now a clergyman's wife in the state of Saskatchewan. Gwendoline described the little town of Avonlea, where they lived, as: 'a town only three years old, but it is growing rapidly'. She placed Avonlea in 'the far west' making it sound like frontier country, but Saskatchewan is in central Canada.

The town's 300 inhabitants comprised Britons, Americans and Germans, yet Gwendoline made no mention of any hostility towards the Germans in this British dominion. The work was hard – ministering to her husband's widespread congregation, travelling by horse and stopping overnight with strangers along the way – but Gwendoline was in her element organising, caring and coping with whatever life threw at her, even after finding 'a young settler frozen to death in his shack'.

Canada lured several nannies to a new life. Nurse Jean Ritchie had married Evelyn Norie on 10 October 1910, followed by fellow Nurse Louisa Cavendish, who married his twin brother. The two Mrs Nories were living together on a farm in British Columbia, with a neighbouring Norlander, Nurse Catherine Manuel, who had started a 'little school in their vicinity'.

Norlanders were spread all over Canada, with nannies working in Toronto, Montreal, Ontario, Alberta, British Columbia and Nova Scotia. However, they had largely left Britain before the war, and apart from the Canadian Government's involvement with the conflict, it appears to have been business as usual for these Norlanders before 1917. Their letters give no hint of understanding the enormity of the European conflict and how it was spreading.

Tucked away at the point where Europe meets Asia Minor, surrounded by warring factions in the Austria-Hungary, Serbia and Ottoman sector of the war, one Norland nurse became simultaneously caught up in revolution and the war, as her letter published in the *Quarterly* described. In southern Europe, the British Government was keen to draw Greece into the war on the side of the Allies. It was a tense situation with the German and Austrian governments using their own tactics to persuade Greece to join the Central Powers. In the midst of this diplomatic skirmish, Nurse Muriel Bois was working for the Calamari family in Athens, where she had been employed since 1913 caring for a nine-year-old boy.

The daughter of a Norwich gentleman, Muriel had qualified at the age of twenty-three in 1908. By Christmas 1916, now thirty-one, she had become an eyewitness to the Greek Civil War, which had exploded in response to the struggle between the Allies and Central Powers for control of Greece.

Greece was suffering an internal struggle on the question of 'benevolent neutrality' between its royal family and its prime minister. King Constantine I was married to Kaiser Wilhelm's younger sister, Sophie, whose mother was the Princess Royal Victoria, which also made Queen Sophie a grand-daughter of Britain's Queen Victoria. Constantine was also first cousin to Tsar Nicholas II of Russia, and his younger brother, Prince Nicholas, had married the Grand Duchess Elena Vladimirovna of Russia. There were too many conflicting loyalties with the European royal families for Constantine to decide with which side he wanted to align his country.

However, his prime minister, Eleftherios Venizelos, wished to join Britain's allies, believing that Greece had a duty to protect Serbia, which was being threatened by Bulgaria, now part of the Central Powers. Greek society was simmering with discontent and 'benevolent neutrality', the policy of keeping out of the war but keeping all parties on tenterhooks, could not be maintained any longer.

In the days leading up to the Greek Revolution of 1 December 1916, Muriel had a front row seat:

At last the Allies could stand it no longer, so a "Note" was handed in to the Greek Government demanding six Greek batteries and certain other things to be handed over to the Allied Forces within a stated time. At the expiration of this time no satisfactory reply was forthcoming. King Constantine and his Government only agreeing to part of this Note.

Then it was that Admiral de Fournet, who had charge of the Allied Fleet in Greek waters, ordered a certain number (about 3,000 I believe) of English and French troops, with a few Italians, to land, in order to take from the Greeks what they would not surrender. The Royalists had sworn that they would rather die at their posts than give in to the wishes of the Allies.

In an attempt to force King Constantine to join the Allies, the British landed a force of marines in Athens' ancient harbour, which then marched to the centre of the city. Muriel nipped out the following morning to see what was going on:

> *On December 1st, about 8.30am, I went to the Zappion, a building originally built for Exhibitions... I there saw English Naval Officers and marines who had marched up from the Piraeus during the night, busily preparing for whatever might happen. They all seemed so business-like with their mitrailleuses that it made one feel that home was the best place!*

Scared by the amount of military activity and the quantity of ordnance hauled into position, Muriel went home and decided against taking out her nine-year-old charge, but he had a drawing lesson after lunch at a nearby house, which they attempted to attend:

> *However, when we arrived for the lesson we were told there would not be one, as all the trains and trams had been stopped and the teacher could not come. Not until then did I realise that fighting was going on not only between the Greek Royalists and Venizelists, but also between our troops and the Greeks.*

Muriel waited for a lull in the fighting before she and her charge rushed home through the streets. She noted shopkeepers hastily boarding up windows, homeowners raising their shutters and gunshots could be heard nearby throughout the afternoon, gradually becoming louder and more persistent:

> *About 4 p.m. a louder report than ever was heard, and we then realized that the Allied Fleet were bombarding Athens from the sea. We all went down to the ground floor of our house (we had no basement) and remained there, hoping and praying that the bombardment would not last long.*

The Allies anticipated that the shelling would force King Constantine to join them. In the ancient city living quarters were intermingled with government offices and military installations, so the bombardment could not be targeted with any accuracy, and indiscriminate shelling of civilians and soldiers was inevitable. Muriel was firmly on the side of the British and forgave the bombardment, writing that if the shelling had not happened the outnumbered British troops in Athens would have been annihilated.

Once the bombardment ceased, the government troops set about massacring the Venizelists, and Muriel risked death if she ventured out:

> *The fighting in the streets, especially around the part I was living in, became furious. We were not allowed to open our shutters because the Reservists were parading the streets and took a shot at any head if they saw one. At one hotel the proprietor sent a waiter to close a window and a bullet was instantly put through his head!*

Muriel heard rumours of the atrocities against prominent Venizelists being 'cruelly maltreated' and dragged off 'to gaol to be the victims of still grosser indignities'. She also witnessed the fate of ordinary Venizelists fighting outside her employer's home: 'I myself saw the bayonet being used pretty freely against the Venizelists as they were being marched off to prison.'

After three days of fighting in the streets, on Sunday, 3 December the civil war had died down, and Muriel dared to go to church as usual along with other English expatriates. Expecting a normal service, she was alarmed to hear the chaplain use his homily to instruct them to prepare to leave at once in accordance with orders received from the British Government:

> *You can imagine my feelings when I tell you that I had been with my boy just over three years and had received every possible kindness and consideration from his people, and now the climax had come, and I had to decide whether to remain or return to England. My first thoughts were to remain.*

Finally, after consulting her employer and other friends, Muriel decided she must leave. She was issued a special emergency passport and a pass, which gave her a berth on a Greek Atlantic liner being prepared for foreign nationals escaping the conflict. There were 500 passengers on board 'under the charge of a distinguished Naval Officer': 'The liner was guarded day and night by British Bluejackets, and if any inquisitive boat came too near a shot was fired to warn them off.'

The crew were all Venizelists, which made the British armed guard essential for the safety of the passengers, but Muriel was very well cared for in the weeks before the ship left Piraeus. A Swedish physical instructor put them through an exercise drill every morning and officers from the British naval fleet entertained them in the evenings. There were nearly 100 children on board and Christmas was celebrated with turkey and plum pudding, and fancy dress and presents for the children from a haphazardly dressed Santa Klaus. After three weeks, they weighed anchor on 6 January 1917: 'Most passengers slept on deck with their lifebelts near them in case of emergency, as one never knew if the wily Hun would take a shot at us, although we were convoyed.'

Escorted by ships of the British Mediterranean fleet, they reached Italy, now on the side of the Allies, where they boarded a train to Paris. Muriel described the struggle to find food at every stop en route. The war was now in its third year and shortages for civilians were widespread. Reaching Paris, their train was plunged into darkness in order to obey the city's wartime blackout, but even then Muriel wondered if it was 'the Hun having an attempt at us!'. At Le Havre the British military took over arrangements and they boarded a ship bound for Southampton, braving the risk of U-boats sneaking into the English Channel.

Muriel did not see her little boy again and she never discovered whether the Calamari family survived the conflict. Safely back home, she joined the ranks of Norlanders finding temporary work with London families. Once recounted to her fellow nurses, the lid had been firmly placed on her frightening escapade.

As 1917 began, Mrs Ward hoped all her nurses who had been in enemy territory and in danger might have arrived safely home, but as Muriel's experience proved the conflict continued to be unpredictable. Russia had been one of the major players in the Allied Forces from the declaration of war in August 1914. Several Norlanders had worked for Russian families or visited Russia before the war, travelling to stay with the relations of their royal charges. In 1917, Nurse Marian Burgess remained there working for the Grand Duchess Kirill, another grand-daughter of Queen Victoria, who was among the Tsar and Tsarina's innermost circle. The Norland Institute's credentials had long been valued among the Russian aristocracy and now another countess about to give birth required a Norland nurse.

Having escaped Germany in 1914, leaving behind her beloved Hesse royal children, Nurse Lilian Eadie had not settled to life at home in Topsham, Devon. She had pined for the Hesse princes and had failed to find distraction in temporary posts. A new position had been advertised at Norland and Mrs Ward was looking for a nurse who was competent with royal children and understood life at court. Now forty-one years old, Lilian decided to take it. The position was for the Osten-Sacken family, who had one boy and a newborn baby on the way. Lilian would be working safely away from the conflict in an environment she understood at Zarskoe Selo.

The imperial village was already home for Marian Burgess, whom Lilian counted among the many friends that she had made during her previous employment with the Hesse family. Lilian continued to receive letters from the Hesse family sent through neutral channels. The constant reminder of what might have been probably led to her early resignation from her new job with the Osten-Sacken family when the new baby was barely a toddler.

When the Bolshevik Revolution began in February 1917, Lilian was ill and living alone in St Petersburg. By 9 November 1917, she had managed to escape to Norway from where she sent a note to the Hesse family in Darmstadt, explaining that she had heard that the Russian imperial family was well. The truth could not have been more different, with the Romanovs in fact imprisoned in Siberia. And so, after another employment in the Russian imperial household, Lilian returned home by boat from Norway to Topsham again, with another fortunate escape from a calamitous world event under her belt.

In the *Quarterly*, Mrs Ward attempted to show that tumultuous international events were not the only kind of war news, by including snippets of news from her earliest Norlanders who were now spread around the world and often married with families of their own. Mrs Donald Ferguson, (formerly Nurse Mary Nicholson), wrote from the Outer Hebrides, describing the straitened circumstances on the islands because of the war and the weather. The cargo-boat bringing supplies normally ran every ten days, but a storm had delayed it and Mary, a fastidious Norlander trained in correct nutrition, had to feed her four-year-old and toddler on potatoes and milk, while they waited to be re-supplied.

Nurse Muriel Symonds had trained at Norland in 1898. Her first job had been with a Mrs Oswell in Chiswick, west London before she moved on to a family in Edinburgh. After seven years as a nursery nurse, by 1906, Muriel had disappeared from the Norland employment register, but the 1911 census records Muriel sharing a house with another single woman in Broadstairs. On the day the census was collected, Muriel and her housemate also listed a student visitor staying with them: Mr Arthur Dann, aged twenty-seven, the son of a retired army captain in the Royal Horse Artillery. Muriel and Arthur were eventually married in December 1913, with Muriel's uncle and Arthur's father in attendance as witnesses.

Muriel had married an ordained missionary. In spring 1916, Mrs Arthur Dann wrote to the Institute from Kabwir on the Jos Plateau in Northern Nigeria, where she was living in a 'bush house amongst nude pagans and an unwritten language'. Despite her discomforts, Muriel was doing what Norlanders do best; she was caring for children 'crawling on all fours into a mud hut to attend to a baby dying of dysentery and bronchitis'. It was not such a far cry from crawling on a nursery floor in London, but the reason the baby was alone in the hut was due to the 'spirits that were troubling it'. The infant's parents had abandoned the child, leaving it in an empty bush hut to which Muriel had been called.

Muriel was short of remedies except administering fluids and care, but she was coping despite 'frogs in the bedroom and a large one in the bed'. She was enthralled by the 'wild scenery' and 'narrow bush paths with tall cactus 12 feet high in parts' and was looking forward to being sent further into Nigeria, to 'open up an untouched part of the country'.

Arthur and Muriel were stationed in a very remote area of Nigeria, but the newly built colonial railway was rapidly advancing in their direction. Muriel may have been too isolated to witness Nigerian troops of the West African Frontier Force being mustered for the conflict in German East Africa, but she must have known it was happening. If her letters could find their way out of the jungle to the railhead and all the way to the Norland Institute, then news could also filter back along the return route.

For some living in Britain's colonies, the war remained a European fight, but its impact as a 'world war' was beginning to reach Norlanders, who had previously felt themselves immune. In spring 1916, Nurse Eileen Godfrey, now Mrs Mackarness, was living in India. A year into her marriage the war had just made its presence felt in her household, as her husband had recently joined up, despite her pregnancy.

Born in 1888, Eileen was the elder daughter of a Scarborough doctor. Aged seventeen, she had travelled to Frankfurt to learn the violin and to practice her German; like many Norlanders, and Britons in general, she had a taste for German culture. Around 1910, she accompanied her father to Melbourne, Australia and on her return in 1912, she accepted a proposal of marriage from Cuthbert George Milford Mackarness, who shortly afterwards joined the Indian Forestry Service and was posted to Assam, leaving Eileen to kick her heels in Scarborough.

Instead, she applied to the Norland Institute, starting her training during 1913, before returning home sick with typhoid fever. Eileen did not manage to complete her probationary period and she was recuperating at home in December 1914, where she witnessed the audacious German shell attack on Britain's East Coast. It is unusual that Eileen was allowed to enter Norland having already accepted a marriage proposal, but as a young woman of some means who had travelled and was obviously educated, Norland was the perfect place for her to finish off her education before marriage, and to gain training in childcare before she started her own family. It is likely Mrs Ward did not know of the engagement, because using Norland in this way was never her intention.

Early in 1915, Eileen set sail on the SS *Khyber* with two of her aunts as chaperones. She sent a postcard to her father from Malta and later, one of his sisters wrote to him with news that they had passed Suez and were out of danger from marauding German submarines in the Mediterranean. By March, Eileen had arrived safely in Calcutta where she and Cuthbert were married.

Writing to Mrs Ward in March 1916, Eileen was halfway through her first pregnancy and Cuthbert was on the North West Frontier training with the Green Howards, prior to joining the 25th Punjabis. Later that year, as the 'Hot Weather' of the Indian summer approached, Eileen escaped to Murree and gave birth to her baby. She did not meet up with Cuthbert until the autumn when he was introduced to his son, Richard, in Amritsar before undertaking a posting to Palestine.

Mrs Eileen Mackarness would not see her husband again until after the Armistice in 1918, when she applied for a free passage and travelled by troopship to Egypt taking baby Richard with her. During her brief stay in Egypt, she conceived her second son, Peter, who was born in late August 1919 in Scarborough, Cuthbert travelling in the opposite direction, having been demobilised and posted back to the Forestry Service in India.

So far, the USA and Latin America had managed to cling on to their neutrality, but nannies on the Eastern Seaboard were involved already in war work. In Canada, the only American country to declare war on Germany in support of its colonial motherland, Norlanders had so far failed to remark on the war. Yet, Nurse Edith Dalzell's letter published in the August 1917 *Quarterly* made Norlanders in Canada finally aware of their country's involvement.

Having worked in Paris with a British family until the outbreak of the war when they were forced to return home, in 1917 Edith was in Canada visiting her brother, who lived in Camrose, Alberta. She was taking time off from Norland work for a while. Having risked the journey across the Atlantic, which was patrolled by German U-boats torpedoing shipping indiscriminately, she had arrived in February in thick snow and bitter cold, to live in her brother's 'little wooden bungalow'. Life in Camrose was taken up with 'cleaning, cooking and sewing', but it was a lonely existence, until March when news reached Edith of a visit by the 151st Battalion (Central Alberta), part of the Canadian Expeditionary Force. With her brother, she prepared for their arrival, putting all their kettles and pans on to boil to make tea.

By 11.30am they were passing Edith's bungalow:

They duly arrived, 3 officers and 125 men. They had their meal picnic-fashion in our field, bringing all provisions with them. At 2.15pm they left, having had a rest, and all said they had enjoyed the outing. We shall always be interested now to hear about the 151st Battalion.

It was a brief glimpse of the war, but for Edith who had seen it first-hand, it appears to have been a welcome reconnection and an opportunity to 'do her bit'. The 151st Battalion would arrive in France in time for the major actions at Vimy Ridge, Passchendaele and Cambrai, which involved huge numbers of Canadian soldiers. Edith did not return to England until 1922, but remained on the Norland register during her sojourn in Canada as a way to keep in touch with her sister nannies.

In spring 1917 the USA declared war on Germany and Norlanders working in the United States were compelled to come to terms with living in a nation at war. During the early years of the war, certain elements of US society had sent money and supplies to both sides in Europe, and Norlanders had contributed to Mrs Ward's column 'War in the Nursery' with their unbiased views on the conflict, but now they began to share news of their own war work.

Writing from a smart new building, The Wyoming on 7th Avenue in New York, Nurse Mary Hough was employed by Mrs Burnes for whom she had worked since 1911. Mary declared her 'sympathies are all with our dear old country', which she had not visited for six years at the time of writing. She had been involved with the British Imperial Club since the beginning of the war and was an early member of the New York branch of Queen Mary's Needlework Guild.

Members undertook either to donate money or to make a garment for the Guild every month, and Mary described huge packing cases full of 'all kinds of garments and bedding and hospital requisites, besides tobacco, cigarettes and pipes for the soldiers'. The cases were sent directly to Queen Mary and the Guild had received numerous appreciative letters from her lady-in-waiting. A Norlander Mary knew had joined the British Overseas Club, collecting money for tobacco before raising her sights higher and embarking on a collection for a new warship. Mary was even involved in the latest craze in America, the chain letter, having received one instructing her to write to four acquaintances after sending a shilling to the charity named in the letter. She hoped it would end 'in big results'.

Mary found 'all Americans generally very ready to help us with donations, their sympathies being entirely with us'. She was moving in different circles from Nurse Hilda Hiley, who had written earlier in the war about the conflicting opinions she heard in the multinational expatriate New York community. Older Norlander, Nurse May Hasler, living in Long Island, was aware of the problems stemming from so many nations now at war having to live peaceably side-by-side in New York:

Those living in a neutral country doubtless do find it anything but easy to enter into the feelings of a belligerent people. We must remember that America was in a very difficult situation, but did they not show their sympathy in a very practical manner when the wealthy American children sent the shipload of toys, garments and food at Christmas to the unfortunate children of Belgium?

May was referring to a shipment of toys collected by Norlanders' charges in New York for Christmas 1914 and sent to Mrs Ward, each parcel individually named for the Belgian refugee children living at Mrs Ward's Lewes home. It was a generous gesture by the privileged for the few, but on a small scale.

May also passed on news from Nurse Annie Hammett in Boston. While her charge was at school, Annie was volunteering at the American Fund for the French Wounded, making surgical dressings and packing them into tin cases before despatching them to Bordeaux. May congratulated Annie on her prowess at bandage-making, 'for she instructs ladies less efficient than herself' in the busy workrooms. America and Norlanders working there were inexorably being drawn into the conflict in the limited ways available to women remote from the theatre of war. As busy working women, with limited time to read the daily newspapers, May recommended Norlanders to read *The Clarion*, a socialist weekly newspaper published in England, which reported the news with comment by the paper's publisher and editor, Robert Blatchford. May had been an avid reader for seven years, spending her weekly 1d on a paper she thought 'Socialist in the best and truest sense of the word'.

It was Christmas 1917 and America had transported approximately 14,000 troops to Europe during the summer, but plans were in preparation for a million men to be in France by May 1918. May was acutely aware that she was living in a country about to undergo radical change. She felt for bereaved families at home, but she and those around her had yet to experience such grief first-hand. She quoted from *The Clarion*:

Men must die that succeeding generations may live in fruitfulness and peace, in wisdom and in honour. This is a bitter and dreadfully sad truth. It seems such a stupid thing that millions of men should die that the world may finally appreciate so plain a fact that light is better than darkness, life than death, love than hate.

May was experiencing the gamut of emotions that had struck Mrs Ward and Miss Sharman in the opening months of the war three years before. For those in America, the confusing sensations that accompanied war were only just beginning. The Allies were hopeful of victory with new American forces behind them, but May was desperate to bring her fellow Norlanders firmly down to earth: 'The difficulty of winning peace by victory is trifling in comparison with the difficulty of securing the peace after it is won.' May's insight into the troubles that would follow victory revealed a higher thinking that few in Europe had yet to consider. With America drawn into the conflict, there were now few Norlanders not directly involved in the world's first total war.

The Russian Revolution had effectively removed the country from the conflict. The war raged on in the Middle East and Africa, but with Russia out of the way, German energies previously focussed on the Eastern Front could now be concentrated on the Western Front. The Ludendorff Spring Offensive of 1918 had begun to make significant incursions into French territory against exhausted Allied troops, but the American Expeditionary Force had just arrived, fresh and ready for action.

The Allies were now hunkering down for what everyone hoped would be a final and decisive victory, yet the Norland Institute was about to experience its worst calamity of the war years. With world events in flux, the nannies were plunged into another round of troubled correspondence.

Chapter 8

Last Push to Armistice

While Nurse Muriel Bois journeyed through the Mediterranean to safety in January 1917, the Norland Institute suffered its first personal blow of the war years. The beloved principal Miss Isabel Sharman died on 11 January 1917 of inoperable cancer. She had been the Institute's first and only principal in its 25-year history. Almost 2,000 Norlanders by the end of 1917 had trained under her tutelage. Their education had been a process of many years' collaboration between Mrs Ward and Miss Sharman, since the latter's own teacher training at Norland Place School.

One of eleven children, Isabel Sharman had helped the family governess and nurse to raise her younger siblings, and had shown an aptitude for working with children. In 1883, her parents had brought her to London to complete her teacher training, and as a student, Isabel's dedication and quiet manner had caught Mrs Ward's eye. She was a natural choice for principal when Mrs Ward decided to open the Norland Institute in 1892.

The two women's relationship had been built on respect, love and an acceptance that they both brought strengths to the Institute despite their extremely different characters. A pillar of her age and class, Isabel was sensitive, nurturing, supremely organised and her iron will remained cloaked in gentility. Where Mrs Ward's approach was direct and often brusque, Isabel was careful not to upset her nurses with diktats published in the *Quarterly*. Her letters were full of advice and gentle rebuke, when necessary.

She had led Norland from its infancy, guiding individual nurses to fulfilling careers all over the world; the motto above her study door read 'In quietness and confidence shall be your strength' encouraging independent young women to achieve their dreams in a thoroughly Edwardian manner. The year before her illness reached a critical stage, she had taken time off 'to rest'. Very few nurses or staff knew the nature of her illness, suspecting only that she was exhausted after long years of tireless service. During her last visit to the Institute before she entered a nursing home, Mrs Ward had watched as 'with methodical care she entered into every detail, handing over her faithful stewardship with gentleness and dignity'. As every Norlander was trained to do when leaving a much-loved nursery and its inhabitants, so Isabel had departed Norland, leaving behind her life's work in perfect order.

The two ladies were close friends beyond their professional relationship, and they had discussed many topics besides childcare. Mrs Ward shared Isabel's views with her nurses: 'Miss Sharman and I often spoke of death, and she always looked cheerfully on that great change. She, in a sense, never grieved for the departed; she always said, "They have finished their work".' Isabel's deep Christian faith and her attitude of dignified restraint had influenced Norland's nannies for over two decades.

Until now, the *Quarterly's* pages had not mentioned personal losses. When nurses died of natural causes, they received a brief mention among the announcements of births and marriages of Norlanders' charges; that was all. Throughout the war, the nurses had not noted the passing of male relations, neither had they spoken of any of their charges, now old enough to fight, who had been killed.

For nearly three years, they had held back, but now loss hit them hard and the spring 1917 edition of the *Quarterly* was dedicated *in memoriam* to Miss Sharman. Years of pent-up anguish filled the *Quarterly's* pages: a stream of tearful letters offering condolences to Isabel's family, to the Institute's staff and to Mrs Ward. Letters from Norland employers contained more restrained sentiments, but they all pointed to the fact that Isabel had become the focus of their constrained war-grief.

In spite of all the other financial requests made on the nurses, they raised a subscription to provide a fitting memorial to Miss Sharman. Suggestions from a crèche cot to a portrait were received, but after much deliberation, the money was dedicated to 'The Isabel Sharman Memorial Fund'. Isabel had inaugurated the Maiden Scheme giving less well-off young women a chance to train at Norland, and so the memorial fund was established to grant money to maidens who were struggling to pay their fees; to nurses who wished to extend their training into areas such as maternity work; and to promising but impoverished students.

Mrs Ward's perceptive decision was based on the privations forced on the nation by the war:

> *Of late years the idea of costly piles of marble has fallen into disrepute, and the utilitarian view has taken its place. I think I voice the views of the Staff and Norlanders as a body when I say that what they desire is to have in a memorial something that shall perpetuate in a useful manner the simple life of love and duty of our beloved late Principal.*

It was the perfect way to keep Isabel Sharman's memory alive, but her death had opened a gap on the staff. Miss Jessie Dawber, who had worked at Norland since before the war, stepped up to the role of vice-principal in the spring. Now acting as principal, Mrs Ward resumed her daily involvement at the Institute, a routine that she had not fulfilled since the start of the war. Mrs Ward declared: 'the future is at present all unknown, but will you have confidence in me, as she had?' In their grief and war-worn state, unhesitatingly the answer was 'yes'.

Norlanders at home and abroad trudged on through the spring of 1917. The war seemed interminable; even Winston Churchill was privately predicting it would continue into 1920. In the press, the horrors of the German offensive in Flanders made hearts sink, and the reports from Russia of revolution and civil war turned Norland's thoughts to the few nurses who continued to work there. Nurse Gwendoline Digby was with Madame Wolkoff in 'Nowozybkow Government of Tchernigow', (today Chernigov in Northern Ukraine). The Wolkoffs were not an aristocratic family and they lived in a quiet town, where Gwendoline stuck out the first year of the revolution until the Wolkoffs departed for the safety of Rome, arriving there during 1919. However, Nurses Lilian Eadie and Marian Burgess had ring-side seats as civil unrest raged in St Petersburg.

Lilian worked for the Osten-Sacken family, who were of less importance than Marian's family. She was not enamoured with her posting and had managed to escape the revolution by November 1917. However, as nanny to the Grand Duke and Grand Duchess Kirill's young children, Marian was working with a family whose father had a claim to the Russian imperial crown; he had a responsibility to stay.

The Grand Duke was the Tsar's first cousin and an officer in the Russian Navy. Marian's life with the Kirills had been a whirlwind of travelling between their home in Germany, their villa in Cannes and the family house in Paris, frequently visiting other royal children, and occasionally meeting Nurse Kate Fox whose royal charges were cousins to the Kirills. Having married in 1905, without the permission of Tsar Nicholas II and outside the Russian orthodox church, the Kirills had spent the first five years of their marriage living in Germany before their reinstatement to Russian royal society in 1910. Since then, the family and Marian had lived in imperial luxury in the royal village of Zarskoe Selo, near St Petersburg.

As the revolution fomented around them, they managed to retain a guard of the Grand Duke's sailors, but the situation was increasingly dire once the Tsar and Tsarina were arrested with the Romanov imperial children in March. Despite orders from the new Russian government to have nothing to do with any members of the imperial family, the British ambassador to the Russian court offered refuge to the Grand Duchess and the children. Under her British title as Princess Victoria Melita, Grand Duchess Kirill was the daughter of the Duke of Edinburgh and a grand-daughter of Queen Victoria, which entitled her to protection within the British embassy. The embassy's offer was not accepted.

Marian was nanny to the Grand Duchess's two daughters and had worked with the family since 1907, earning her the coveted Norland badge for long service in a single household. Now the Grand Duchess was four months pregnant with her third child. The women were as close friends as a grand duchess and a nanny could be, having endured the ignominy suffered by the Kirills since the Grand Duchess's controversial marriage. At Easter 1917, Marian was ill and the Grand Duchess along with Lady Buchanan, the British ambassador's wife, visited her in hospital; it was all terrible timing.

In June 1917, four months after the initial revolutionary uprising, the Kirills decided to depart St Petersburg for a time. The Grand Duke had recently sworn allegiance to the new government, despite his life-long bond of loyalty to the Tsar as a member of the Romanov family. It was an act of expediency that won the Kirills the necessary documentation to leave the country without any confrontation. Leaving the royal nurseries in Zarskoe Selo behind, Marian departed the palace with only a few personal possessions. The government had forbidden anything of value to leave Russia, and her employers took only clothes, with the family jewellery concealed on their persons.

They took a train to Finland, then still part of Russia, expecting to be able to return to their palace when the trouble had abated. Marian continued unwell, caring for ten-year-old Maria and eight-year-old Kira, as they travelled into what would become exile. At Christmas 1917, Marian gave her address in the *Quarterly's* employment register as 'c/o Palais Wladimir, Zarskoe Selo, Russia'. Clearly, she hoped for the return of better times.

The altered focus of the war, created by the withdrawal of Russia from the conflict and the promise of the arrival of the American Expeditionary Force, injected new life into Norland's 'war in the nursery' column. The row apportioning blame raised its ugly head once more, however as the notion of bravery and courage against the foe wore thin, Nurse Cicely Colls was again at the forefront, voicing opinions that had begun to leak into the wider public conscience:

Surely the idea, consciously or unconsciously instilled into us during childhood that war is noble and glorious, and soldiers the bravest men – is fundamentally false! Volunteers at least in these days, were brave before they joined the army! By all means extol self-sacrifice and endurance, which includes moral and physical courage – but the noblest example of these was not a soldier, and He opposed physical force!

Casualties from the Western Front and Middle East had been convalescing at home for some time; the horrific results of war displayed for all to see. As the parameters of conscription widened to include married men up to the age of forty-one, more and more families had direct personal experience of the war. The public mood was changing, aligning itself more closely with Cicely's view that war was not a moral or honourable act, but a ghastly mistake engineered by governments. However, Cicely's grasp of what had started the war came straight from the cosseted environment of the nursery as she continued: 'There have been big mistakes and quarrels, and it is a terrible muddle everyone is in now, and we are all very angry with one another.'

Nurse Kate Jolly was engaged in war work in Glasgow, where its citizens were fighting for workers' rights in the numerous munitions factories in the city and along the Clyde. They remained steadfastly supportive of 'the boys at the Front' and so was Kate, who responded hotly to Cicely's simplistic explanation:

> *What about the 40 years' diabolical, cold-blooded systematic preparation on Germany's behalf? … Germany knew exactly what she wanted – and went straight for it. We, in our utter unpreparedness (thanks to our futile statesmen) have muddled and made mistakes enough, God knows!*

Kate had never taken up a German nursery posting and remained uninfluenced by friendships made there. Her views were mainstream, and her anger stemmed from attitudes towards German Unification in 1873 and four decades of the new state's growing confidence and militarism. She also caught the whiff of pacifism in Cicely's letter:

> *Is Miss Colls a "conscientious objector"? Is not he who voluntarily lays down his life for his country, the truest, noblest follower of Christ?... Miss Colls does not realise we are fighting for the greatest cause this world has ever known. Let our children realise that – that their fathers are laying down their lives to uphold the good – against the powers of evil and might.*

Kate believed firmly that Germany had taken its opportunity because Britain had been distinctly un-military in the decades before the war: 'Germany would have thought twice before she struck – probably never

would have struck at all – if we had been a nation of 'national servists'.'
Kate referred to the argument that Britain, without national service on
the outbreak of war, had not benefited from a trained body of young men
readily available to be called-up, unlike France and Germany.

From New York, Nurse Hilda Hiley, who had taken up the original
argument with Cicely, replied again to her latest letter. With American
forces on their way to Europe, Hilda's views looked towards the future
when the war might be over:

> *What it is we hate so much in this war – not the whole German nation,
> but that terrible Prussian military spirit which has dominated it and
> turned it into a machine with no soul. It is a spirit which wishes to
> tyrannise over and dominate Europe which we hate, and which we are
> fighting ... I think too that it is no good to encourage hatred and isolation
> when the war is over. We are fighting not so much to defeat Germany
> as the hopelessly wrong philosophy of life which has led her into war.*

Hilda's thoughts for policy after the war were the stuff on which
governments might build a lasting peace.

August 1917 was the last time the *Quarterly* would indulge the nurses'
'war in the nursery' argument. Mrs Ward had returned to the helm and
she closed the matter summarily:

> *This topic has been the subject of many letters, but with the two in
> this issue, the matter is closed for further discussion. All the nurses who
> have written show deep patriotic interest. We would beg these earnest-
> minded nurses to turn their thoughts now to "The times to come", the
> beautiful days after the war.*

Her concentration on matters after the war had ended was plain to see
in her seasonal address in the Christmas 1917 edition, in the tasks she
set herself and her nurses for 1918:

> *What lies before us as a corporate Institute? What lies before us as
> individual members? ... We have to review the Past and make plans*

for the Future. We have to re-consecrate ourselves to our glorious work!

It was a messianic rallying cry, which boiled down to 'the training of girls to take care of little children, their health, their habits, their intellect, their spiritual well-being'.

On the surface it appeared that it was business as usual, but Mrs Ward was thinking of her responsibility to the British Empire:

We have to bring ourselves well up to date, and to provide for each generation the nurse that will be required to bring up a race of heroes in the strife between good and evil; a race of citizens alive to responsibilities and Duty. These are the principles that must underlie the teaching given to our students.

The new vice-principal, Miss Dawber, picked up Mrs Ward's refrain:

An immense responsibility rests upon those women who now have in their hands the power of developing and strengthening the characters of the next generation, and of inspiring noble aims and high ideals in the future citizens of the world ... This, as Norland Nurses and educated women, is surely our [sic] *war-work.*

Although she was in agreement with Mrs Ward in this matter, Miss Dawber's relationship with her employer did not stem from the same depth of mutual respect that Miss Sharman had enjoyed. Continuing her Christmas letter to the nurses, Miss Dawber stepped into disputed territory:

At the same time we fully realise the many other claims of the nation, and have great sympathy with those nurses who feel that for the time being they must take a more active share in England's struggle than life in a nursery affords.

While Mrs Ward's attitude towards Norlanders leaving nursery employment to go into war work had always been ambivalent, Miss

Dawber's hearty support for nurses who might not wish to return to childcare signified that she was at odds with Mrs Ward's values. In March 1918, after a year as vice principal, finally Mrs Ward promoted her to the status of full principal, but by November 1918, Miss Dawber had resigned. She had failed to manage Mrs Ward and seemed to lack Miss Sharman's tact.

Mrs Ward expressed their conflict privately, writing: 'She speaks to me as if I were the enemy of my own work.' Miss Dawber had desired to see Norland moving with the times, not left adhering to the childcare philosophy of the nineteenth century, which was no longer sufficiently forward-thinking to lead childcare practice in the new world order anticipated once the war was over. Ostensibly she left Norland to nurse her ageing mother, but the following year, Norland's biggest rival, The Princess Christian Nursery Training College in Manchester, appointed Miss Dawber as their principal. Obviously, she possessed the right qualities to lead, but not the diplomatic skills required to survive at Mrs Ward's new Norland Institute.

Between Christmas 1917 and autumn 1918, there were no further editions of the Norland *Quarterly*. Paper was a costly commodity and there had been occasional letters from nurses in North America complaining that their copies were 'not getting through'. However, an edition replacing the Christmas 1918 publication arrived a month early, with the banner heading 'War and Peace'.

On 11 November 1918, Armistice was declared. Europe was on its knees and many millions of displaced people now had to find a way home, both physically and in rapprochement. However, Mrs Ward's editor's letter failed to mention the Armistice, instead she concentrated on Norland's future, particularly on balancing its books. The war had affected others through suffering and death, but its primary effect on Norland had been financial. Mrs Ward laid out the state of affairs: 'Since 1914, although we have had a full staff and all the financial responsibilities of two large houses, we have never had a full term, and, on one occasion, we had only two entries.'

Many trained Norlanders had been forced to quit the Institute during the war. With a general shortage of domestic staff across the country, some families had asked their unmarried daughters to return home to care for elderly parents and convalescing soldier relations. Their hard-earned education and new-found independence counted for little among their families.

Nurses no longer working through the Institute's register did not attract agency fees for each new employment contract. Equally, there had been a dearth of new students with sufficient savings to pay the fees and so, since July Mrs Ward had been forced to sublet the Institute as a hostel to the National Training School of Cookery. She retained two large bedrooms as eight cubicles for visiting nurses and the staff offices, but it had been a squeeze, and now she posed to her nurses a pressing question: 'Shall the Institute with all its activities be wound up, or is it to take a part in the great schemes of reconstruction that will inevitably be brought forward before the close of 1919.'

Mrs Ward went on to answer her own question; she had just the fleet of young women in mind to save the day and perhaps even the British Empire:

The work must be carried on in a healthy environment, with strong healthy girls, for the benefit of well-born healthy children, who are destined to become the parents of a healthy race – children who in time are to be healthy citizens and rulers of a freeborn race.

It was fighting talk and the 735 nurses currently on the Institute's register, she hoped, would flock to the flag: 'Dear Nurses, come to the monthly At Homes, and also tell me by letters whether you intend to support the Institute or whether you feel that you would rather work as isolated, independent units.' Underlining just how straitened the Institute's finances were, Mrs Ward regretted 'that this year I have not had either time or money to spend on sending you the usual pages of Nurses' addresses'. November 1918's *Quarterly* was rather a thin affair with which to mark the peace.

Mrs Ward had opened the doors of her beloved Institute to a cohort of Norlanders she had last known at the start of the war. The deluge of letters from supportive and newly-opinionated Norlanders responding to her appeal consumed the winter of 1918. Nurse Winifred Ward took time out of her Christmas festivities to write to Mrs Ward on Boxing Day 1918. Winifred had no ideas for 'reconstruction', but she was appalled at the thought of the Institute's closure:

> *Just when good nurses are more sorely needed than ever before! For a little time there will surely be fewer children, and these more precious than ever, many fatherless, and most of them highly strung and nervous from the abnormal, and often times agonising circumstances of their birth. We must gird ourselves afresh, and take lovingly and skilfully in hand this new, and handicapped generation.*

A Norland employer, Mrs Enid Bagley, wrote to extol the virtues of the two Norlanders she had employed over the past three years. Mrs Bagley acknowledged the loneliness felt by children's nurses and the self-sacrifice they made, but begged Mrs Ward to 'carry on'. Everyone was in favour of Norland's survival. Norlanders' eagerness to share their vision for a post-war Institute reinvigorated the war-weary nannies. The nurses took Mrs Ward at her word, their letters bursting with suggestions for Norland's re-development, including some bold attempts at refreshing the training regime.

Nurse Doris Wolf prized her three months' hospital training as 'inestimable value to the would-be nursery nurse', but the three months spent in Norland's Nurseries had not gone so well. She claimed she lacked hands-on experience with the smallest babies:

> *And speaking from my personal experience, the other six months' training was not sufficient to be practical. The time we spent in writing essays, clay modelling etc., pardon me for saying so, would, in my opinion, have been more profitably spent in a crèche.*

Having trained during the first decade of the century, Nurse Kate Viall had several years' experience under her belt. She described a Norlander as 'a lady trained for the care and education of young children', but felt that the exalted position of a Norland nurse within a household meant that parts of the current curriculum were unnecessary:

I consider that all cooking, except invalid cookery, is a waste of time from a nurse's point of view. We always live in houses where a cook is kept, and our one year's training is too precious to be wasted over things we shall not want.

Equally, the Institute's staff had always encouraged extended training post-qualification, such as the Red Cross or midwifery, but Kate could not see how this was to be achieved: 'We cannot afford, having paid nearly £100 for our Norland training, to stop work after a few years, and earn practically nothing while we take some other training – for example in an Infants' Hospital.' Kate recommended cutting cookery from the course and adding more medical nursing experience, as at some point in their career all nannies would have to care for sick children.

Twelve nurses in New York, including May Hasler and Hilda Hiley, wrote to ask for greater clarity in the running of the Institute. They wanted to know who owned the buildings that housed the Institute and the Nurseries in Pembridge Square; and they felt that with entrance fees at their current rate, not only did they wish to know how the profit was spent, but they proposed a pension fund should be set up 'for those who have given the best years of their life to Norland work'.

Most Norlanders lived with their employers, but only the highest salaried were able to put away sufficient savings for their retirement. The situation of Nurse Ethel Gilbert was telling. Ethel was among one of the first cohort to train at Norland. However, by Christmas 1917 she was living in 'a boarding-house in Hampstead' with a 'lovely sunny room with a beautiful view over London, stretching from Crystal Palace to Epping Forest on a clear day'. She continued to work with children, helping Sir Arthur Pearson, the founder of the charity St Dunstan's, to organise his Christmas Appeal for the children of 'soldiers and sailors blinded in the War'.

Moving from a nursery suite to a single room was not every nurse's dream retirement, although it sounded comfortable enough for a single woman, if a little lonely. Ethel signed off her letter asking 'friends who are near enough to come and see me one day'. Many Norlanders who read Ethel's letter could easily envisage a similar fate and the idea of a pension fund was appealing.

Across Europe, nannies' wages had not increased during the four years of the war, although the cost of living had rocketed. The New York nurses, who had been protected from the economic impact of the war, suggested that the Institute demand higher salaries 'even for probationers':

> *Out here we have always found that intelligent employers are quite willing to pay well for the privilege of having for their children those who have had a Norland training, and as we have to pay well for that training we are entitled to get good salaries.*

Nurse Netta Middleton raised a hot debate about pay scales for probationers and Badge nurses. Traditionally, the Institute had negotiated the delicate matter of wages with employers, and Netta suggested that they write to the employers on the register stating there would be an increase in salaries.

Criticism of the Institute came from outside the ranks of nurses too. Norlanders were now deemed costly by middle- and upper-class families whose incomes had declined during the war. Younger Norlanders could earn between £36 and £40 a year, while more experienced nurses were asking £50 to £100 (£16,380 to £32,770 in today's terms, still less than the sums commanded by some modern Norlanders). With board and lodging paid for, estimated at a cost of £100 per annum to the employer, there was a growing feeling among employers that a lower salary of around £60 was sufficient for a young, single woman to live comfortably.

In some cases, clients were reverting to pre-1900 habits, employing cheaper untrained girls to staff their nurseries. Mrs Ward was quick to draw her nurses' attention to the damage to the Institute their demands for better pay were doing:

> *For this reason some of our very nicest applicants have told us recently that they cannot afford the luxury of a Norland Nurse and they have gone elsewhere, while the nurse, perhaps, obtains a highly paid position and gains in money what she loses in comfort and happiness.*

In spring 1919, with men returning from the front, the women who had filled their roles in wartime now found themselves out of work. The war had opened up previously unheard of opportunities for women and forged new confidence and independence, but the peacetime reality was the prospect of unemployment and a return to life as second-class citizens. For Mrs Ward, the security of a long-term post, albeit on reduced pay, was better for her nurses than a short-term well-remunerated fix without prospects. She anticipated that once circumstances improved her nurses would then be well-placed to name their price.

However, there was one suggestion for which she could never have prepared herself. The war had changed the nannies; the politics of the war and the tumultuous revolutions being enacted across Europe had influenced them. While the New York nurses thought 'it would be helpful to have a Norlander on the Staff', Nurse Cicely Colls went even further. Not only did Cicely wish to reduce the entrance fees at the Institute, in order to make the training more affordable to every type of young girl, she suggested that Mrs Ward form a 'nurses council'. The idea was tantamount to revolution to Mrs Ward, who was not ready for the new workers' committees.

Mrs Ward responded with reasons for and against all the nurses' suggestions, giving the impression that all had been given due consideration, but there was a note of pique in her replies. To the proposal to remove cookery from the course, she replied: 'Nurse Kate Viall's letter is pregnant with useful hints, and her remarks on delicate children are excellent.' She was damning with faint praise.

Cicely she declared: 'alive to the requirements of the present day, and a Socialist of the highest order'. Mrs Ward's words were not intended to be complimentary; her response to a nurses' council invoked the obedient relationship to their matron that Norlanders experienced during their hospital training: 'I ask all you nurses who have been in Hospital, can you imagine the Matron under whom you have worked being dictated to by a Committee of their own or former nurses?'

The demand for temporary nurses had increased during the war and the need did not abate in the first months of 1919. The Institute received forty to fifty requests daily for nurses, but potential employers tended to request younger Norlanders. Not only did they command a lower salary, but they were less likely to demand 'the services of two housemaids' and did not 'resent the visit of parents to their nurseries'. Older Norlanders had established themselves as a class of their own. Neither servants nor members of the family, they had carved out their status by requiring servants to help run their nurseries under a strict regime, leaving nanny to focus on the children.

In the Christmas 1915 *Quarterly*, Mrs Ward had asked her nurses to take note of an advertisement for nursery maids studying at the Birmingham Nursery Training School at Edgbaston. She encouraged her Norlanders to employ these students, because a properly trained nursery maid was preferable to a young girl one had to train oneself and on completion of their course, these girls were only fifteen years old, thus still malleable and willing to take instruction from an experienced Norlander. These were the very young women who might now take the place of Norlanders in homes that were struggling to maintain a staff.

Nurse Winifred Ward had noted that there would be fewer children in the immediate post-war years because of the lack of men, but for a decade already greater awareness of and access to family planning had created a trend for middle- and upper-class couples to produce smaller families, which older Norlander, Nurse Kate Fox, deplored. Kate felt that upper-class families had a responsibility to have large families and the help of a Norland nurse to care for them would encourage parents to produce more offspring. Kate had recently tried to find a Norlander to care for her cousin's four children, but had drawn a blank: 'I was told it was quite impossible to get any nurse to go permanently where there were more than two, and even that is very difficult as most of them refuse to go where there is more than one.'

Kate felt that the current cohort of Norlanders were 'an unpatriotic body of women', who did not realise the 'seriousness of the dwindling population'. If mothers could not find nurses 'of the domestic class', as Kate put it, because they had gone into munitions work, then surely they should be able to rely on Norland, but 'because they are patriotic and are having families of more than one child, no Norland nurse will help them'. Kate promoted the latest thinking from Dr Truby King, the

New Zealand children's healthcare pioneer: 'I wish nurses would go to hear Dr. Truby King, then perhaps they would realise that by refusing to help mothers of large families they are being a grave hindrance to the national well-being of the country.'

With nurses preferring an easier life caring for a single child instead of a large family, and attitudes like Kate's circulating at Norland, the Institute's nurses had acquired a reputation for being the *crème de la crème* for the best and worst reasons.

During spring 1919, Mrs Ward felt under mounting pressure to clarify the Institute's financial arrangements and uncharacteristically, she succumbed to the nurses' demands. Addressing the New York nurses' comments on the Institute's profits, it appeared that these had not been nearly as large as they had hoped:

Because money was needed for rent, taxes, food, washing, uniform, hospital fees and the salary of a large staff, stationery, postage, telegrams, wages of charwomen at £1 per week and in addition four meals a day.

In an attempt to keep up appearances for the sake of her employers, whom Mrs Ward believed expected nothing less from Norland, she had maintained the administration of the Institute during the war without any curtailing of the staff or daily running costs, despite the lack of funds being collected from prospective students. Having to explain Norland's finances put her on the defensive: 'If you imagine that either I, Mr Ward or Miss Sharman have ever participated in any share of the profits you are mistaken. Indeed, had it not been for my husband's most generous help we should many a time have been in a tight place.' The two ladies had taken a salary from the Institute, but had also ploughed any profits back into the establishment, and Mr Ward had topped up their shortfall when necessary.

It transpired that Mrs Ward owned the freehold of 7 Pembridge Square, where the Nurseries were housed, which she rented to the Institute at a lower than market value rate. 11 Pembridge Square, the Institute building, was owned by Mr Ward, who rented it back to the Institute for £240 per annum. Mrs Ward had also paid for 10 Pembridge Square (now let to the Cookery School) mainly from personal funds, except £1,600 taken from the Institute's savings. All the houses had been maintained and furnished from profits frequently supplemented by Mrs Ward's and Miss Sharman's private purses. As to the future ownership of the buildings on Mrs Ward's demise, she was not prepared 'to reveal the contents of my Will'.

Any thoughts of closure were now in the past and in fact Norland had plans for expansion. As young women left their wartime employment seeking training and a future career, Norland began to see an increase in probationer applications. Mrs Ward had listened to suggestions for the improvement of the course and now students received more practical childcare training and hands-on time in the Nurseries. The theory element of the course had been extended from twelve weeks to twenty-two and the buildings were adapted to what today we would recognise as a private training college.

However, in one area of Mrs Ward's Norland spring cleaning she went against the grain of all that Norland had stood for in maintaining the elevated status of her nursery nurses. She lengthened the training in domestic chores, and with good reason:

The average Norland Nurse will not be altogether a blessing in a household if she expects the mother and one or two servants to do the rest of the home making, in addition to waiting on the Nurseries, and I am convinced that in future every home will have to do with half the number of servants that it had in pre-war days.

She had recognised the need for economy in every aspect of life, even asking nurses to state the main rail line on which they would most like to find employment: 'For I regard it as a pure waste of your employers as well as your own money, to take work as far away as you can possibly find it from the place where your home and life interests lie.'

But some standards had to be maintained and outward appearance was foremost if Norland's public reputation was to continue unsullied. Not only a handful of employers, but also older Norlanders had complained about the unkempt appearance of many younger nurses when walking their charges in London's parks. Remarks had been received on the wearing of: 'Holland dresses without a cloak, going about without gloves, or wearing hats instead of bonnets on Sundays, to say nothing of uneven hems, heels worn down, grubby ties, low necks, and wispy bonnet strings.'

One nurse had even seen a 'probationer wearing *blue and black striped* [sic] stockings!' Nurse Dorothy Sanders hoped that all nurses would remember their beloved Miss Sharman every time they looked in the glass, remembering 'to put her bow straight, to see if there were a speck on collar or cuffs, to give a final pat to her hair'. Several nurses retorted that they were busy enough these days without having to fuss about their appearance, but Mrs Ward remained adamant.

For a Victorian upper middle-class lady still engrossed in her life's work in the second decade of the twentieth century, Mrs Ward had come a long way towards accommodating her newly modern, post-war nurses. Their ideas no longer sat as comfortably with her pre-war dictatorial leadership; their suggestions put her on the defensive and on the subject of Norland's uniform, she would not budge. Her lengthy editor's letter in the March 1919 *Quarterly* was signed off with a stinging remark concerning dress. The material for the nurses' uniforms had increased in price due to wartime shortages, and Mrs Ward was at a loss to understand how nurses were maintaining their personal wardrobes:

> *I cannot see how ... you can make both ends meet if you carry out the practice, which has been steadily on the increase, of keeping your private dress up to date in every detail that fashion dictates and your Norland uniform as well. We are all observing that this practice has resulted in a showy attempt to look pretty and fashionable to the detriment of your simple, neat uniform.*

Across the country, spirits were rising as well as living costs, and the weight of the war had lifted. Working Norlanders were revelling in the brave new world ahead of them, but in Finland a life of luxury had descended into one of penury and hardship for Nurse Marian Burgess, who was now caring for three royal Kirill children. The new baby, Prince Vladimir Kirillovich had been born in August 1917. It had been a difficult birth in exile, but correspondence to royal relations reported that mother and infant were in fine form, and at eighteen months old, Vladimir was a rare joy to his family and nanny.

Marian and the family had spent all of 1918 at Haiko, relying on the hospitality of friends and enduring the Finnish civil war, which had broken out in response to the Russian Revolution. Life was terribly hard, food was scarce and the family suffered several searches of their home by Finnish and Bolshevik troops. Every time, the Kirills feared they would be captured and forced to return to Russia to face the fate of the imperial family.

A Red Cross parcel arrived, sent by Lady Buchanan the wife of the British ambassador to Russia. Clothes for the children, jam, butter and tinned milk were gratefully accepted. The tables had turned and the condensed milk that Marian had hoped to send to the Belgian refugees at the start of the war was now part of her own charges' meagre diet. Marian was suffering the same plight as the many displaced families struggling to come to terms with the true impact of the Armistice.

The Kirills had been in Finland for nearly two years and finally, Marian managed to send a message to the Institute stating her address for the foreseeable future as: 'Societathauset, Borger, Finland'. She intended to remain with the Kirills whatever their future held.

Having spent the war in Vienna holed up in the safety of the German embassy, Nurse Kathleen Wanstall had returned home to Kings Lynn. She was the last to escape from behind enemy lines, four years behind most of her fellow nurses. Gradually, Norland and Norlanders began to accept the altered circumstances of immediate post-war society. While revolution and civil war continued to rage across Europe, and the terms of the peace treaty were negotiated in Versailles, it appeared that from summer 1919, peace reigned at last.

Chapter 9

Peace in the Nursery

Since 1914, Norlanders had passed the war years embroiled in charity committees, first aid training, petty economising and mending, and upholding the values of their beloved Institute wherever the war had taken them. However, overnight the Armistice removed all requirements for such hectic activity on the home front. Norlanders could return to their daily duties without the constant nagging thought: what can I knit this evening; whom should I pray for tonight?

At the Norland Institute, life continued without interruption – no one had paused to mark the cessation of hostilities. In the *Peace Quarterly* Mrs Ward's focus had been entirely on the Institute's future. Looking back appeared a pointless exercise, when renewal was pivotal to survival in the unfolding new world.

The political and social landscape for women had changed irrevocably over the course of four years of conflict. The Representation of the People Act 1918 had introduced universal suffrage for men over twenty-one. For women, the right to vote was restricted to those over thirty and they had to be property owners to boot. Many Norlanders qualified to vote on age, but there is no evidence that any owned property and therefore, only Mrs Ward was eligible to vote in the December 1918 General Election.

In the workplace, the nation's women, among them a handful of Norlanders, had entered employment in wartime industries, gaining a degree of financial independence, albeit fleeting, because in many cases, their employment was 'for the duration'. Men returning from the theatres of conflict expected to be able to return to work in their previous occupations. While some women factory workers found new outlets for their labour in the immediate post-war period, a large proportion of war workers were compelled to return to the family sphere.

Yet, there was hope for emancipation from the drudgery of a domestic existence. In 1918, Marie Stopes published *Married Love*, dedicated to young husbands and men intent on betrothal, encouraging them to recognise their wives' sexual needs. The sequel *Wise Parenthood*, a birth control manual, soon followed. Norland's spring 1919 *Quarterly* did not mention the civil disturbances in Britain's port cities; no one discussed women's suffrage; and sexual independence and contraception were beyond the Institute's horizon. Their business was raising the Empire's children, as Isabel Sharman had always taught. When Mrs Ward described her beloved principal's sentiments, months after her death, they still held true:

> *Miss Sharman regarded work with little children, the development of character, the physical care of them, their moral education, as some of the highest duties that women can undertake, and never was such work more important than now when the children are the most valuable asset of the nation.*

No longer raising officers to line the trenches, Norland nurses could now look forward to bringing up future politicians and economists, who would ensure that the Great War had been truly the 'war to end all wars'.

The threat of Zeppelin and Gotha aeroplane attacks behind them, Mrs Ward announced the resumption of the Institute's monthly 'at home' social evenings. She requested nurses to wear their full uniform and their badges. Held from 7pm to 9pm, the evening gatherings were designed to fit round every Norlander's nursery routine, based on the assumption that their charges would be in bed and either parents or nursery maids would watch the children.

Mrs Ward estimated that seventy to eighty nannies had left Norland to get married during the war years, making new applications from student nurses very welcome. According to Mrs Ward, applications continued to 'pour in' and, despite her previous worries about nurses' pay, she declared that 'salaries remain as high as ever'. It was a volte-face on her rallying cry in November 1918's *Quarterly*, but with postal difficulties now removed, Mrs Ward's publication was reaching over 800 nurses and their employers around the world; putting a positive spin on the Institute's circumstances could only be good for business.

In recognition of Norlanders' dedication to their posts during the war, plans for Norland's first reunion since its twenty-first anniversary gathering in 1913 forged ahead, with the event beginning on 25 September 1919. The first fortnight of the autumn had seen record temperatures in London reaching the high twenties, but by the time of the reunion, the Indian summer had waned and temperatures had plummeted to the low teens. Prepared for a heat-wave and a deluge, nurses began to arrive in London the day before, 'not to secure a particular bed, or a front seat, but to miss not a minute for talk, and in order to show off photographs of charges'. One married ex-Norlander even brought along her own baby.

The first evening was spent discussing Mrs Ward's plans for Norland's future and a committee of eight nurses was elected, among them Cicely Colls, who had previously requested the formation of a students' council. The minutes of the meeting note against Cicely's name 'if willing', acknowledging her disgruntlement that Mrs Ward had gone so far in electing a committee, but would not extend to a council of representatives.

Nevertheless, the reunion was a success in many other areas. The following day, Norland Badges were distributed, among them one to older nanny Nurse Ianthe Hodges for her record twenty-one years in one situation. Mary Faulconer recently home from Oporto, Portugal and Muriel Bols, who had escaped Athens at New Year 1917, received Badges for ten years' service, along with Beatrice Moxon and Constance Sadler, who had fled Schloss Schwerin in the first weeks of the war. Working in Russia and unable to attend in person, Marion Burgess's brother had written asking for his sister's Badge to be kept 'until such time as she will be able to come and receive it'. Another Norlander employed on the Continent had written expressing the belief that 'United we stand – divided we fall', a refrain Mrs Ward picked up, heartily adding 'and in our patriotism join together in the great work in which we all have our share'.

Amongst the self-congratulatory festivities, the real work of Norland's cohort of nurses was also celebrated. The headline speaker, who had helped to draw the nurses from all over the country, was Madame Montessori.

Her presence was a personal coup for Mrs Ward, whose teaching methods had always embraced the very latest theories in children's education. Inviting Madame Montessori, Europe's leading educationalist, to their reunion certainly placed the Norland Institute at the forefront of post-war thinking on child welfare. For the first time, care of the whole child – its physical, emotional and educational well-being – was on the agenda.

Heavy rain brought the reunion to a hurried end, its success further marred by news that a railway strike would begin at midnight: 'It was indeed damping to the spirits, and some hurried straight from the Hall to stations, others came to the Institute to look up trains and snatch their hand luggage, while a few brave ones hoped for the best.' It was the first inkling that the after-effects of the war and the increasing economic troubles affecting the wider world could have an impact on those within Norland's walls.

Rejuvenation of the capital, even amidst economic decline, was vital to keep London alive and there were plans for redevelopment of the East End's bomb sites. Day nurseries that had thrived during the war years while women replaced men in the factories were now closing, as mothers returned to the home, but Norland's Bethnal Green mission nursery, funded by subscriptions from the nurses, was immune from such council-enforced closures. However, it was being forced to move site. The London County Council wanted the existing building for an infant school and new premises had been found.

The day nursery secretary was now seeking donations to fund the building of a brand new nursery on an air raid site, which consisted of two derelict buildings. Plans included a nursery 'on modern lines and would also provide a comfortable flat for the staff'. She also sought a new matron for the current nursery and appealed to Norlanders newly released from war work, who were 'free and longing for the babies again'. It took time to find the right person, but Nurse Mary Emerson took up the reins during early 1920 and shortly after assuming her post, Mary had the nursery 'in a flourishing condition' with thirty 'fat rosy babies who spend their days there [and] have sprung from the deplorable slums of Bethnal Green'. Yet by Christmas, Mary was reporting to the *Quarterly* on the desperate unemployment she was witnessing in the East End.

Men were roaming the streets, queuing in hope of a day's work outside the dock gates. Women had been forced to return to work, placing their babies in Mary's nursery, which was now bursting at the seams.

Just as her predecessor had during the first Christmases of the war, Mary appealed for small gifts of garments and toys for the children. Previous requests had been for infants and toddlers with fathers at the front; barely a year later, the need was for babies whose fathers had returned to a city unprepared for so many heroes. The appeal extended beyond Christmas presents, because £1,200 to construct the new nursery was sorely required. The mission secretary had negotiated a two-year reprieve with London County Council to remain at their present premises and she reminded Norlanders that their mission fund had been started in 1906 to alleviate poverty in the East End. It was their duty to continue.

Economic depression was pinching all levels of society. Mrs Ward again tackled the subject of pay, asking nurses to consider the rising daily expenditure on food and coal for families, before they thought about demanding pre-war salaries. However, simultaneously she advertised for a matron for the Norland Nurseries at a salary of £80, 'rising at the rate of £4 a year'. The Nurseries were a lucrative business taking in the children of the well-to-do and council-funded wards of court, and only the best nanny matron would do. Mrs Ward's only stipulation was for a non-smoker, taking the opportunity to reinforce her regulation of no smoking in the Institute's nurseries or in public while in uniform. Smoking as a female pursuit had taken off among munitions workers free to spend their wages on luxuries and it was also fashionable among the upper-classes. Nice, thrifty young ladies like Norlanders were not encouraged to partake of such frivolous vices, but young women had changed during the war and evidently, a smoking Norlander was no longer a rarity.

At the beginning of the war, Mrs Ward had listed 576 trained nurses on her register, of whom 43 were employed by titled families and 66 were working overseas, mostly in Europe. By Christmas 1921, 573 trained Norlanders remained on the list, but now only 28 worked for titled families and the number of German royal clients had greatly diminished. Nurse Marie Hinman had returned to work in Europe during 1920, accompanying Princess Christian of Hesse, a German aristocrat and her four children, to the Hotel Beau-Site in Paris. There were a handful of other Norlanders in Paris and some in Italy, but few had really yet to venture back to Europe. Seventy-three nannies were posted further overseas, with many more working in New York than before the war. Yet, the most telling figure is the number who were now at home: 177 Norlanders were unemployed or in temporary roles, whereas at Christmas 1914 only 94 had been out of work.

Families who might have managed to afford a Norlander during the conflict were now feeling the post-war pinch. Many parents of Norlanders had also requested their daughters to return home, either to care for them in their old age or to nurse brothers who had returned wounded from the war. It was a significant change but on the surface everything appeared the same and Mrs Ward simply did not acknowledge her Norlanders' altered circumstances.

For those who had newly started work overseas, the gloss of foreign employment was undiminished. Nurse Kathleen Tweedie had taken three years between 1910 and 1913 to train at Norland, starting out as a maiden. She had spent the war working in England for several families, but had taken the first opportunity for a foreign appointment after the cessation of hostilities. At Christmas 1920, she wrote from Ligne de Rosette, Egypt, describing the festivities from a warmer climate. Her employer's house, El Tarh, was situated on a vast, flat expanse of fertile soil reclaimed from a salt lake beside the sea. In every direction, the land was green, but monotonous and Kathleen described the risk of inundation:

Inroads of the sea are prevented by a strong sea wall, and in winter it is strange to see breakers dashing over it, a line of white along the horizon; the sea itself being invisible except from the roof. A tidal wave would wipe us out entirely.

Ligne de Rosette was 20 miles from Alexandria, an hour's drive in summer, but a world away during winter when heavy rain could make the roads impassable. Holed up in El Tarh, Kathleen had the company of two other English families and between their four children and her three charges, Christmas was rather jolly. Her employer, John Camplin, had dressed as Father Christmas, distributing presents to everyone. Kathleen remarked on the behaviour of her youngest charge: 'Joyce, a very prudent maiden aged three, quietly collected all hers, and a few extras, and marched off into the day nursery, where I saw her examining them in peace!'

Kathleen enjoyed the adults' party, dancing to a jazz band on the lamp-lit balcony. That night, her household accommodated two nurses and five children in one room, but she assured her readers that although 'it sounds dreadfully unhygienic, it is a huge room, and I think we had our proper allowance of air'.

Since 1882, Egypt had been under British occupation and had provided a staging post for soldiers being redeployed to the Western Front in the retreat from Gallipoli. From Kathleen's letter, it is clear that British culture among the expatriate community had not been dented by the war. Apart from the jazz band, Kathleen was describing British life in north Africa as it had been for decades. There were several other Norlanders also employed by families working in Egypt or officers stationed there at the close of the conflict, who enjoyed similar lifestyles.

However in rural France, Nurse Margaret Evans was experiencing a very different way of life, confronted by the appalling detritus of the war. She had spent the years after 1914 ministering to refugees, first in Holland and then in France as part of the Quakers' Society of Friends. In March 1921, Margaret was still on the Continent and was no longer supported by the Friends, as they had pulled out in spring 1920 to concentrate on the post-war collapse of social infrastructure and civil war in Central Europe. Margaret had decided to stay in France, continuing to work in villages scarred by years of shelling. Her self-proclaimed aim was to 'help France help herself'. Having spent four years watching the sacrifice of others, Margaret had assumed the role of district nurse and lay-woman, ministering to ailments and souls. She estimated that there were 2,500 people in her care, spread out across five communes and seventeen villages. Her charges ranged in age 'from one day to about 95 years'.

The local government had refused to lodge or maintain her, but had allowed Margaret a meagre salary, which was proving insufficient.

Margaret had been accustomed to deprivation since the start of the war, but her description of her existence in war-torn France was heart-rending to her fellow nurses in their comfortably furnished nurseries. Margaret was subsisting on hand-outs from the local populace. In return for her medical help, she might receive whatever money they could afford, but generally her patients paid her in kind. She carried out her visits 'on my bicycle, regardless of weather, and there will come a time, I suppose, when I have to give up – physically worn out'. Margaret appears not to have taken up Norland employment again, although remaining on the register published each Christmas 'c/o Miss Sharpe', in Tunbridge Wells, so as to maintain contact with the Institute.

A year after the war, Nurse Mignon Miller, who had fled with the Countess Apponyi from Belgium to Hungary, was still working with the same family. They had survived the war and, after a brief sojourn in London during 1919, she and the countess were again travelling, as were so many Norlanders now that civilians could travel without risk. Having qualified in 1908, Nurse Winifred Buckwell had spent the war working with families around the home counties, unable to enjoy the benefits of travel in the first years of her career due to the hostilities. In early 1921 she had taken a position with the Dundas family in Lansdowne, United Provinces, India. She had travelled by ship through the Mediterranean and the Suez Canal and arrived in the far north of India without mishap. As the hot months from April through the summer approached, Winifred and her family took the train to Rawalpindi, before entering Kashmir, a province where railways had yet to be built due to the difficult mountainous terrain.

In May 1921, Winifred wrote to the *Quarterly*, describing their 200-mile onward journey by 'motor lorry' to Srinagar, a hill station, where they had come to enjoy the cool mountain air. Winifred described the treacherous drive along Himalayan roads:

> *Sometimes we went for several miles through such a narrow gorge that there was only just room enough for the rushing river and our road, which had been cut out of the side of the mountain ... In some parts of the road we had to drive actually* through [sic] *the rocks, long jagged tunnels, in the centre of which it was quite dark.*

In 1921, Kashmir was one of the remotest, most isolated regions of the British Empire and yet, when they arrived, Winifred was not at all surprised to see a camp already set up for them, each private tent equipped with its own bathroom and a large dining tent, where she ate goat for the first time. It was illegal to slaughter cattle in the province, but Winifred declared that she did 'not miss beef as much as one might expect, for the mutton and goat are delicious!'.

Despite being under canvas, there was no lowering of domestic standards and there was no evidence that the war had affected her employer's finances. Equally, her observations of the canals and using water transport to go shopping for silks and Kashmiri shawls in Srinagar do not include any mention of returning Indian soldiers wandering the town. Winifred described 'wooden houses, many of them beautifully carved' and meadows of mauve irises and red roses with the mountains reflected in the waters of Dhal Lake where they picnicked. If the war had touched anyone here, the effects were private and hidden. Winifred's letter to the Institute, published belatedly at Christmas 1921, was a fabulous advertisement to her fellow nannies, that if work might be scarce in Europe and salaries squeezed, then the colonies still had need of Norland nurses.

In New Zealand, Nurse Anna Miller was also reaping the rewards of travelling. She and her sister had departed for Canada on 19 November 1919, arriving in Halifax from where they enjoyed a month's sight-seeing at Niagara and Toronto, before continuing overland to Vancouver. They had hoped to take a boat straight to New Zealand, however, a sailors' strike had kept them in Canada for four months and with their purses emptying rapidly, they were obliged to find employment at a Women's Labour Bureau. Both nannies were placed quickly with families and Anna noted that 'Chinamen' provided the services of nursery maids in her household. Anna's employer had not heard of Norland, but on her departure the lady had already applied to the Institute for another Norlander to replace her.

Nursing the children through influenza, Anna succumbed herself, which further delayed their onward journey, but finally they had arrived in Auckland 'three days before our Prince'. Edward, Prince of Wales, the future King Edward VIII, was visiting New Zealand to thank the population for their contribution during the war, but Anna and her sister headed straight to South Island, where Anna was engaged at an orphanage and her sister as matron at a boys' school. Their employment was short-term because Anna describes several moves around South Island, working for families and in hospitals on children's wards dealing with measles and an epidemic of whooping cough, and a sheep station in the country near South Canterbury. She handed over her post with a doctor in Christchurch to a newly arrived Norlander, before moving on during late 1921 to Auckland to explore the North Island.

Anna and her sister were operating as temporary nurses, although finding their own opportunities without the aid of the Institute's employment register. Positions materialised by word of mouth, and Anna was happy to work on short engagements because it gave them both a chance to see New Zealand. There were drawbacks as she noted: 'this multiplies partings that do not grow easier by repetition'.

Temporary work and salaries were again hot topics among Norlanders in the early 1920s. While Anna and her sister were happy to hop voluntarily from job to job, the financial crisis at home was having a terrible impact on newly qualified nurses. Probationers entering their first posts would begin by filling-in for experienced Norlanders taking a holiday. They would temporarily enter the older nanny's nursery, where everything was as they would expect, leaving it in the same state a month later. It was the perfect way to gain experience before taking a first full-time position.

However, salaries for such short postings had become an issue. Not only did a family have to continue to pay their regular Norlander, but there were extra fees for her replacement during periods of leave. With fewer Norland probationers coming through the Institute to fulfil such postings, families could not afford the fees for one of the more experienced nurses to cover leave and therefore, incumbent nannies were unable to take their holiday.

Nurse Jacoba Watson complained that she had not taken her full leave entitlement in six and a half years, because a temporary replacement nurse was not affordable for her employer. She described the circumstances of one family she 'knew':

An officer's wife, who has already been badly hit by the war, who has three sons to educate, and perhaps a husband more or less an invalid from wounds received in the war, although she endeavours to keep a nurse for the children, cannot afford an extra three guineas a week while her nurse has a holiday.

Jacoba had tried to be discreet, but she was obviously very angry about the situation. It seems she was in fact describing her own employer; she went on to give very specific details about the mother of the household being unable to care for her own children, because she was constantly required to tend to her war-wounded husband.

Other families were in need of temporary childcare at the Norland Nurseries, having newly arrived from overseas, like Mrs Wood and her family who were home on leave from her husband's foreign posting. Mrs Wood had left her children at the Norland Nurseries on arrival in London, being 'too weary and nerve-wracked to cope with the training of our children'. She and her husband had headed for their vacation, knowing that: 'It makes our holiday a holiday indeed, to be able to hand over the welfare of our little ones with every confidence, while we rest and recuperate our energy.' Short-term care of small children was still an affordable luxury for some families.

The discussion on the merits of temporary work and salaries continued in the *Quarterly* until Christmas 1921, when Mrs Ward declared she was introducing a new system for temporary engagements. She informed the nurses in her editorial column that the chief aim of the Institute was: 'To bring Employees into touch with those who seek permanent employment, where they may settle down and become happy contented nurses in a permanent and happy home.'

However, she was prepared now to recognise that temporary work was not necessarily the nurse's preferred choice of engagement, as economic circumstances had altered since the end of the war. In future, there would be three classes of temporary nurse: those in Class I were nannies with more than five years' experience and aged over twenty-five, who would be required to travel anywhere within the British Isles at two hours' notice, for a weekly wage of £2, 12s. 6d; the remuneration for Classes II and

III would decrease according to experience, and the degree of urgency or difficulty of the position.

Class I nurses were her 'emergency nannies' prepared to cope with anything a nursery could throw at them. Mrs Ward described an example of what they might face:

A nurse arrives at her post to find the following conditions prevailing – the mother is dangerously ill, so are two of the children, and there is a tiny infant to care for; the servants are good but out of hand. Again, Grandmama hates the very sound of the name "Norland Nurse," yet she has taken possession of the house and family and the distracted father comes to us for help.

It was a ghastly description, but too often the reality temporary nurses faced. However, temporary work still did not count towards the prestigious bar that so many of the older nannies were now wearing attached to their Badge. Nurse Mabel Lister, who had trained in 1905 and by 1920 might have been wearing the coveted blue bar for fifteen years' service, had been an exponent of temporary work. In 1919, once again she was engaged for a few months while a family 'just home from India' settled into life in England. The only recognition of her long service in short-term employment was accorded when Mrs Ward suggested a new section for the nurses' testimonial books. From 1921 onwards, there would be a new page pasted into their books entitled 'Special Recognition' on which temporary posts would be listed, but the bar would remain elusive, despite the changing economic conditions imposed by the war.

As the Institute marked 'Obligation week', the new term for the Armistice commemoration in 1920, the nurses were reminded in the *Quarterly's* editorial of what they owed to the nation:

We surely have a very special privilege and duty in this way, to which we must keep ourselves ever more widely awake. Our work lives by the strength of the ideal which inspires and invigorates the whole – making us realise that it is the tone of our character and the spirit with which we are imbued, that form two of the fundamentals of a right success.

The sentiment was true enough, but as the 1920s got underway, the nurses were moving away from an Edwardian sense of duty and obligation to the *alma mater*. Mrs Ward lamented the cost of printing the *Quarterly*, now at twice the pre-war expense; she repeated Norland's strict dress code, demanding that white gloves be worn when working with infants and velvet shoes must never be worn when in uniform. The details were lengthy and the uniform was becoming outmoded, with stringed bonnets and hems a regulation 8 inches from the ground, when fashionable young women were hitching their skirts to skim the knee. However, Mrs Ward had entered into the spirit of the times in one respect. She had accepted the position of president of the Norland League of Nations Union, an organisation established after the war to promote future peace amongst all peoples. She requested that Norlanders join the Union in order to educate their charges about the importance of peace.

Norland's mission work was still going strong in London's East End. The Bethnal Green Children's Day Nursery had moved to its new premises and the latest matron, Nurse Linda Kemp, declared the playground 'a veritable suntrap, and a priceless asset to the Nursery'. She was caring for thirty-two babies and had just received gifts to display beneath the Christmas tree, one of which was a bottle of hair oil 'which a thoughtful child brought, labelled "For baldness and greyness"'.

In India, Nurse Mary Faulconer's spirits were equally buoyant. Having returned home from Portugal in the later years of the war, she had arrived in Delhi during 1921, where she had a front row seat at the Prince of Wales's visit to the city in 1922. Her ebullient letter began 'it has been a very memorable week and all passed without any trouble from the natives – much to everybody's relief'. The massacre at Amritsar only three years previously still marred the colonial power's perception of Indians gathering as a crowd. Mary had a 'splendid view of everything from the balcony of an Hotel' giving her a magpie's view of the diamonds, emeralds, pearls and 'most wonderful clothing' of the royal participants.

That evening there was a dance at the Delhi Club and the Prince appeared 'in the uniform of a Seaforth Highlander with kilts'. The following day, the Prince opened the Delhi Durbar, a mass assembly of India's royal personages, which thrilled Mary:

Everybody went into the grounds [Delhi Fort], *which were illuminated with thousands of coloured lights in the buildings, bushes, and trees, and even under the water, and in the waterfalls; it was just like being in fairy land.*

There was sword-dancing and displays of horsemanship, and the Prince handed new colours to both British and Native regiments. It was the kind of spectacle organised only for visiting royalty touring the colonies to offer grateful thanks for their support during the war and at which, of course, Norlanders would ensure their presence. As Nurse Cicely Colls wrote, the Norland nurse 'should be like the British Navy, "Able to go anywhere, and do anything" and therefore never beaten!'

Despite financial difficulties in the closing year of the war and the changing patterns of employment, Norland was thriving. Many of the earliest nurses continued to work, notching up year after year of faithful service and proving how necessary Mrs Ward's decision to start the Institute had been. Families did need nannies, either long- or short-term, and whether they were wealthy or recipients of charity at Norland's mission crèche.

It appeared that Norland nurses were unstoppable, and obdurate in their service. Nurse 33, Ianthe Hodges, had trained in 1894. At the 1919 reunion aged fifty-three, she had been awarded her green bar for twenty-one years' service with a single family. Ianthe had worked for the Earl of Dudley throughout his time as Lord Lieutenant of Ireland and as the fourth governor-general of Australia, caring for his five older children before twin boys arrived in 1907. Ianthe's long relationship with the family became particularly invaluable when the Countess drowned in the summer of 1920. Although her older charges were now adults, as someone who knew them all intimately, Ianthe was able to support them in their grief. Ianthe's was a life-long service and sacrifice that Mrs Ward viewed as a 'gift from God'. By 1925 Ianthe had moved to the Earl's eldest son's household to care for the next generation.

Nurse Edith Sperling, nurse 20 on the Norland admissions register, had trained alongside Ianthe in 1894 and also remained in employment. She was now matron at Marlborough College, Wiltshire.

However, not all the old guard proved to be as resilient as Ianthe and Edith. Nurse Florence Newman, nurse 157, who had trained in 1895 and had been instrumental in the introduction of the Norland Badge, died in July 1921 having worked through the Institute until 1916, when she had been appointed superintendent of a munition girls' colony, a camp erected purely to accommodate unchaperoned young female war-workers. Mrs Ward remembered Florence's cheerfulness and easy way with children, and how she had been ill for a year, commenting that she thought her 'end was a release from suffering', aged only forty-four.

Nurse Edith Rowell had completed her training in 1897. She was a blue bar nurse, having served eighteen years in the Rea family nursery. After a serious operation and short recuperation, Edith had returned to work, but five weeks later, she suffered a recurrence of her illness and died 'in bed in her night nursery'. While Mrs Ward believed Edith would be a great loss to the Institute, her focus turned to the family left without a nurse: 'what the loss must be to her Employer and the children whom she trained solely by love, is not easy to imagine'. It was another example of the deep connection forged between a nanny and her charges, and often the lady of the house too.

The Institute did not pass through the war without casualties. Already, Mrs Ward had reported the death of Nurse Evelyn Trenchard, who had drowned in the wreck of the liner *Florizel*, which had sunk off the coast of Newfoundland in February 1918. Aged thirty, Evelyn had been travelling first class to a new appointment in New York. The *Florizel*, an extremely robust ship, which doubled as an icebreaker in the winter months, had run aground in a storm 250 yards from shore. Unable to lower the lifeboats on to the rocks surrounding them, the passengers were advised to find a safe place on-board and await rescue. Ten minutes after grounding, the ship's power failed leaving passengers to flounder in the darkness. Evelyn was one among the seventy-nine who perished, with forty-four survivors spending thirty hours on-board, watching as the ship broke up around them in the pounding seas.

During the years of the conflict, a handful of probationers had died. This was not unusual for the period, with complications arising as the result of minor operations or after catching diseases from the children in their care. Evelyn's death, although not attributable to the war, was the first mention of the death of a young nanny in service.

Another was Nurse Viola Josa, who had worked through Norland's register since gaining her certificate in 1908 and who had once been keen to teach all Norland charges geography, had recently become Mrs Roffe-Silvester. She became the first Norlander to succumb to the influenza epidemic that swept Europe in the last year of the war. Her husband, Reverend Roffe-Silvester wrote to Mrs Ward, telling her of his wife's 'short illness and much suffering, influenza with acute complications, aggravated by looking after her two sick babies'.

After a largely healthy existence during the war, tucked away in safe nurseries or taking care of themselves and others on the Continent, Norlanders could not remain immune to the pandemic that would claim an estimated 3 to 5 per cent of the world's population, nearly 100 million people. Of all the Norlanders who quietly nursed charges through the 'flu pandemic and who themselves contracted it, the suffering of royal Nurse Marian Burgess was the most sorely felt.

Marian had fled St Petersburg in 1917 with the Grand Duke and Duchess Kirill and their two daughters, with a son, Grand Duke Vladimir, being born in exile in Finland. Their meagre existence was gossiped about in correspondence between royals across Europe, who were all related by blood and marriage, and many of whom feared revolution in their own countries. During 1919, the two princesses, now aged twelve and ten caught the 'flu. Already ill with nearly two years' existence on starvation rations, giving extra food to baby Vladimir rather than sustain herself and forced to accept aid from the Red Cross, Marian nursed the princesses Maria and Kira through their illness. Finally, Marian's remaining stamina ebbed away; contracting influenza was inevitable in her impoverished state of health and, after a short illness, she died on 28 December 1919.

Along with Nurse Kate Fox, Marian was one of the Institute's most highly regarded nannies. She had fulfilled a royal appointment for over ten years, at one of the wealthiest and most resplendent courts in the world. She was an impressive example to Norland's cohort of nannies of what hard work, diligence and quiet manners could achieve. She had behaved selflessly in her last years of service to the Kirills and had died in the course of her duty. Mrs Ward could ask no more of her nannies, and Marian's obituary in the *Quarterly* was a fitting memorial.

It described the extensive travel that Marian had enjoyed with the Grand Duchess and her children, criss-crossing Europe, staying at royal palaces and the continent's smartest hotels, always in the company of other royal children and their glamorous parents. Marian had not taken leave in six years and when offered a holiday in 1918, she had refused to leave her employers during their plight.

When the end came, the Grand Duchess had written to Mrs Ward, telling her that she had been with Marian at the very end, sitting beside her hospital bed. Grand Duchess Kirill had also written to Marian's family offering her condolences and sharing her grief for the loss of a devoted nanny and much-loved companion. The Grand Duchess had organised Marian's funeral and offered a romantic description for Mrs Ward to share with her fellow Norlanders: 'The snow was lying thick on the ground, and the coffin was taken on a sledge to a little church on the top of a steep hill, by moonlight. The light of the church window seemed to take the form of the cross and to be beckoning them on in their journey.' The Grand Duchess had written the annual testimonial for Marian six weeks before her nanny's demise:

> *During these last two years Nurse Marian Burgess has remained faithfully at her post in spite of the greatest dangers, privations and miseries which we have had to endure. Weeks of sleepless nights – surrounded as we were by bloodshed and murder and terror – her courage never gave way. Living for nearly a year on starvation rations she managed by her untiring devotion to keep our three children in good health. By miracles of ingenuity she contrived to keep them clothed and fed. To me she has been a comfort and a friend such as one rarely meets. God bless her for all she has been to us during nigh upon 13 years.*

Every nanny dreamed of such a testimonial. This final entry in Marian's testimonial book had become a hallowed memorial to a children's nurse who had worked through the first two decades of the twentieth century, and who had enjoyed a life of luxury at the Russian imperial court. But she had felt fear and witnessed savagery that few Norlanders, even those like Kate Fox who had escaped Germany in the early weeks of the war, had experienced.

Marian's demise was the last war news to reach Norland. Another royal Norland nurse would step into Marian's place and the business of childcare would start afresh. The old guard was retiring and Nurse Kate Fox was imminently to return to the Greek royal family. Europe's nobility had been decimated by the war and post-war revolutions. Territorial boundaries had been redrawn, but Norland had proved it could move with the times. With Mrs Ward at the helm, the Institute set about finding new clients – movie stars were emerging in the USA and the highly sought after oil resources in the Middle East were building wealth among Arab princes. It was a new world, with new opportunities and Norlanders had the spirit to take advantage of all that their training and hard-won prestigious name afforded them.

Epilogue
Nurse Kate Fox
The Return of a Royal Children's Nurse

Having been dismissed from her situation with the Greek royal family in spring 1913, Kate Fox was indignant at her dismissal as well as distraught at the loss of the princesses, whom she had grown to love dearly during ten years' service.

In the immediate aftermath, unable to persuade the Princess to intervene, Kate wrote to her employer's husband who was in London. The Prince did not respond, but he did inform his wife of Kate's request for his intervention. For the first time, Kate had crossed the line of royal companion and nanny, and compelled the Princess to respond to her as a servant. A letter was despatched swiftly with a strong admonishment: 'I think it was quite sufficient for you to know through me how he felt for you.'[1] In a single sentence, Princess Nicholas told Kate that nursery matters were her affair; the Prince was not to be bothered with such fripperies, and that they both felt terrible about Kate's predicament. However, in the same letter, finally Kate learned why she had been sacked.

While the Prince had been on a visit to Russia, his sister-in-law, the Grand Duchess Kirill, had explained to him that a letter sent from his wife to Kate had fallen into the wrong hands and the contents had angered the mistaken recipient. Addressed clearly to Kate at the Palais Vladimir, as numerous previous correspondence had been, the letter had been taken straight to the Grand Duchess, Princess Nicholas's mother, and as the letter contained advice to Kate on how to manage the children's grandmother it had infuriated the older lady. Not only was it obvious that her daughter held unpalatable opinions about her, but she was prepared to share them with a mere servant. From that moment on, any relationship

Kate may have forged with the princesses' grandmother began to unravel. Princess Nicholas explained to Kate: 'That is why she always had the idea that I was much more intimate with you than I was with her! ... Of course I never believed that you betrayed my confidence, but it <u>was</u> told to me that you boasted of my friendship to you.'[2]

Apparently, the storm had been brewing since 1910, when the Princess calculated the letter had fallen into the wrong hands; Kate's dismissal had not been as spur-of-the-moment as originally thought. Although the letter was not her fault and fundamentally her dismissal had been unjust, the nanny had flaunted her status among other royal nannies and lorded it over other servants at court. Crowing about her close friendship with the Princess to any of them, as well as to lesser royals she might meet, did not earn Kate many friends when the time came for her to need their help.

Enclosed with the letter was a cheque for £5 5s, so that Kate could replace her sewing machine which had been left behind in Athens, as well as news that Greece and Turkey had just signed a peace agreement. The momentous and personal news explaining Kate's dismissal, wrapped in the minutiae of domestic life in Athens and reports of international significance were typical of the Princess's style. Given the two women's long term friendship, it is unlikely that Kate understood it as undermining the importance of the part of the letter concerning herself; this was how a close bond with royalty worked.

Towards the end of the summer, the Princess requested that Kate send her testimonial book to Athens so that she could write the annual report in it. Evidently, Kate was putting her professional life in order and had told the Princess that she was working again through Norland, because the Princess's reply was heartfelt: 'And so you have taken up work again? How can you do it, I mean look after other children when yr heart is aching all the time for these darlings?'[3]

In order to protect them, and in the hope that Kate might be reinstated soon, the Princess had not told her daughters that Kate was never coming back, but by the end of September she had been forced to tell the girls. Princess Olga, the oldest, was the hardest hit by the news: 'When Nursie said good-bye to us, she said she would never leave us; I always thought that even if Nursie didn't look after us anymore, she would come back & live with us.'[4]

By autumn 1913, further details emerged of Kate's behaviour at the royal court. A French governess had been engaged for the Princesses, whom Kate had nicknamed 'Mademoiselle Olala'. The governess had heard about it and had been offended.[5] It was another detail that added to the character portrait of Kate as a haughty children's nurse, who now appeared also to be divisive, wishing to keep the princesses to herself. Her high-handed tone to her fellow nurses through the pages of the *Quarterly* during the war certainly paints a picture of a woman used to being in authority and receiving respect.

During a visit to Paris in early winter with a new family, Kate did not manage to meet the Princess also in the French capital, neither did she see Burgie who was accompanying the Kirills. Yet, Princess Nicholas did send her a charming note informing her that Burgie 'is quite on your side & you don't know how nicely she and the Grand Duchess Kirill spoke of you & the whole sad affair'.[6] It was a generous note allaying Kate's fears that she was being gossiped about by her friends in her absence.

Shortly after the Paris posting, Kate was sent by Norland on an emergency engagement. A baby had been born prematurely to a British soldier's wife in Nowshera, a military station on the Afghan–Indian border and a nursery nurse was required to attend as quickly as possible. Kate sailed on the first available boat from Liverpool. Writing of her exploits to Norland later in the year, Kate described the sights as her ship anchored off shore along the Indian coast. Natives joining or leaving the ship were forced to crawl in and out of the portholes used for coaling. From Karachi, she took the 'Punjaub Express' to Lahore and another train onwards to Nowshera, where she was advised not to travel alone at night 'without a revolver'. Employing her authoritative manner, Kate obliged a policeman to lock all her windows and door so that she could go to bed.

The following morning, she arrived at her remote destination. Apart from the terrific heat, Kate mentioned also the dearth of water, 'which cannot be used in the lavish manner it is at home, so that life is a little difficult with a tiny baby'. With tissue paper pasted at her bathroom window for privacy and newspaper used instead of a cloth to clean the nursery pans, Kate was a far cry from the palace at Zarskoe Selo, but she had something important to report to Norland. Of all the nurses on Mrs Ward's list, Kate had been singled out to cope with this adventure, to escort the sickly baby and mother home to England.

Kate had also written to Princess Nicholas during her trip. Unable to wait until Kate was back in London, the Princess wrote to her on the return journey, her letter addressed to the ship *City of Calcutta* expected in Port Said in mid-March. Evidently, Kate had written from Nowshera explaining how lovely the family was. Fearing Kate might be distancing herself, the Princess's reply described a Greek family that needed a Norlander. They lived in Alexandria, which would have made it possible for the two women to meet.[7] However, Kate's request for £100 per annum for the job turned out to be too much for the Greek family to afford. The Princess let Kate down gently and continued with news of the Greek monarch's silver anniversary, writing that it 'rather upsets the autumn'; she had plans to visit Russia as well as make a trip to Berck Plage for Baby's foot.[8]

However, the Princess's travel plans across Europe were squashed for the next four years. In June, she told Kate about 'thousands of miserable refugees from Thrace and Asia Minor' fleeing further persecution in Greece and how much she feared another Greco-Turkish war.[9] The Princess was unable to countenance the cataclysmic event about to occur in Sarajevo in a few days. The assassination of Archduke Franz Ferdinand would ensure the two women's separation at opposite ends of Europe until the conflict ceased.

In August 1914, the Princess had managed to fit in a visit to Russia, from where she wrote to Kate complaining that she was 'cut off from the rest of Europe'. The declaration of war had caught her out, a very long way from home. She described Grand Duke Kirill's appointment to the navy and how she was planning to leave Russia returning to Athens via Roumania, Serbia and Salonika, a safe route for a royal lady with her family connections in those territories. Knowing that Kate was now employed by a member of the German royal family, she hoped that she had 'got out of Germany safely as you must have been there when the war broke out'.[10]

Between August and October 1914, letters continued to pass between the two women despite the hostilities. However, it was not until Christmas 1914 when the *Quarterly* published Kate's description of her escape from Germany, that the Princess realised fully how close Kate had come to arrest behind enemy lines.

As disruption to international communications increased, post from opposite ends of Europe was slowed from their usual daily correspondence to a monthly trickle. The Princess sent news of Russian relations Kate knew, who had been killed already in the war and described her views on the importance of a recent Russian victory in Poland 'as it may mean the turning point of the whole war'.[11] Similar hopes were attached to each battle in the early months of the conflict; the Princess's naivety was nothing extraordinary.

A month later, the Princess had learned that Kate's luggage had all been safely returned to her, but there was still no sign of the testimonial book Kate had entrusted to a Greek doctor, and she offered to help trace it through Greek diplomatic channels. The war news from Athens concerned the Greek Queen Sophia, a younger sister of the Kaiser, whom the Princess declared 'continues to live in fools paradise & thinks the Germans are Angels!' Princess Nicholas continued 'she does not know the truth, she only reads German papers & sees German people from the Legation'.[12] Again, the Princess was imparting confidences to Kate, without knowing who might intercept her mail. The British war censor was only one of several who might open the letters en route from Athens and use the more political elements to their advantage.

Despite her generous pension from Princess Nicholas's mother, a sum equivalent to many Norlanders' annual salary, Kate had returned to full-time work in early 1915 at the Mothers' Hospital in London. She was living in the nurses' quarters, where letters reached her discussing the Princess's indignation at hearing gossip around Athens that the behaviour of Princesses Olga and Elisabeth had improved since Kate's departure.[13] The argument over Kate's ability to raise the princesses to their grandmother's standards was obviously lingering.

Throughout 1915 into 1916, the Princess's replies to Kate's letters nearly always mention her attempts to trace Kate's testimonial book, as well as her efforts to locate Kate's pension. It was unclear whether the money was to be paid from Schloss Schwerin in Germany or from Russia, but Baron Offenburg was sorting it out. Having been the royal official who dismissed Kate, he was duty bound to carry out his orders to pay her pension, but wartime embargoes on monies arriving from enemy countries would have created difficulties. Only when her husband was staying in London at Claridge's in September 1916 on a diplomatic mission was the Princess able to confirm that Kate would get her money.[14]

The Princess also never failed to send reports concerning her children's latest exploits, from Princess Elisabeth's horse-riding abilities to Baby's pink celluloid dolly and dolls' house.[15] The Princess could not find riding gloves to fit Princess Elisabeth and had asked Kate to locate a pair in London because she had smaller hands, closer to the child's size and might try them on before purchase. The Princess told Kate 'please don't do it if you find it too expensive',[16] but Kate had recently received a Christmas gift of money from the Prince and Princess with which to 'get something nice for your dear self' so she was not in a position to refuse, although her personal finances were not as buoyant as they had once been.[17]

Working at the Mothers' Hospital was not as lucrative as being a royal nanny and in June 1915, the Princess had offered Kate a loan with which to pay for her midwifery training.[18] There had been a plan afoot between the two women to establish a 'foundling house' in Athens. Now it was becoming a bigger project and the Princess asked Kate to send catalogues from London with samples for nurses' uniforms. She was also keen to find a matron to set up the home on English lines, to be 'the first of its kind in Greece', but Kate was not her immediate choice for the role. Ever protective of her friend and nanny, the Princess wanted the establishment to be up and running smoothly before Kate arrived to take over, because she did not want anyone to be able to blame Kate if it failed in any way.[19]

The project did not come to fruition, but the Princess continued to entice Kate to return to Athens. She had offered her former nanny another engagement with a friend, but with Kate requiring upwards of £80 and annual holidays, the Princess was compelled to explain that the war was forcing everyone to make small economies and the family could not afford her. A letter from Kate to Princess Elisabeth had mentioned a position in South Africa, and the Princess noted that the family must be offering a big salary for Kate to contemplate travelling so far. She was saddened that 'the Institute doesn't send anyone out just now after all such a lot of people travel about just now and this way there is really no danger'.[20]

While Kate remained oblivious to the restrictions the war was placing on wealthy families, Princess Nicholas seems to have been unaware of the increasing tension surrounding Greece's non-intervention in the war. Her husband was in London negotiating on behalf of his brother, the King, while around her, the Princess's way of life was crumbling as the Greek monarchy fought off the republican forces of the Venizelists.

By December 1916, there had been a three-month gap in correspondence, which the Princess attributed to 'one of the many ships that have sunk lately or [sic] kept back by Censor at your foreign office'. Princess Nicholas's Christmas letter illustrates her lack of understanding of the political forces at work. The ultimatum offered to the Greeks by the British and French, the first note, required complete demobilisation of the Greek Army. While they waited for a response, the parties had retired to the safety of their ships: 'All the legations have left and are sitting on various ships ready to leave at any moment. Why they didn't come back after their first note was accepted is what we can't understand... We are all in a state of dreadful anxiety.'

Meanwhile, the Greeks endured the violence described by Nurse Muriel Bois before her escape from Athens that month, which the Princess witnessed from the palace: 'The bombardment of Athens was dreadful. The poor children were so frightened. Baby cried and clung to me... Nearly all the shells fell around the King's palace... It does not feel like Christmas under these conditions.'[21] The Princess's allowance from Russia had not arrived and she apologised to Kate for not being able to send her usual Christmas money. The pressing need for household economies had even reached the Greek royal family; presents for a long departed nanny were now a luxury.

After Greece's entry into the war on the side of the Allies under Venizelos's leadership, Princess Nicholas and her family went into exile in Switzerland during 1917. She wrote from her hotel outside Zurich, describing the cold rooms and enclosing news from Burgie of Grand Duchess Kirill's impending confinement. The gossip around Europe was that it would be a difficult birth due to the circumstances in which the Kirills now lived.[22]

Perhaps it felt too far to travel now that she was in her late forties or the war made the journey seem too risky, but in 1917 Kate declined the position in South Africa in favour of working as matron at the Norland Nurseries. In the aftermath of Miss Sharman's death, in Kate's view Norland had been plunged into turmoil. It greatly displeased her to see her *alma mater* in such a state and she wrote to the Princess with a plan to set up an alternative institution. Kate asked if she would fund the venture, but the Princess admitted that her Russian income had been confiscated: 'With very little hope of getting it back, at least for the present. You can imagine what that means for us! It is quite dreadful & I don't know what we are going to do – life seems hopeless at times.'[23]

The Princess was consumed with worry for her relations in Russia. News had arrived that the birth of Prince Vladimir had not been easy, but that mother and baby were now doing fine; her mother and brothers, whom she had not heard from in over a year, had no money: 'one can't believe it after all that luxury.'[24] She worried too for Kate's future and was appalled that she contemplated leaving Norland to resume temporary work, which Kate did in spring 1918: 'I quite understand that yr situation must have become difficult with so much jealousy & envy all round you at the Institute, & that you were glad to leave!'[25] Whatever Kate had described was going on at Norland and her part in it, it sounds very similar to her behaviour in the royal nurseries in Russia.

That summer, the princesses suffered chicken pox and not only had Princess Olga grown taller than her mother, but she had started her periods, a subject discreetly covered in Princess Nicholas's letter.[26] Kate's girls were growing up without her.

In Russia, the imperial family had been executed, but the details were infuriatingly scanty with only formal reports in the papers to rely on, and the Kirills' departure from Finland had been refused. The royal village outside St Petersburg had been over-run, which particularly upset the Princess: 'do you know that our dear old house in Zarskoe has been completely plundered & that it is inhabited by those fiends.' And to add further insult, Nurse Margaret, Kate's replacement would be departing soon. They could no longer afford her and there had been trouble between the nanny and French governess again.[27]

Shortly after Armistice was declared, Kate had written speculating on what the future held for them all. As usual, the Princess's reply encompassed the global and the private in a single letter. Princesses Olga and Elisabeth had both caught the 'flu that was spreading across the world. The Princess had nursed them herself until she could find a medical nurse. They were staying at a hotel in Lausanne, where coping with a dangerous illness in alien surroundings was concerning the Princess further: 'how I longed for you & N. Margaret to nurse the darlings instead of being obliged to hire a stranger.'

In response to Kate's thoughts on the end of the war, the Princess's reply is ambiguous and it is unclear whether she was alluding to the morass of suffering of the people of Europe or her personal circumstances and all she had lost in Russia and Greece:

Yes indeed it does seem a blessing that the dreadful fighting is over. God give that it may really mean peace to the world in general & that those who have suffered unjustly during this dreadful war will be recompensed.[28]

She was desperate to return home, was fearful for the lives of her relations and hated the new world in which they lived. Now that the Allied Fleet was in the Black Sea, she was hopeful that her mother and brothers might escape Russia, but there were others who remained in prison in St Petersburg and who faced the same punishment as the Imperial family.

As Europe returned to some normality, Kate's letters began to mention a future date when she might return to the Princess's service, or at least when they might meet again. For six years, their correspondence had been unbroken by the war. However for the moment, the Princess was unable to fulfil Kate's dream:

> *I too would love to have you somewhere near, as you know, but for the time being, I don't see how that could be done – of course one never knows, something may suddenly turn up – how lovely it would be if you could go to my "grand-children".*[29]

The princesses were a long way from producing heirs, but Princess Nicholas had an eye to the future and a plan to reintroduce her friend into their lives.

Again Kate asked the Princess to fund another nursery idea, this time in partnership with a Miss o'Brien, but it remained too big a request.[30] Kate was at a loose end, taking unfulfilling temporary engagements until a family in London sent for her. The Wardells' newborn baby was fighting for his life and only a Norlander would do. She was quick to despatch the details to Princess Nicholas and the Princess said she was overwhelmed by how Kate had 'saved that poor baby's life'.[31]

Occasionally, Kate spotted royals around the capital with whom she had once been familiar. On the news from Russia of the death of the Imperial family, Kate had taken it upon herself to write to another of the Princess's sisters-in-law who was in London. Grand Duchess George replied 'I agree with all you wrote & it was revolting to see the unpardonable indifference to that unfortunate family.' She accepted Kate's condolences on the death of her husband and Grand Duke Paul: 'it makes one's heart & soul ache to think of the mental torture they had to go through'.[32]

Kate was maintaining her royal acquaintances because the connection to her old life held great importance for her, as well as the possibility of future royal employment. Previously, she had asked Princess Victoria, who had once invited her to Buckingham Palace, to visit the Mother's Hospital, which had illustrated to her fellow midwives how well-connected she was, and now she wrote to the Princess asking for advice on how to approach Grand Duchess George should she see her again after church. The answer was to maintain her distance unless the Grand Duchess approached her first.[33] However, Kate managed to orchestrate 'a little walk & a chat' having 'bumped' into the royal lady.[34]

Kate remained with the Wardell family at Welbeck Street throughout 1919, but simultaneously she entered into correspondence with a family in India, who were anxious to engage her. Meanwhile, the Princess rebuffed a request from Kate to holiday at her current home in Villeneuve. As the Princess explained:

> *I am afraid it would be, very difficult for you to come here on a holiday; things are not what they used to be & travelling, what with passports & all the formalities has become very complicated; it isn't as simple as it used to be.*[35]

Kate was completely unaware of the impact war had had on Europe's royal families and how they too were now forced into straitened circumstances. She had been accustomed to travelling freely with her royal employers without the necessity of passports, but borders were now strictly controlled. Many royals could not afford to travel even if they had properties left to visit.

Throughout their separation, the Princess had encouraged her daughters to maintain their relationship with Kate, and the princesses wrote frequently to their 'own darling Nursie'. They had not seen one another in over six years and yet the Princess was able to write: 'The other day they were saying "how lovely if Nursie could be here with us, we could do such a lot of things together; Nursie could do everything so well". They mention you constantly.'[36]

It must have been gratifying to Kate to know that she remained so highly regarded by the family. Realising that Kate's ship might pass through the Mediterranean on her way to India if she took the position, Princess Nicholas invited her former nanny to visit them at their new apartment in Villeneuve – in this case Kate would be passing through with her travel papers already in order. However, despite the years apart, royal protocol still took precedence: 'Any time after October will be right for your visit, try not to arrive just on 14th as that is our new year's day & we may have to spend it with the queen or something.'[37]

Discussion of the visit continued throughout the summer, but in the end, Kate decided to stay with the Wardells in London. Baby Simon needed her still and she reported she had had a small accident. Ultimately, tiredness, the discomforts of travel and trepidation at starting yet another appointment may have overwhelmed her. She was forty-nine years old and India may have seemed too much for her to cope with in middle-age. The long-awaited visit was off.

In her final letter of 1919, the Princess wrote that she had received news of Kate via a personal friend, who had reported that 'she didn't think you altered only a little stouter'. Princess Nicholas offered Kate an open invitation to visit at any time she might pass through. Kate had forwarded a letter from Burgie in Finland which had gone astray. News of Burgie's recent death would take time to reach them and the Princess concluded her letter:

> *Did Burgie write anything interesting? How they live & if the children have all they want in the way of clothes – they say the baby is a beauty! How I long to see them. [ ] Fondest love Foxie dear from your loving Ellen...*[38]

* * *

During the war, they had both suffered on a small-scale relative to the misery of others, but the changes it had brought them had deeply affected both women. The luxurious lives they had led could not be recovered because the war had changed everything. Theirs had been a remarkable friendship both before and during the conflict. One a commoner, the other one of the highest ranking royal ladies in Europe; their friendship had been cemented by their mutual love for three princesses and a genuine companionship in the demanding, gossip-ridden life of Europe's royal courts.

Kate's life among Europe's royalty had been the promise Norland had hinted at during her training. However, through her overt delight in her royal engagement and self-appointed seniority over her fellow Norlanders, she had displayed evidence of her manipulative nature; she had been divisive, but throughout the war she had remained fiercely loyal to <u>her</u>

royal family. Despite her dismissal, she had retained her ties with Princess Nicholas and her daughters; her friendship and support was sincere; they had been friends, equals in an age that had rarely allowed such disregard of protocol.

Ill-suited to temporary work and pining for the Princess who had returned from exile to Greece, in 1921 Kate went to live with her beloved Princess Nicholas and her daughters as their companion, caring for the next generation before returning to England in old age.

Torn from them in 1913, Kate had managed to find temporary engagements to fill her war years, but she had never been able to replace the princesses with a family for whom she felt equal affection. Having enjoyed the true and innocent love of three children, and the close companionship of a royal lady, Kate had experienced the harsh lot of the professional nanny: separation, a broken heart and life-long yearning for something her own life had not delivered – children of her own.

Nurse Kate Fox died on 19 November 1949, aged seventy-nine. Her obituary published in the *Quarterly* was matter-of-fact, but listed her early accomplishments as well as her more recent successes. Kate had attended the weddings of all three princesses and in a final demonstration of love and respect for her, Princesses Olga and Marina had attended their nanny's funeral.

Kate had become a legend among Norlanders, the last of the cohort that set Norland on the international stage.

Notes

PROLOGUE

1 RA/MDKD/OUT/FOX Letter 30 October/12 November 1905. Almost without exception, Princess Nicholas used both old style and new dates in her correspondence with Kate
2 RA/MDKD/OUT/FOX Letter 14/27 November 1905
3 RA/MDKD/OUT/FOX Letter undated from Hotel Bristol, Paris
4 Shepacat, more usually Chefakat, the order of mercy: a green and red enamelled five pointed star set on a pentagon decorated with gems hung from a commemorative ribbon
5 RA/MDKD/OUT/FOX Letter 19 October/1 November 1907
6 RA/MDKD/OUT/FOX Letter 19/30 August 1908
7 RA/MDKD/OUT/FOX Note 5 September 1908
8 RA/MDKD/OUT/FOX Letter 3/16 March 1909
9 RA/MDKD/OUT/FOX Letter 11/24 March 1909. As Grand Duchess Elena Vladimirovna of Russia, the princess had Anglicised her first name to Ellen
10 RA/MDKD/OUT/FOX Letter 3/16 June 1909
11 RA/MDKD/OUT/FOX Letter 21 June 1910, Prince Christopher was Princess Nicholas's brother-in-law
12 RA/MDKD/OUT/FOX Letter 5/18 July 1910
13 RA/MDKD/OUT/FOX Letter 5/18 July 1910
14 RA/MDKD/OUT/FOX Letter 31 October/13 November 1911
15 RA/MDKD/OUT/FOX Letter 17/30 January 1913
16 RA/MDKD/OUT/FOX Postcard 3 January 1913
17 RA/MDKD/OUT/FOX Letter 3/16 January 1913
18 RA/MDKD/OUT/FOX Letter 8/21 January 1913
19 RA/MDKD/OUT/FOX Letter 3/16 January 1913
20 RA/MDKD/OUT/FOX Letter 11/24 January 1913
21 RA/MDKD/OUT/FOX Telegram 1913
22 RA/MDKD/OUT/FOX Letter 25 March/7 April 1913
23 RA/MDKD/OUT/FOX Letter 10/23 May 1913
24 RA/MDKD/OUT/FOX Letter 10/23 May 1913
25 RA/MDKD/OUT/FOX Letter 17/30 May 1913
26 RA/MDKD/OUT/FOX Letter 21 June 1913
27 RA/MDKD/OUT/FOX Letter 28 June/11 July 1913

EPILOGUE

1 RA/MDKD/OUT/FOX Letter 25 July/7 August 1913

2 RA/MDKD/OUT/FOX Letter 25 July/7 August 1913
3 RA/MDKD/OUT/FOX Letter 1/14 September 1913
4 RA/MDKD/OUT/FOX Letter 24 September/7 October 1913
5 RA/MDKD/OUT/FOX Letter 8/21 October 1913
6 RA/MDKD/OUT/FOX Letter 14/27 November 1913
7 RA/MDKD/OUT/FOX Letter 3/16 March 1914
8 RA/MDKD/OUT/FOX Letter 4/17 April 1914
9 RA/MDKD/OUT/FOX Letter 6/19 June 1914
10 RA/MDKD/OUT/FOX Letter 12/25 August 1914
11 RA/MDKD/OUT/FOX Letter 11/24 October 1914
12 RA/MDKD/OUT/FOX Letter 25 November/8 December 1914
13 RA/MDKD/OUT/FOX Letter 11/24 April 1915
14 RA/MDKD/OUT/FOX Letter 25 September/8 October 1916
15 RA/MDKD/OUT/FOX Letter 1/14 March 1916
16 RA/MDKD/OUT/FOX Letter 5/18 January 1916
17 RA/MDKD/OUT/FOX Letter 1/14 December 1915
18 RA/MDKD/OUT/FOX Letter 17/30 June 1915
19 RA/MDKD/OUT/FOX Letter 11/24 March 1916
20 RA/MDKD/OUT/FOX Letter 4/17 August 1916
21 RA/MDKD/OUT/FOX Letter 7/20 December 1916
22 RA/MDKD/OUT/FOX Letter 8/21 October 1917
23 RA/MDKD/OUT/FOX Letter 7/20 December 1917
24 RA/MDKD/OUT/FOX Letter 15/28 January 1918
25 RA/MDKD/OUT/FOX Letter 17/30 April 1918
26 RA/MDKD/OUT/FOX Letter 16/29 June 1918
27 RA/MDKD/OUT/FOX Letter 20 July/2 August 1918
28 RA/MDKD/OUT/FOX Letter 8/21 November 1918
29 RA/MDKD/OUT/FOX Letter 14/27 January 1919
30 RA/MDKD/OUT/FOX Letter 23 February/8 March 1919
31 RA/MDKD/OUT/FOX Letter 14/27 March 1919
32 RA/MDKD/OUT/FOX Letter 22 March 1919
33 RA/MDKD/OUT/FOX Letter 19 July/1 August 1919
34 RA/MDKD/OUT/FOX Letter 3/16 August 1919
35 RA/MDKD/OUT/FOX Letter 9/22 July 1919
36 RA/MDKD/OUT/FOX Letter 29 April/12 May 1919
37 RA/MDKD/OUT/FOX Letter 28 August/10 September 1919
38 RA/MDKD/OUT/FOX Letter 26 November/9 December 1919

Acknowledgements

Without the assistance and friendship of two Norland principals this book would never have come to life. Thurza Ashelford first showed me the Norland Archives, nestled in boxes in an ottoman outside the College's conference room in 2005, when I was filming *Nanny School* for Discovery Channel. I knew then that I would find something unique among the papers and *Quarterlies*, but it was Thurza's successor, Liz Hunt, who suggested a history of Norland in the twentieth century. My thanks extend to both ladies for their indulgence and impetus to get this project off the ground, and to the College staff, who have tolerated my frequent visits during their working day, particularly Abby Searle.

The Great War history of Norland took various forms until a cup of tea and a good chat with documentary history producer Steve Humphries, who gave me the final kick I needed to realise that this book should not encompass the entire twentieth century, but would be much tidier and more interesting if it concentrated on Norland's Great War experiences. Thank you so much Steve for the tea and for recommending Pen & Sword. And thanks too to Jen Newby, then commissioning editor for social history at Pen & Sword, who was so quick to respond to my proposal that the pain of waiting only lasted overnight.

My appreciation also to the team at Pen & Sword, especially commissioning editor Eloise Hansen, who picked up the reins in the last few months of writing and has seen me and the book through the production process with ease.

Several archives, both official and familial, have indulged me and to them I owe my gratitude. Firstly, I must acknowledge the permission of Her Majesty Queen Elizabeth II to quote extensively from Princess Nicholas of Greece's correspondence with Nurse Kate Fox, and to Miss

Pamela Clark and the staff at the Royal Archives, Windsor for their assistance during my days in their comfortable research room.

My thanks also to Ken Osborne, archivist at the Church Mission Society who did not hold the records I sought, but introduced me to Harry Stephens at the School of Oriental and African Studies, who unearthed details of the Danns in West Africa; to Aileen Anderson and Barrie Duncan at South Lanarkshire Leisure and Culture for their searches through the records of the 5th Battalion Scottish Rifles to find Ian Mann; to Carol Leadenham archivist at the Hoover Institute Archives, Stanford University for information on the Friends' War Victims Relief Committee and Kevin Pooley at the Salvation Army; to Eleanor Cracknell, archivist at Eton School and Angharad Meredith, archivist at Harrow School for searching their records for evidence of Norlanders in the schoolmasters' family homes; and to Dorothy Goldsack for an informative tour of Sherborne Girls' School, as well as showing me their archive. Lastly, my thanks to Ann Smith at Sherborne Castle for entertaining an unsolicited email asking for news of a Norlander turned matron and nurse.

The internet can be a wonderful resource, most especially for tracing family names, which is how I found the descendants of many of my nannies, who have answered emails landing in their inboxes out of the blue with speed and great detail. Thanks must go to Andrew Jennings for information concerning the Jennings family in Oporto, where Nurse Mary Faulconer spent the early part of the war; to Tim Chambers at Oporto Cricket and Lawn Tennis Club for indulging my lateral thinking when trying to trace Mary's employers, and similarly to Josephine Carrapato, warden at St James's Anglican Church in Porto, and Terrence Weineck for sifting through parish records.

My gratitude must also extend to the Mackarness family and their fabulous family history website, which Patience, Eileen Godfrey's granddaughter, gave me permission to plunder.

Several members of the Molteno family responded to surprise emails from me with research on their family history in South Africa, where Nurse Beatrice Moxon was a nanny. Thanks to Robert, Catherine and Gill for sharing their family history and for suggesting alternative sources to contact in Cape Town. So my gratitude extends to Alison van Rensburg at Rondebosch Boys' High School, to Lionel Smidt at the University of Cape Town and Andre Landman in the University Library's special collections.

And finally, to family, friends and colleagues who not only read the initial proposals, but also have pandered to my endless need to talk about Norland's nannies, most especially Eric and Louis who have lived and breathed little else for the past two years. Your patience is admirable, but think – you know almost as much about Norland's Great War adventures as I do!

Select Bibliography

Adie, K., *Fighting on the Home Front: The Legacy of Women in World War One*, (Hodder & Stoughton, 2013).

Bourke, J., *Working-class cultures in Britain 1890-1960: Gender, Class and Ethnicity*, (Routledge, 1994).

Burnett, J., *Destiny Obscure: Autobiographies of Childhood, Education and Family From the 1820s to the 1920s*, (Allen Lane, 1982).

Cahalan, P., *Belgian Refugee Relief in England during the Great War*, (Garland, 1982).

Carpenter, H., *Secret Gardens: The Golden Age of Children's Literature*, (Allen & Unwin, 1985).

Cunningham, H., *The Invention of Childhood*, (BBC Books, 2006).

Droege, A., *Diary of Annie's War – The Diary of an Englishwoman in Germany During WWI*, (Grosvenor House Publishing, 2012).

Fletcher, A. & Hussey, S., *Childhood in Question: Children, Parents and the State*, (Manchester University Press, 1999).

Gathorne-Hardy, J., *The Rise and Fall of the British Nanny*, (Weidenfeld, 1993).

Hardyment, C., *Dream Babies: Childcare Advice from John Locke to Gina Ford*, (Frances Lincoln, 2007).

Heren, L., *Growing up poor in London*, (Phoenix, 1996).

Horne, J. & Kramer, A., *German Atrocities, 1914: A History of Denial*, (Yale University Press, 2001).

Kingsley-Kent, S., *Making Peace: The Reconstruction of Gender in Interwar Britain*, (Princeton University Press, 1993).

Llewelyn Davies, M., *No One but a Woman knows: Stories of Motherhood Before the War*, (Virago, 2012).

Marlow, J., ed., *The Virago Book of Women and the Great War*, (Virago, 2014).

Mills, J. & R. eds, *Childhood Studies: A Reader in Perspectives of Childhood*, (Routledge, 2000).

Pember-Reeves, M., *Round about a Pound a Week*, (G. Bell & Sons, 1913).

Powell, A., *Women in the War Zone: Hospital Service in the First World War*, (The History Press, 2009).

Read, D., *The Age of Urban Democracy: England 1868-1914*, (Routledge, 2014).

Sacks, J., *Victorian Childhood*, (Shire Publications, 2010).

Stallings, L., *The First World War, A Photographic History*, (Daily Express Publications, 1933).

Steinbach, S., *Women in England 1760-1914: A Social History*, (Weidenfeld & Nicholson, 2004).

Stokes, P., *Norland: The Story of the First One Hundred Years 1892-1992*, (Norland, 1992).

Van der Kiste, J., *Princess Victoria Melita: Grand Duchess Cyril of Russia 1876-1936*, (Sutton Publishing, 1991).

Van Emden, R., *The Quick and the Dead: Fallen Soldiers and Their Families in the Great War*, (Bloomsbury, 2011).

Weir, A., *Britain's Royal Families: The Complete Genealogy*, (Pimlico, 1996).

Wielinga, M., *Het Engelse kamp in Groningen: de geschiedenis van 1500 Engelse militairen tijdens de Eerste Wereldoorlog*, (Profiel BV, 2014).

Zeepvat C., *From Cradle to Crown: British Nannies and Governesses at the World's Royal Courts*, (Sutton Publishing, 2006).

Primary Sources:

Norland Quarterlies, (1897-1922).

Miscellaneous papers, Norland College Archive.

Royal Archives, Windsor – letters from Her Royal and Imperial Highness Princess Nicholas of Greece to Nurse Kate Fox, RA/MDKD/OUT/FOX.

Online Resources:

Calculator for historic monetary values: www.measuringworth.com/ppoweruk

Dutch Refugee camps: www.wereldoorlog1418.nl

Friends' Fourth Report of the War Victims Relief Committee, published 1917.

Molteno family archive: www.moltenofamily.net

Mackarness family archive: www.mackarnessplace.co.uk

'Report on Sanitary Condition and Vital Statistics during the year 1914 together with the report of the Chief Sanitary Inspector, Bethnal Green', George Paddock Bate, MD FRCS, Metropolitan Borough of Bethnal Green 1914, p.25 http://wellcomelibrary.org

Women's War Economy League, *New Zealand Herald*, vol. LII, Issue 16034, 28 September 1915, p.8: http://paperspast.natlib.govt.nz

Newspapers:

The Times, 16 October 1914 Letters to the Editor: 'Prospect of Invasion by Air'
The Times, 16 October 1914 Letters to the Editor: 'The Cheviots in Wartime'
The Times, 5 September 1917, p.6: 'Air Raid on London'
The Times, 25 September 1917, p.8: 'London Air Raid'
The Times, 23 July 1915, p.11: 'The Dearth of Servants'
London Gazette, 24 June 1916, p.6299

Index